# Creative Design and Innovation

Using many real-world examples and cases, this book identifies key factors and processes that have contributed to the creation of successful new products, buildings, and innovations, or resulted in some failures. Such factors include the creativity of individuals and groups, their sources of inspiration, the processes of creative design and innovation, and the characteristics of the products, buildings, and innovations themselves.

Much has been written about creativity and innovation, but what helps to foster creativity, enable creative ideas to be translated into practical designs, and ensure those new products or buildings succeed as innovations on the market or in use? This book discusses these elements through the author's origination and analysis of examples and case studies ranging from the revolutionary innovation of the smartphone, through radical innovations in domestic appliances and sustainable housing, to creative designs of contemporary jewellery. The broad range of examples and cases include product and fashion design, filmmaking and fine art, as well as industrial design, engineering, and architecture, offering lessons for creatives, designers, and innovators from many subject backgrounds. Analysis of the different factors, successes, and failures are presented in text boxes throughout the book to allow readers to easily understand the key lessons from each example or case, with numerous colour visuals, diagrams, and charts for illustration.

This book is a must-read for a broad audience interested in creativity, design, and innovation, including practitioners in design, engineering, architecture, and product management, and students and instructors of those subjects.

**Robin Roy** has a BSc in Mechanical Engineering and an MSc and a PhD in Design Technology from the University of Manchester. After engineering apprenticeships in the UK and Sweden, and a short period of teaching in the USA, he joined the Open University in 1971 as one of the first lecturers in Design. At the OU he has contributed to many courses and led many research projects on design, innovation, and the environment, and in 1999 was awarded a personal chair in Design and Environment. After retiring in 2012 as one of the longest serving OU academics he became an Emeritus Professor and is still active in teaching, writing, and research. Website: http://www.open.ac.uk/people/rr4

# Creative Design and Innovation
## How to Produce Successful Products and Buildings

**Robin Roy**

Routledge
Taylor & Francis Group

LONDON AND NEW YORK

Designed cover image: Daniel Ging © Unsplash

First published 2024
by Routledge
4 Park Square, Milton Park, Abingdon, Oxon OX14 4RN

and by Routledge
605 Third Avenue, New York, NY 10158

*Routledge is an imprint of the Taylor & Francis Group, an informa business*

*British Library Cataloguing-in-Publication Data*
A catalogue record for this book is available from the British Library

*Library of Congress Cataloging-in-Publication Data*
Names: Roy, Robin, author.
Title: Creative design and innovation : how to produce successful products and buildings / Robin Roy.
Description: Abingdon, Oxon : Routledge, 2024. | Includes bibliographical references and index.
Subjects: LCSH: Product design. | New products. | Technological innovations.
Classification: LCC TS171 .R688 2024 (print) | LCC TS171 (ebook) | DDC 658.5/752—dc23/eng/20231107
LC record available at https://lccn.loc.gov/2023038932
LC ebook record available at https://lccn.loc.gov/2023038933

ISBN: 978-1-032-40710-4 (hbk)
ISBN: 978-1-032-40708-1 (pbk)
ISBN: 978-1-003-35440-6 (ebk)

DOI: 10.4324/9781003354406

Typeset in Univers
by codeMantra

Printed in the UK by Severn, Gloucester on responsibly sourced paper

For June, Alex, Linda, Ella, Joe, and Olivia

# Contents

## Contents

# Figures

# Preface

Writing this book has been on my list of ambitions for a long time. Most of my career has involved producing courses and doing research on creativity, design, innovation, and the environment at the UK's Open University (OU). The OU is one of Europe's largest universities and teaches its over 200,000 current students through specially produced, multimedia distance learning courses. OU courses, originally produced as printed books, are now mainly presented online. Its students, most of whom work, continue to be supported by local tutors and now also through online tutorials and peer group discussions.

I was one of the first academics to join the Design group in what was then the Faculty of Technology (now STEM Faculty) at the OU. During my career from a young lecturer to Emeritus Professor I gradually assembled a substantial collection of print and electronic material on creativity, design, and innovation in product and engineering design, sustainable design, architecture, the arts, and media. I drew on this collection for my OU teaching and research but planned to use it one day to write a book on general principles and processes for creative design and innovation across these different fields. Producing courses and doing research at the OU also gave me good access to many people and organisations. This enabled me to interview designers, design engineers, managers, and others for OU/ BBC television, video, and audio programmes and to produce research reports for bodies like the Design Council and the Energy Saving Trust. Armed with all this material I made a proposal to the editor of my previous Routledge book, *Consumer Product Innovation and Sustainable Design,* which was accepted.

The opportunity to work on the book came with the COVID-19 pandemic and the lockdowns when, as well as tackling some long-delayed jobs in the house and garden, I had time at home to write. And when the lockdowns eased, I could also read and write in local coffee shops and was able to carry out the original interviews with a few designers, architects, and others for the book. Friends kindly invited me to stay for some very enjoyable writing retreats in trendy parts of London and Manchester, and in beautiful remote Dorset, the latter in return for looking after my host's dog.

I hope that the book's readers, whether a professional, educator, or student, find the many examples and case studies on which the book is based interesting and engaging and the guidance on successful creative design and innovation useful.

# Acknowledgements

Firstly, I want to thank the individuals who agreed to be interviewed for this book's case studies – architect, inventor, and engineer, Dr Derek Taylor; product entrepreneur, Debbie Greaves; architect, Robert de Grey; and designer and art teacher, Nichola Clarke. Thanks are due to the Open University *Design Thinking* course students, Jacqueline Quinn, Rhiannon Davies, Tom Gibbard, and Ellie Wright, who provided me with images of the T-shirts printed with graphics they had designed and an account of the creative process they used to design them. I also want to thank the friends who provided me with space for enjoyable writing retreats in London, Manchester, and Dorset. I am grateful to my editors at Routledge, Grace Harrison and Matthew Shobbrook, who were most encouraging and helpful, and to the organisations which provided images for the book's illustrations. Finally, I want to especially thank my partner, June Payne, for proofreading and her very helpful comments on draft chapters and for patiently supporting me during the long authoring process.

# 1 Creativity, design, and innovation
## Introduction and framework

### INTRODUCTION: CREATIVITY, DESIGN, AND INNOVATION

So much has been written about creativity and innovation, what more is there to say? The importance of creativity and innovation to business, the economy, the arts, and culture probably does not need repeating. Bill Gates in his book *How to Avoid a Climate Disaster* (2021, p. 14) argues further that radical innovation is urgently needed to avoid disastrous climate change, stating, 'When it comes to climate change, I know innovation isn't the only thing we need. But we cannot keep the earth liveable without it.' But what are the best ways to foster creativity, translate creative ideas into practical designs, and for the new or original arte-facts which may result to succeed as innovations on the market or in use? These questions have been the subject of several fields, including psychology, business and management, design and innovation studies, and the histories of science and technology, sometimes illustrated by examples and case studies often of creative breakthroughs by well-known historical or contemporary figures.

The focus in this book is on innovations in physical objects rather than in services, processes, or systems. The main content of the book comprises many specially written examples and case studies, mainly of products and buildings. These span the range from revolutionary technological innovations, such as the smartphone and the iPhone, through radical innovations in sustainable and eco-logical housing, and innovative products such as a purpose-designed bag for dog walkers, to creative product designs such as an item of contemporary jewellery and graphics for T-shirts. For comparison there are also a few examples of crea-tive innovation in the arts and media. I have tried to make these examples and case studies as readable, engaging, and thought provoking as possible.

The main aim of the book is to identify common factors, processes, and lessons for success in creative design and innovation through an analysis of these examples and case studies. In the final chapter I attempt to distil these factors, processes, and lessons into general guidelines for designers, engineers, architects, product managers, and entrepreneurs aiming to produce successful product and building innovations, and to reduce the risk of failures. The book is also aimed at teachers and students of those subjects.

As the book is about creativity and innovation, I will first distinguish between these terms. I will then discuss the role of design as the bridge between creativ-ity and innovation.

DOI: 10.4324/9781003354406-1

### Creativity – An ability or an activity?

Creativity may be viewed as an ability or an activity. In the first meaning it has been defined as the *ability* of individuals, teams, or organisations to conceptualise or imagine new, unusual, or unique ideas and concepts and to embody them in creative works – inventions, designs, plans, artworks, etc. – which are considered useful or valuable. Thus Margaret Boden (2004, p. 1) says,

> Creativity is the ability to come up with ideas or artefacts that are new, surprising, and valuable. 'Ideas' includes concepts, poems, musical compositions, scientific theories, cooking recipes, choreography, jokes ... and so on. 'Artefacts' include paintings, sculpture, steam-engines, vacuum cleaners, pottery, origami, penny whistles.

Boden then distinguishes between *historical* (H) creativity – the ability to create ideas and artefacts that are completely new to the world and so are of historical significance – and *psychological* (P) creativity – the ability to create ideas and artefacts similar to those which already exist and are only 'new' to an individual or group.

Turning now to creativity viewed as an *activity*, two definitions are,

> Creativity is ... a novel and appropriate, correct, useful or valuable response to the task at hand (Amabile, 1996, p. 35).

> Creativity is an imaginative activity fashioned ... to yield an outcome that is of value as well as original (National Advisory Council on Creative and Cultural Education, 1999, p. 29).

A narrower definition of creativity as an activity that is of particular value to business is offered in the *Cox Review of Creativity in Business* in the UK (Cox, 2005, p. 2),

> Creativity is the generation of new ideas – either new ways of looking at existing problems, or of seeing new opportunities, perhaps by exploiting emerging technologies or changes in markets.

That the outcome of creative ability or activity should be 'valuable' is stated or implied in the above definitions. This of course begs the question: valuable to whom – individuals, society, government, the nation, humanity? So, while most people might agree that a new medical device is a valuable outcome of creativity, not everyone would agree that a creative idea leading to a new deadly weapon is valuable. However, the definitions seem to sidestep that issue and only say that the outcome of creativity must be of value to at least someone or some group of people. Indeed Weisberg (1993, p. 246) challenges the idea that a novel work must be valuable to be creative; only that it is the outcome of an individual's *goal-directed* activity even if no one else values it at the time. Its *value* comes from assessment by other people in the field, which may only come years later. If considered of great value, the creative work may also have *influence* by being incorporated into the works of others. So, when the public are encouraged to 'get creative' by producing a painting or a poem, few expect their work to be valued by art, literary, or other experts or to have a lasting influence. Someone producing a novel work for their own satisfaction Weisberg argues is creative.

However, in this book I shall be considering creativity as an essential element of the innovation process, and so its outcome has commercial or social value, rather than as an activity undertaken for its own sake. I shall also focus on creativity as an ability or activity leading to outcomes or innovations that people would generally consider benign. Although, of course, few innovations are without implications and impacts.

### Innovation – An activity or outcome?

Like creativity, innovation may be viewed as an *activity* or as the *outcome* of that activity.

In the first meaning innovation is the activity that transforms creative ideas into new products, buildings, services, or systems, launched on to the market, introduced into practical use, or made known in the world.

Thus, a dictionary definition of innovation as an *activity* is, 'The introduction of something new' (Merriam Webster Dictionary, 2020).

A widely used academic definition of innovation as an activity is that by Tidd and Bessant (2020), 'Innovation is the process of turning opportunity into new ideas and of putting these into widely used practice'.

The *Cox Review* (Cox, 2005, p. 2), mentioned above, defines innovation as,

> the successful exploitation of new ideas. It is the process that carries them through to new products, new services, new ways of running the business or even new ways of doing business.

Other definitions state that innovation, whether as an activity or its outcome, has occurred when something new is *first* introduced rather than after it has been widely adopted or used. Thus, in his classic work on innovation, Christopher Freeman (1982, p. 7), says,

> We owe to Schumpeter the extremely important distinction between invention and innovation … An *invention* is an idea, sketch or model for a new or improved device, product, process or system. … An *innovation* is accomplished… only with the *first commercial* transaction involving the new product, process, system or device, although the word is also used to describe the whole process.

Viewed as the *outcome* of the innovation activity or process, an innovation is simply, 'A new idea, method, or device' (Merriam Webster dictionary, 2020). For example, foldable screens are the latest innovation in smartphone technology.

The *Oslo Manual*, which is used to help measure scientific, technological and innovation activities in OECD countries, provides a general definition of an innovation as an outcome (OECD/Eurostat, 2018, p. 20),

> An innovation is a new or improved product or process (or combination thereof) that differs significantly from the unit's previous products or processes and that has been made available to potential users (product) or brought into use by the unit (process).

The *Oslo Manual* explains that the term 'unit' means the actor(s) responsible for innovation. It refers to any institutional unit, including households. The *Oslo Manual* then identifies two classes of product innovation – goods and services – and six classes of business process innovation, including production, distribution, and marketing.

In common with Boden's distinction between historical and psychological creativity there is the distinction between innovations which are new to the world and those that are new to an individual or organisation. In his classic work *Diffusion of Innovations*, Everett Rogers (2003, p. 11) considers an innovation, from the viewpoint of an individual or organisation considering adopting it, to be anything that is new to that individual or organisation, even if it is already widely known in the world,

> An innovation is an idea, practice, or object that is perceived as new by an individual or other unit of adoption. It matters little … whether the idea is 'objectively' new … if the idea seems new … it is an innovation.

In this book I shall be mainly focusing on innovations that are new to the world – or at least new to a nation, society, or culture – rather than just perceived as new by individuals or organisations. As noted above, I shall also focus on products and buildings while recognising that such artefacts are often dependent on new services and systems.

### *Relationships of creativity and innovation*

Given that creativity is part of the broader innovation process, an individual or group can be creative without producing an innovation if the outcome of the creative activity is not introduced into the world. But the innovation process cannot happen without creative work.

As Bettina von Stamm (2003, p. 1) says,

> creativity is an essential building block for innovation. This is reflected in the now widely accepted definition of innovation equalling creativity plus (successful) implementation. … Implementation – putting ideas into practice – is made up of … idea selection, development, and commercialization, and of course creativity is needed here too.

Figure 1.1 is one of the many models that have been produced to show phases or stages of the innovation process. This so-called 'Funnel-Bugle' (Fugle) model was developed by Schultheiss (2018) based on reviews of five earlier generations of innovation process models (Rothwell, 1994; Preez et al., 2006) plus a sixth-generation model proposed by Barbieri and Álvares (2016). As the Fugle model shows, creative idea generation, selection, and prototype development occur during a convergent 'funnel' part of the innovation process. Then, if a potentially worthwhile innovation has been identified within a portfolio of possibilities, the process moves to a divergent implementation and exploitation 'bugle' culminating when the innovation is introduced on to the market or into use. The 'gates' represent management reviews to approve or deny progress to the next phase.

Although the Fugle model provides an overview of the innovation process in a business, it has two deficiencies. Firstly, a *divergent* phase of problem definition, exploration and idea generation usually comes *before* the convergent 'funnel' phases begin. Secondly, creative idea generation is shown occurring at the beginning of the innovation process whereas, as von Stamm noted above, creativity is required at every stage, as each phase of the innovation process will throw up new problems which require creative solution.

**The role of design**

Where does design fit into this picture? Design may be viewed as the bridge between creativity and innovation. For example, von Stamm (2003, p. 12) says,

> Design is the conscious decision-making process by which information (an idea) is transformed into an outcome, be it tangible (a product) or intangible (a service).

Likewise, the *Cox Review* (Cox, 2005, p. 2) said, '[design is] what links creativity and innovation. Design shapes ideas to become practical and attrac-

Figure 1.1
The Funnel-Bugle
(Fugle) business-
oriented innovation
process model
(Schultheiss, 2018,
p. 3). Courtesy of
Frank Schultheiss.

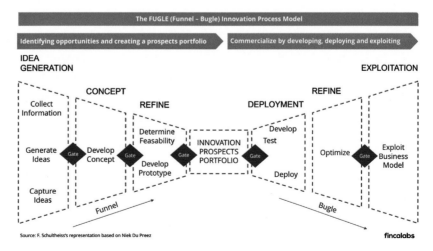

tive propositions for users or customers.' For example, the concept, refine, deployment, and second refine phases in Figure 1.1 all involve the activity of designing.

Dubberley (2004) has catalogued over a hundred models of design and development processes. One of the most widely used is the Double Diamond model originally produced by the UK Design Council in 2004 (Figure 1.2), expanded to a Framework for Innovation model in 2019 (Design Council, 2023). The Double Diamond is essentially another model of an innovation process moving from problem to solution but labelled as a design process. It starts with the important divergent problem exploration and convergent definition phases resulting in a defined problem or task: the design brief. The process then diverges again with the creative activity of generating potential solutions before converging on workable solutions and choosing one to be implemented.

The Double Diamond design and innovation process has four distinct phases,

- *Discover* – the process starts by questioning the challenge and quickly leads to research to identify user needs.
- *Define* – the second phase is to make sense of the findings, understanding how user needs and the problem align. The result is to create a design brief which clearly defines the challenge based on these insights.
- *Develop* – the third phase concentrates on developing, testing, and refining multiple potential solutions.
- *Deliver* – the final phase involves selecting a single solution that works and preparing it for launch.

This design model, thus, provides more detail of the funnel part of the Fugle model, where creativity and design are most important, and less detail of the business-oriented bugle part, when design has a smaller role, although, as

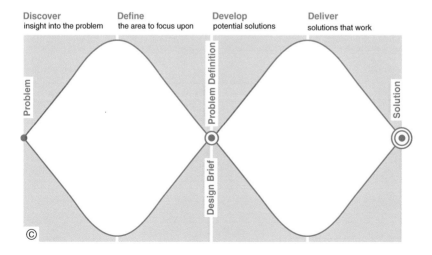

**Discover**
insight into the problem

**Define**
the area to focus upon

**Develop**
potential solutions

**Deliver**
solutions that work

Problem

Problem Definition

Design Brief

Solution

Figure 1.2
Design Council
Double Diamond
model of the
design process
(Taylor 2021). The
Double Diamond by
the Design Council
is licensed under a
CC BY 4.0 license.
(www.designcouncil.
org.uk).

noted above, creativity is required throughout the whole innovation process. The Double Diamond model also has two phases of divergence and convergence rather than the single converge/diverge sequence of the Fugle model.

Another useful generic model of the product design and development process is one produced for teaching graduate industrial design, engineering, and management students at MIT (Figure 1.3). A strategic product planning stage precedes the process, which starts with concept development when customer and user needs are identified and alternative product concepts are created, then evaluated, and one selected for development. The process continues with the selected concept and its method of production developed in increasing detail until the product and its production process are finalised and ready for launch.

For new buildings the Royal Institute of British Architects *Plan of Work* (RIBA, 2020) describes a planning, design, and development process that has a similar set of phases to the product design and development process in Figure 1.3 but continues to handover of the building and its use. Box 1.1 shows the Plan's phases which, in common with the other models, moves from an exploration of possible design concepts to satisfy a brief to a design for the building in sufficient detail for it be to be constructed.

---

**BOX 1.1 RIBA *PLAN OF WORK* FOR PLANNING, DESIGN, DEVELOPMENT, AND CONSTRUCTION OF A NEW BUILDING (RIBA, 2020).**

**0 Strategic Definition>>1 Preparation and Briefing>>2 Concept Design>>3 Spatial Coordination>>4 Technical Design>>5 Manufacturing and Construction>>6 Handover>>7 Use**

---

A difference between the Fugle innovation process and the other models is that the resultant output may or may not count as 'an innovation' depending, in the words of the *Oslo Manual*, on whether it 'differs significantly from previ-

Figure 1.3 MIT product design and development process model (Roy, 2010, p. 23 adapted from Ulrich and Eppinger, 2000, p. 16). Courtesy of the Open University.

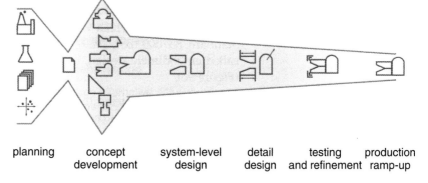

planning    concept development    system-level design    detail design    testing and refinement    production ramp-up

ous products or processes'. The output may simply be an updated version of an existing product, a new but conventional building, or a product that is a variation of products that already exist. As Figure 1.4 below shows, such 'non-innovative solutions' comprise most new products, designs, and buildings.

As this book is about creative design and innovation, the examples and case studies in Chapters 2 to 7 all involve some level of innovation but, as I noted in the Introduction, were chosen to represent the full spectrum of change from revolutionary innovations to creative product designs.

### Types and degrees of innovation

Many scholars and others have attempted to categorise innovations according to how novel and significant they are or turn out to be. There is a confusing variety of labels. For example, revolutionary, transformational, and 'first to the world' are all terms for innovations involving technologies, such as the internet or the smartphone, that have led to new industries and transformed ways of life.

Von Stamm (2003) provides a table of levels and categories of innovation, which I have adapted to include some of this book's case studies (Table 1.1).

Two widely used categories in the above table are 'radical' and 'incremental' innovations. The UK Design Council, for example, distinguishes incremental innovations – improvements in the function or form of an existing product, such as a redesigned kitchen tool – from radical innovations, such as the smart

*Table 1.1* Levels of innovation in products, services, and processes.
Adapted from von Stamm (2003, p. 6)

|  | *Products* * | *Services* * | *Processes* * |
|---|---|---|---|
| Revolutionary | *Integrated circuits/ microprocessors* Smartphones e.g., Apple iPhone 2G/3G | The internet/World Wide Web Artificial Intelligence | The assembly line *Global supply chain production (e.g., iPhone)* |
| Radical | *Dyson cyclone vacuum cleaners* Rover Safety bicycle Dunlop pneumatic tyre | Media streaming and downloading services (e.g., *iTunes*, Netflix) | Pilkington float glass *Prefabricated housing* 3D printing |
| Incremental | *Apple iPhone generations 4 to 15* Dyson Ballbarrow wheelbarrow Welch's detachable pneumatic cycle tyre Purpose-designed dog walking bags Customised greeting cards | *Smartphone apps* (e.g., weather forecast and transport timetables) *Compare the Meerkat advertising campaign* | Chilled and frozen ready meals Local authority kerbside recycling schemes |

* The items in italics are some of the case studies included in this book.

watch, which created a new category of product and market (Fullagar, 2015). 'Discontinuous' and 'continuous' innovation are terms sometimes used to distinguish between the same two types of innovation.

Henderson and Clark (1990, p. 12) argue that the radical/incremental classification is too simple and proposed four innovation categories. *Incremental* innovations are existing designs with improved components, such as a cooling fan with more efficient propeller blades. *Architectural* innovations have existing components arranged in a new way, such as a new design of fan with radial blades. *Modular* innovations use new technology applied in an existing concept, such as a fan with a novel type of motor. While *radical* innovations involve new technology applied in a completely different product, such as air conditioning replacing cooling fans.

Other often used categories are 'sustaining' and 'disruptive' innovations (Christensen, 2016). Sustaining innovations sustain an existing business by improving products in ways that people already value, such as the successive generations of Apple smartphones. Disruptive innovations disrupt existing businesses by creating an entirely new market through the introduction of a new kind of product or service. The disruptive innovation may initially have some drawbacks compared to existing products, but has unique features or benefits that people value, such as Apple's original 2G touchscreen iPhone. 'Evolutionary' and 'me-too' innovations are further terms sometimes used for products that are minor improvements on, or variants of, existing products or innovations.

For this book I have made use of some of the existing terms and categorised innovations into five levels, dependent on three criteria:

Their **originality** – how novel, non-obvious or surprising they are to the world.

How **successful** they are – in terms of commercialisation and/or adoption into society or use (plus sometimes other measures such as user satisfaction or environmental sustainability).

Their **impact** – how valuable people and society consider them to be and their long-term significance and influence on knowledge, thinking, and understanding, and in enabling further ideas and innovations.

My five levels range from rare, completely original, and world-changing innovations to the countless variants on what already exists. They are:

1. **Revolutionary innovations** (rare)
2. **Radical innovations** (infrequent)
3. **Major innovations** – radical, but sometimes with limited success or impact (occasional)
4. **Innovative products and buildings** (moderately common)
5. **Creative product designs** (very common)

This classification has similarities to the so-called 'iceberg of innovation' (Figure 1.4), which shows that the rare, but often well-known, revolutionary, and radi-

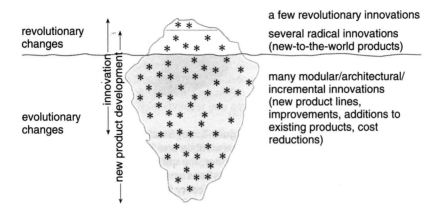

revolutionary
changes

evolutionary
changes

a few revolutionary innovations

several radical innovations
(new-to-the-world products)

many modular/architectural/
incremental innovations
(new product lines,
improvements, additions to
existing products, cost
reductions)

Figure 1.4
The iceberg of
innovation (Roy,
2010, p. 13).
Courtesy of the
Open University.

cal innovations are greatly outnumbered by the often-unknown evolutionary changes or incremental innovations, new and improved products, and design variants.

## SOURCES FOR THE EXAMPLES AND CASE STUDIES

Given that this book is based on examples and case studies from each of the above five levels, my first task was to identify and choose a suitable set to represent the spectrum from revolutionary innovations to creative product designs. I drew up a list using the literature, internet searches, and my previous research and archive of examples and case studies and chose those which I could develop using a mix of available primary, secondary, and tertiary sources.

### Primary sources

The primary sources included interviews and audio and video recordings carried out by me or others. I conducted five interviews with designers, engineers, architects, and entrepreneurs for the case studies. Other primary sources were interviews conducted by others; for example, interviews carried out for the Design Museum, London with Jonathan Ive, head of design at Apple from 1997 to 2019, and with the fashion designer, Paul Smith (Design Museum, 2014a; 2014b). Primary sources also included autobiographies, articles, patents, registered designs, unpublished documents, lectures, and online material produced by the designers, engineers, architects, and others involved in creating the products, buildings, and innovations discussed in the case studies. The autobiographies of James Dyson (Coren and Dyson, 2001; Dyson, 2021) are examples. Dyson is an inventor/designer and engineer, and the company he founded was one of the manufacturers of the radically innovative cyclone vacuum cleaner the story of which provides one of the Chapter 4 case studies. Other primary sources, used to supplement my interviews, included presentations about his life and work by renewable energy engineer and architect, Derek Taylor; and a business plan by Debbie Greaves, written for her and her partner's purpose-designed dog walking bags enterprise.

### Secondary sources

Secondary sources included academic and popular books and articles, online material and broadcasts about my chosen products, buildings, and innovations and/or their creators. A significant example is *The One Device,* by Brian Merchant (2017), a book about the conception and development of the Apple iPhone. Merchant spent ten years researching the iPhone project during which he interviewed managers, engineers, and designers inside and outside Apple as well as consulting historians, journalists, museums, publications, and patents. Clearly, I could not match Merchant's research, but so as not to rely on a single source I checked his account against other material by academics, science writers, and technical journalists (referenced in the iPhone case study in Chapter 3). Other secondary sources I drew upon for the case studies included websites and documents produced by the architectural practice, Rogers, Stirk Harbour and Partners (RSHP) and reports on the *Design for Manufacture* low-cost housing competition for the Oxley Woods eco-housing case study in Chapter 5; and for Chapter 6 a BBC TV *Dragons' Den* programme in which Debbie Greaves and her partner pitched for investment in their dog walking bags enterprise. I also drew on my previous publications on creativity and innovation (e.g., Roy, 1993; 2013; 2016).

### Tertiary sources

Tertiary sources included encyclopaedia entries, for example on cellular radio systems, and Wikipedia articles on several topics, which were also used to identify further primary and secondary sources as well as to obtain creative commons licenced images for this book.

### Strengths and limitations of a case study approach

My use of an inductive case study approach, of course, has strengths and limitations. Its main strength is that it is based on analysing empirical information, even if second or third hand, rather than deriving from theory. Its limitations are that even first-hand accounts, unless they are recorded during actual creative work (in so-called protocol studies), are likely to be incomplete and subject to deficiencies of memory and recall, bias, and self-justification. If a team or one or more organisations are involved, different people will often have different memories of the same events and individual opinions of others may affect what they say or remember (Wegener and Cash, 2020).

In addition, analysis of a limited number of examples and case studies can only identify factors, processes, and lessons that may be *associated with*, rather than provide scientific or statistical proof of the *causes* of, success and failure in creative design and innovation (see e.g., Weisberg, 1986).

## SOURCES FOR THEORY AND ANALYSIS

The book, however, does not rely just on its examples and case studies. I also drew upon the creativity, design, and innovation literatures and on attempts by others to synthesise general patterns associated with successful and less successful creative design and innovation to provide a conceptual framework for my analysis of the examples and case studies.

It is important to note, however, that the book does not provide detailed coverage of several relevant fields. They include the psychology of creativity, creativity techniques, and design methods since these fields are the subject of many existing publications. Examples include Ochse (1990); Csikszentmihalyi (1996); Boden (2004); VanGundy (1988); Sawyer (2013); and Cross (2021). Nor does the book discuss in any detail the strategic, organisational, marketing, or financial aspects of design, new product development, or innovation as these topics are well covered in the business and management literature. Examples include Nayak and Ketteringham (1986); Thakara (1997); Utterback (1994); Dodgson et al. (2008); Brown (2009); Christensen (2016); Hands (2017); Tidd and Bessant (2020); and Fadell (2022).

In the sections below I summarise some elements from the creativity, design, and innovation literatures that helped with my analysis of the examples and case studies and in providing guidelines and lessons for successful creative design and innovation.

### *Creativity*

One of the most useful summaries of what is known about creativity and innovation from a similar perspective to this book is *Creativity in Industry* by Raymond Whitfield (1975), an experienced engineer with a degree in psychology. Whitfield reviews different theories of creativity, discusses the creative individual and the innovation process, and provides case histories of five distinguished engineering innovators.

Whitfield begins with one of the best-established theories of creativity – that original ideas are produced in the mind by forming new associations between different areas of existing knowledge or objects. Koestler (1964) for example says that the creative act involves 'bisociation', making connections between two unconnected objects or frames of reference, giving the example of Gutenberg's invention of the printing press by making a connection between casting letters like coins and using a wine press to apply pressure. Creative ideas produced through such 'associative thinking' may arise in ways other than through bisociation, including use of a physical or biological analogy, by transfer of one area of knowledge to another, or by adapting existing solutions. James Dyson, for example, conceived the idea for a cyclone vacuum cleaner by transferring the principle of an industrial cyclone to a domestic appliance.

Associative thinking is related to the process of inspiration. There are countless examples of how an idea was inspired by an individual or group seeing, hearing, reading, recalling, or discovering something that triggered a creative thought. An example from Chapter 3 is Martin Cooper, saying he had the idea of developing the first portable mobile phone by recalling the image of a two-way wrist radio in the Dick Tracy cartoon strip.

Another theory discussed by Whitfield is that creative ideas may occur unexpectedly to someone in a 'lightbulb moment'. This is based on the creative process first formulated by Wallas (1926) in which an individual is trying to solve a problem through focused thinking and research ('preparation'), then setting it aside by doing something else or sleeping on it ('incubation') and the idea for a solution suddenly occurs in a flash of insight ('illumination'). Transforming that idea into a practical solution ('verification') may then take years. Whitfield emphasises that the moment of creation is more likely when someone has become 'immersed' in a problem with a 'burning desire to solve it'.

Whitfield also discusses creative individuals and summarises key elements of their nature; including possessing a store of general and specialised knowledge; a mind that is imaginative and open to ideas; being capable of dedicated hard work; tolerant of uncertainty; and often non-conforming.

The American cognitive psychologist Robert W. Weisberg has criticised and built upon the above theories and identified principles about the nature of creativity by carrying out detailed case studies of ground-breaking creative works – meaning radical innovations. Weisberg's case studies include Picasso's *Guernica*, the Wright Brothers' aircraft, and Frank Lloyd Wright's *Fallingwater* house (Weisberg, 1986; 1993; 2003; 2011). Weisberg concludes that such creative breakthroughs come not from 'geniuses', but through the processes used in ordinary thinking by building on pre-existing information. Extraordinary creativity, he argues, arises from being critical of what exists – including the creator's own work, drawing on existing ideas and objects produced by the creator and others – combined with the creator's store of general and specialised knowledge accumulated over many years, and their motivation and dedicated hard work. The creative act is then often triggered by an external idea or object or an analogy. More modest examples of creativity, Weisberg says, arise from similar ordinary thinking processes, but the material on which they draw, and the creative leaps are much smaller. Figure 1.5 is a model of the creative process based on Weisberg's theory of creativity derived from his case studies of creative breakthroughs.

Another study of exceptional creativity is Howard Gardner's book *Creating Minds* in which he examined the lives of great 19th and 20th century innovators, including Freud, Einstein, and Picasso. He proposed three related factors that determine who makes fundamental creative advances. The *individual* – the development of a talented child into an accomplished master of a given domain; *the work* – the ways in which the individual masters, labours in, and then makes fundamental advances in one or more domains; and *other people* – including the family and teachers of the child and the collaborators, rivals, and judges of the mature individual (Gardner, 1993, p. 8). Another book, *The Element* by Ken

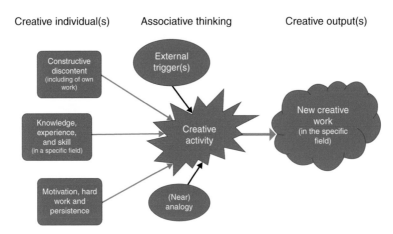

Creative individual(s)　　Associative thinking　　Creative output(s)

Constructive discontent (including of own work)

External trigger(s)

Knowledge, experience, and skill (in a specific field)

Creative activity

New creative work (in the specific field)

Motivation, hard work and persistence

(Near) analogy

Figure 1.5
Model of the creative innovation process based on Weisberg's case studies and theory of creativity. Diagram by the author developed from Fowles (2004).

Robinson (2009), presents the stories of several creative people from ex-Beatle Paul McCartney to celebrity hairdresser Vidal Sassoon. He concludes that highly creative individual work results from a combination of a person's natural talent driven by their passion to achieve in a specific field. 'The Element' is 'The place where the things you love to do and the things that you are good at come together' (Robinson with Aronica, 2009, p. 14).

Such studies raise the issue of the role of innate ability or talent. This is part of the nature vs. nurture debate and so is highly controversial. Without a detailed discussion of this question, it seems that with sufficient learning, training, and practice ordinary people can become highly creative. As noted above, Weisberg strongly argues against the view that geniuses are born, while Malcolm Gladwell (2008) popularised the '10,000 hours rule' – the hours of practice needed for anyone to become a renowned expert in a particular field, provided they had opportunity to practise for that long. But for *exceptional* levels of creativity and achievement it does seem necessary to have an innate ability to start with and acquire expertise through many hours or years of focused training or practise (Hambrick et al., 2016).

### *Design*

There is also a large literature on creative product design, engineering, and architecture, such as Brian Lawson's book *How Designers Think* (1980) and *Design Thinking* by Peter Rowe (1987). These studies point to the importance in creative design of the use of analogies, an ability to generate alternative concepts, of guiding principles and big ideas, of attention to detail design, and usually the need for teamwork. Eugene Ferguson's book *Engineering and the Mind's Eye* (1992) uses examples from historic water pumps to the Hubble Space Telescope to argue that engineers must rely as much on observation, hands-on knowledge, visual thinking, sketches, drawings, and physical models as on scientific and technical knowledge when designing innovative products. Another valuable study is Nigel

Cross's book *Design Thinking* (2011), which includes case studies of Gordon Murray's design of the McLaren F1 sports car and Kenneth Grange's design of an improved sewing machine. Cross discusses Murray's innovative redesign of the steering column of the F1 as a lightweight structure instead of heavy linked steel bars by creative application of his knowledge of engineering principles. Grange's redesign of a sewing machine arose from his dissatisfaction with conventional electric machines in which the mechanism is located at the centre of the base while the user needs more space in front of the needle. By moving the mechanism back Grange created an off-centre layout with more space for the user to manipulate the fabric. These and other examples discussed by Cross emphasise the central importance of being able to 'reframe' problems from a new perspective and of sketching, drawing, physical, and increasingly computer, models in the creative design process. My previous publications containing case studies, including Moulton's small wheel bicycles and the Brompton and Strida folding bicycles, confirmed the role in successful design and innovation of the elements identified by Cross plus other elements. These include 'constructive discontent' with, and questioning of, the design of existing products; domain knowledge of, and immersion in, information about a problem to be solved; use of different forms of associative thinking; a big idea or 'primary generator' that drives the process; and the making and testing of prototypes, followed by a process of detailed design requiring further creativity (Roy, 1993; 2009; 2013).

User- or human-centred design (Kelley, 2001) and design for sustainability or eco-design (Ceschin and Gaziulusoy, 2016) are important approaches discussed in the design literature, including in my previous book, which examined the sustainable design of innovative consumer products (Roy, 2016). A focus on a user-centred and/or sustainable design approach is illustrated in several case studies in this book, including Dyson's product innovations, Taylor's integrated renewable energy buildings, the Oxley Woods eco-housing development, and Greaves's dog walking bags.

### Innovation

As noted earlier, I will not be covering the management, finance, or marketing of new product development and innovation in this book. However, there are publications in the field that were useful for analysing the examples and case studies and compiling the guidelines and lessons for innovators.

A classic study of success and failure in industrial innovation was Project SAPPHO which compared pairs of commercially successful and unsuccessful scientific instrument and chemical process innovations (Freeman et al., 1972). The project was subsequently updated to compare a total of 21 scientific instrument and 22 chemical process innovations. For the scientific instrument innovations, the most significant differences between success and failure were that: the successful firms had a better understanding of user needs through contact with users throughout development and produced designs which met those needs; they paid more attention to marketing and sales; had a senior person overseeing and promoting the innovation; and had good internal communications between different specialist areas, especially development and marketing, plus good communications with external experts and organisations (Rothwell et al., 1974). A later review by Rothwell (1994) confirmed these findings, adding that the innovation process was aided and speeded through parallel working within a company on research, development, marketing and production, greater networking between organisations, and use of electronic systems such as computer simulation and computer-aided design.

The book by von Stamm (2003), referred to earlier, is another study of innovation success and failure containing ten case studies of innovations in products, services, and systems. The cases included a multipurpose power tool, a new HIV drug, a sports car, and a recycled plastic construction material. Von Stamm emphasises the crucial importance of business leadership to innovation success. She also stresses the need for organisations that have an innovative culture, are willing to experiment, value the contributions of creative people and employ them in multidisciplinary teams, and collaborate with customers and suppliers. Her case studies also illustrate the need for organisations to understand the wider social, market, and technological context in which they are attempting to innovate, the role of patents, and the need for models and prototypes in innovation process.

Walter Isaacson's book *The Innovators* (2014) is a study of the conception and development of products and systems behind the digital revolution, including the computer, the microchip, and the internet. The book concludes with some lessons and conclusions from the history of these innovations. Among these are, 'creativity is a collaborative process' and that 'Innovation comes from teams more than from the lightbulb moments of lone geniuses' (p. 479).

Isaacson also concludes that 'the digital age … was based on expanding the ideas handed down from previous generations' (p. 480) and that both governments and private business were involved in creating these revolutionary and radical innovations. Other lessons drawn by Isaacson are that 'the most productive teams were those that brought together people with a wide range of specialities' (p. 480) and that the successful innovators and entrepreneurs he studied were not marketers or financial types but were 'product people … They cared about and deeply understood the engineering and design' (p. 485).

Tony Fadell is a hardware and software engineer with extensive experience of creating, developing, and managing the production of radically innovative digital products and systems, including the iPod and the iPhone (discussed in Chapter 3). In his book *Build. An Unorthodox Guide to Making Things Worth Making* (Fadell, 2022) he offers the lessons learned from his innovation successes and failures. The first lesson arose from working in the 1990s on the invention and development of a touchscreen pocket computer with telephone, email, and other functions called the Sony Magic Link. The Magic Link failed because it was a premature innovation. It did not solve a problem perceived at the time by potential users; the technologies on which it depended were insufficiently developed; and the infrastructural systems to operate the product did not exist and had to be created by the innovators. Another lesson was the need to target the correct market. The Magic Link was intended for the public, but Fadell realised that it was for business users willing to pay its high price. He managed to persuade Philips to develop two business pocket computers, the Velo and Nino, based on some Magic Link hardware and Windows software. These were moderately successful, but the smaller Nino only really succeeded when it could play audiobooks. This led Fadell to realise that a product that could also play digital music could be even more successful. When invited to join Apple he led the team that created the iPod series. Fadell attributes the iPod's enormous success to it satisfying a genuine desire felt by consumers to have a portable device that could store more digital music than any other product in a beautifully designed and easy to use device linked to Apple's iTunes online music store. In other words, an innovation will succeed if it meets a real need, offers a unique advantage, is well designed, and has the infrastructure to support it.

These books all argue that creative teams in one or more organisations are usually required to produce significant innovations, even if the process started with one individual. But a few examples and cases in this book, such as the jewellery designer discussed in Chapter 7, show that for some products and artistic works an individual will often carry out all or much of the process from creative idea, through design, development, and making, to introduction to the world.

In the chapters that follow I will attempt to discover whether there are common patterns across the spectrum from revolutionary innovations to creative product designs from which to distil useful guidelines and lessons for successful creative design and innovation.

## REFERENCES

Amabile, T.M. (1996) *Creativity in Context*. Boulder, Colorado: Westview Press.

Barbieri, J.C. and Álvares, A.C.T (2016) 'Sixth generation innovation model: description of a success model', *RAI Revista de Administração e Inovação*, 13, pp. 116–27.

Boden, M.A. (2004) *The Creative Mind: Myths and mechanisms* (2nd edition). London: Routledge.

Brown, T. (2009) *Change by Design: How design thinking transforms organizations and inspires innovation*. New York: Harper Business.

Ceschin, F. and Gaziulusoy, I. (2016) 'Design for Sustainability: An Evolutionary Review', in P. Lloyd and E. Bohemia (eds.) *Future Focused Thinking – DRS International Conference 2016*, 27–30 June, Brighton, UK.

Christensen, C.M. (2016) *The Innovator's Dilemma: The revolutionary book that will change the way you do business*. Boston: Harvard Business Review Press.

Coren, G. and Dyson, J. (2001) *Against the Odds: An autobiography* (2nd edition). London: Texere Publishing.

Cox, G. (2005) *The Cox Review of Creativity in Business*. London: HM Treasury.

Cross, N. (2011) *Design Thinking: Understanding how designers think and work*. Oxford: Berg.

Cross, N. (2021) *Engineering Design Methods: Strategies for product design* (5th edition). Chichester: Wiley.

Csikszentmihalyi, M. (1996) *Creativity: The psychology of discovery and invention.* New York: Harper Collins.

Design Council (2023) *The Double Diamond. A universally accepted depiction of the design process.* Available at: https://www.designcouncil.org.uk/our-resources/the-double-diamond/#msdynttrid=LY_8W1rdBldoARdz-SImRL0cBI5C3i1xNX3Eufqfghw (Accessed: 3 July 2023).

Design Museum (2014a) *Profile. Jonathan Ive.* London: Design Museum. Available at: https://designmuseum.org/designers/jonathan-ive (Accessed: 3 July 2023).

Design Museum (2014b) *Profile. Paul Smith.* London: Design Museum. Available at: https://designmuseum.org/designers/paul-smith (Accessed: 3 July 2023).

Dodgson, M., Gann, D. and Salter, A. (2008) *The Management of Technological Innovation.* Oxford: Oxford University Press.

Dubberley, H. (2004) *How do you design? A compendium of models.* San Francisco: Dubberley Design Office. Available at: https://www.dubberly.com/wp-content/uploads/2008/06/ddo_designprocess.pdf (Accessed: 3 July 2023).

Dyson, J. (2021) *Invention: A life.* London: Simon & Schuster. Videos of chapters from the book available at: https://www.dyson.co.uk/james-dyson/invention-a-life (Accessed: 3 July 2023).

Fadell, Tony (2022) *Build. An unorthodox guide to making things worth making.* London: Bantam Press.

Ferguson, E.S. (1992) *Engineering and the Mind's Eye.* Cambridge, Mass.: MIT Press.

Fowles, M. (2004) The inception of technological innovation (Lecture). Department of Design and Innovation, The Open University, Milton Keynes, April.

Freeman, C., Robertson, A.B., Achilladelis, B.G. and Jervis, P. (1972) *Success and Failure in Industrial Innovation.* Report on Project SAPPHO. London: Centre for the Study of Industrial Innovation, University of Sussex.

Freeman, C. (1982) *The Economics of Industrial Innovation* (2nd edition). London: Frances Pinter.

Fullagar, P. (2015) *Incremental vs. radical: What's the future of product innovation?* Available at: https://www.designcouncil.org.uk/news-opinion/incremental-vs-radical-what-s-future-product-innovation (Accessed: 3 July 2023).

Gardner, H. (1993) *Creating Minds.* New York: Basic Books.

Gates, W. (2021) *How to Avoid a Climate Disaster.* London: Allen Lane.

Gladwell, M. (2008) *Outliers: The story of success,* London: Allen Lane.

Hambrick, D Z., Ullén, F. and Mosing, M. (2016) 'Is Innate Talent a Myth?', *Scientific American*, 20 September. Available at: https://www.scientificamerican.com/article/is-innate-talent-a-myth/ (Accessed: 3 July 2023).

Hands, D. (2017) *Design Management. The essential handbook.* London: Kogan Page.

Henderson, R. and Clark, K. (1990) 'Architectural Innovation: The Reconfiguration of Existing Product Technologies and the Failure of Established Firms', *Administrative Science Quarterly*, 35, pp. 9–30.

Isaacson, W. (2014) *The Innovators. How a group of hackers, geniuses and geeks created the digital revolution.* London: Simon and Schuster.

Kelley, T. with Littman, J. (2001) *The Art of Innovation: Lessons in creativity from IDEO, America's leading design firm* (2nd edition). New York: Bantam Doubleday.

Koestler, A. (1964) *The Act of Creation.* London: Hutchinson.

Lawson, B. (1980) *How Designers Think.* London: Architectural Press.

Merchant, B. (2017) *The One Device. The secret history of the iPhone.* London: Bantam Press.

Merriam-Webster Dictionary (2020) *Innovation.* Available at: https://www.merriam-webster.com/dictionary/innovation (Accessed: 29 May 2023).

National Advisory Council on Creative and Cultural Education (1999) *All our Futures: Creativity, culture and education*. London: Department of Education and Science.

Nayak, P.R. and Ketteringham, J.M. (1986) *Breakthroughs! How leadership and drive created commercial innovations that swept the world*. London: Mercury Books.

Ochse, R. (1990) *Before the Gates of Excellence. The determinants of creative genius*. Cambridge, UK: Cambridge University Press.

OECD/Eurostat (2018) *Oslo Manual 2018: Guidelines for collecting, reporting and using data on innovation* (4th edition). OECD Publishing, Paris/Eurostat, Luxembourg. Available at: https://doi.org/10.1787/9789264304604-en (Accessed: 22 July 2023).

Preez N.D., Louw, L. and Essmann, H. (2006) 'An Innovation Process Model for Improving Innovation Capability', *Journal of High Technology Management Research*, 17, pp. 1–24.

RIBA (2020) *Plan of Work 2020 Overview*. London: Royal Institute of British Architects.

Robinson, K. with Aronica, L. (2009) *The Element: How finding your passion changes everything*. London: Penguin.

Rogers, E. M. (2003) *The Diffusion of Innovations* (5th edition). New York: Free Press.

Rothwell, R., Freeman, C., Horlsey, A., Jervis, V., Robertson, A. and Townsend, J. (1974) 'SAPPHO updated – SAPPHO phase II', *Research Policy* 3(3), pp. 258–91.

Rothwell, R. (1994) 'Towards the fifth-generation innovation process', *International Marketing Review*, 11(1), pp. 7–31.

Rowe, P. G. (1987) *Design Thinking*. Cambridge, Mass.: MIT Press.

Roy, R. (1993) 'Case studies of creativity in innovative product development', *Design Studies*, 14(4), pp. 423–43.

Roy, R. (2009) 'Creativity and concept design', T211 *Design and Designing*, Block 3 (2nd edition). Milton Keynes: The Open University.

Roy, R. (2010) 'Products: New product development and sustainable design', T307 *Innovation: designing for a sustainable future*, Block 3 (2nd edition). Milton Keynes: The Open University.

Roy, R. (2013) 'Creative design', T217 *Design essentials*, Book 3. Milton Keynes: The Open University.

Roy, R. (2016) *Consumer Product Innovation and Sustainable Design. The evolution and impacts of successful products*. Abingdon, Oxfordshire, UK: Routledge.

Sawyer, K. (2013) *Zig Zag. The surprising path to greater creativity*. San Francisco: Jossey-Bass.

Schultheiss, F. (2018) *The Agile Innovation Framework: A Next Generation Innovation (Process) Model*. Available at: https://www.researchgate.net/publication/323110631_The_Agile_Innovation_Framework_A_Next_Generation_Innovation_Process_Model (Accessed: 29 May 2023).

Taylor, B.P. (2021) *The Double Diamond as an example of some challenges of attribution in the history of ideas*. Blog, 5 May. Available at: https://chosen-path.org/2021/05/05/the-double-diamond-as-an-example-of-some-challenges-of-attribution-in-the-history-of-ideas/ (Accessed: 28 May 2023).

Thakara, J. (ed.) (1997) *European Design Prize Winners! How today's successful companies innovate by design*. Aldershot, UK: Gower Publishing.

Tidd, J. and Bessant, J. (2020) *Managing Innovation: Integrating technological, market and organizational change* (7th edition). Chichester: Wiley.

Ulrich, K.T. and Eppinger, S.D. (2000) *Product Design and Development* (2nd edition). New York: McGraw Hill.

Utterback, J.M. (1994) *Mastering the Dynamics of Innovation*. Boston: Harvard Business School Press.

VanGundy, A.B. (1988) *Techniques of Structured Problem Solving* (2nd edition). New York: Van Nostrand Reinhold.

von Stamm, B. (2003) *Managing Innovation, Design and Creativity*. Chichester: Wiley.

Wallas, G. (1926) *The Art of Thought.* New York: Harcourt.

Wegener, F. and Cash, P. (2020) 'The Future of Design Process Research? Exploring Process Theory and Methodology', in S. Boess, M. Cheung and R. Cain (eds.) *Synergy – DRS International Conference 2020*, Brisbane, 11–14 August, pp. 1977–92.

Weisberg, R.W. (1986) *Creativity: Genius and Other Myths.* New York: W.H. Freeman.

Weisberg, R.W. (1993) *Creativity: Beyond the Myth of Genius.* New York: W.H. Freeman.

Weisberg, R.W. (2003) 'Case studies of innovation', in L. Shavinina (ed.) *International handbook of innovation.* Oxford: Elsevier, pp. 204–47. Available at: http://cachescan.bcub.ro/e-book/v06/580689_2.pdf (Accessed: 3 July 2023).

Weisberg, R.W. (2011) 'Frank Lloyd Wright's Fallingwater: A Case Study in Inside-the-Box Creativity', *Creativity Research Journal*, 23(4), pp. 296–312.

Whitfield, P.R. (1975) *Creativity in Industry.* Harmondsworth: Penguin.

## 2  Creativity and innovation in engineering, design, architecture, arts, and media

### INTRODUCTION

As I noted in Chapter 1, a main aim of this book is to identify factors, processes, and lessons associated with the development of successful products, buildings, and innovations, ranging from revolutionary innovations, such as the smartphone, to creative product designs , such as a piece of contemporary jewellery, and to reduce the risk of failures. Chapter 1 explained that these success and failure factors, processes, and lessons are derived from an analysis of examples and case studies of new products, buildings, and innovations specially written for this book.

In the book a 'successful' new product, building, or innovation means that it meets one or more of the following criteria:

- It is successfully introduced or built and adopted into use, preferably widely or long term.
- It is commercially successful in terms of sales, profitability, or market share.
- It meets the needs of end users and other partners after introduction or construction and/or satisfies other objectives, such as improving environmental sustainability.
- It gains recognition through design or innovation accolades, awards, or prizes after introduction or construction. (Although this would not normally be sufficient on its own.)

An unsuccessful new product, building, or innovation is one that fails to be introduced, or has limited success if introduced, or requires significant modification or redesign after introduction or construction.

In this chapter I will present short examples from different creative fields – engineering, industrial design, architecture, product and fashion design, media, and fine art. These examples illustrate some of the factors, processes, and lessons associated with the creation of successful new products, buildings, or innovations, or which resulted in a few failures. Some of these factors, processes, and lessons are summarised in Table 2.1 at the end of the chapter.

DOI: 10.4324/9781003354406-2

Chapters 3 to 7 then provide extended case studies of successful, and a few less successful, new products, buildings, and innovations to expand upon and verify these success and failure factors, processes, and lessons. Finally, in Chapter 8 I will try to identify general patterns of success and failure and summarise those patterns as guidelines for individuals, teams, and organisations attempting to produce – or for those teaching and learning how to produce – successful new products, buildings, and innovations and avoid failures. The approach adopted is like that of my previous book which drew on case studies of the evolution, introduction, and successful adoption of innovations in consumer products such as washing machines, domestic lighting, and television (Roy, 2016).

> **In boxed text – like this – following each example in this chapter I attempt to identify the main factors, processes, and lessons about creativity, design, and innovation that the example illustrates.**

## ENGINEERING

### Charles Draper – The Thames Barrier

The origins of the *Thames Barrier* lie in severe flooding events in 1928 and 1953 which resulted in deaths and flooded homes in London and major financial losses. These events led to a rethink of London's flood strategy which had previously consisted of building higher river walls and embankments. By the mid-1960s, a report by Sir Herman Bondi put forward the idea of a flood barrier with movable gates built across the Thames which allowed shipping to use the river and prevent the losses caused by flooding.

Many concepts were considered before one was chosen for development. The chosen concept of gates with a D-shaped cross-section that could rotate to allow or block the river flow and shipping was created by an engineer, Charles Draper. Draper was inspired by the D-shaped shutoff mechanism of a gas valve in his parents' house (Stoughton, 2019) – *a direct analogy*.

In 1969 Draper built a working model, which was just the beginning of a major project. There followed five years of mathematical and physical modelling, testing, and refinement by engineering and design consultants before construction began in 1974 and a further eight years before the barrier became operational in 1982. The Barrier's six main gates are 19 metres high and normally lie in recessed sills in the riverbed allowing river traffic through the barrier. Each gate is pivoted between concrete piers, which contain operating machinery and control equipment. When a flood threat is imminent, the gates are swung up through 90 degrees to a vertical position and form a continuous barrier across the river (Figure 2.1). By 2021 this had occurred nearly 200 times since the barrier was built (Bruton, 2017; Rendel Ltd., 2022).

Figure 2.1
The Thames Barrier with its D-shaped cross-section gates in closed position. 'Thames Barrier 03' by Andy Roberts licensed under CC BY 2.0. (https:// commons. wikimedia.org/wiki/ File:Thames Barrier 03.jpg).

**What does the *Thames Barrier* example illustrate about the factors and processes of creative design and innovation?**

There was a clear need and hence strong *motivation* to solve the problem of flooding in London.

A new way of *'framing'* the problem was conceived by a group of experts – an openable flood barrier rather than higher river walls – resulting in many barrier ideas and concepts being created and assessed.

The *creative idea* of rotating gates to allow or block the river flow was conceived by an engineer through use of a *direct analogy* – the mechanism of a gas shutoff valve – a form of *associative thinking*.

This breakthrough initiated a *major engineering design project* to develop and implement the rotating gates concept, itself requiring creative solutions to numerous tasks and problems.

### *Peter Fraenkel – River and marine current turbines*

Inventions can be inspired not just by physical objects, but by a knowledge of engineering, mathematics, or science. An example is the river and tidal stream turbines invented by mechanical engineer Peter Fraenkel. Fraenkel was working for the Intermediate Technology Development Group (ITDG) and considering the problem of water pumping in developing countries. While developing low-cost water-pumping wind turbines, he had the idea of an *'underwater windmill'* with the turbine's rotor placed in a fast-flowing river to pump water from the river for irrigation. Fraenkel's idea derived from his knowledge of fluid dynamics, namely that the power output of a turbine depends on the rotor diameter, the fluid flow, and the fluid density. He reasoned that since water was some 800 times denser than air, he could get a much higher turbine output from the river flow than from a wind turbine (Fraenkel, 1997).

ITDG therefore developed a river current turbine for pumping irrigation water out of the Nile in Southern Sudan. This had a three-metre diameter rotor driving a pump mounted under a pontoon. It proved capable of pumping 50 cubic metres of water per day and ran for nearly two years during the early 1980s until the project was curtailed by a civil war.

Subsequent developments of the underwater rotor idea by IT Power, a company founded by Fraenkel, radically changed the application from simple water-pumping river turbines to complex marine and tidal current electricity generating systems with the aim of creating an innovative major renewable energy source. IT Power in partnership with two other engineering organisations developed and demonstrated a 15kW axial-flow tidal turbine system at the Corran Narrows on Loch Linnhe, Scotland. This proved the concept to be viable, but also highlighted numerous technical challenges including the difficulty of reliably mooring floating tidal turbines.

A series of increasingly large demonstration tidal current turbines from 300kW up to 1.2MW output (Figure 2.2) were then developed by Marine Current

Figure 2.2
The 1.2 MW commercial SeaGen tidal stream generator, installed in Strangford Narrows in Northern Ireland in 2008, with blades raised for maintenance. 'SeaGen tidal power plant, Strangford, County Down, Northern Ireland, June 2011' by Ardfern licensed under CC BY-SA 3.0. (https://commons. wikimedia.org/ wiki/File:SeaGen, _Strangford, _June_2011_(02)).

Turbines (MCT), another company founded by Fraenkel, working with major engineering consortia (Fraenkel, 2007). The technology is becoming the basis of a commercially viable *non-intermittent* renewable energy source – alongside offshore wind turbines – pioneered by Atlantis Energy, which took over MCT from Siemens in 2015. A large-scale tidal stream system was installed by Atlantis in 2016 off the north coast of Scotland to demonstrate the technology's technical and commercial viability. By 2020 the project's four undersea turbines had delivered 37GWh of electricity to the National Grid with several other tidal stream systems under development, construction, or completion. The technology can therefore be considered to have become a commercial innovation.

> What does this marine current turbine example illustrate about the factors and processes of creative design and innovation?
>
> Fraenkel's creative idea for an *'underwater windmill'* involved *transferring the technology* of a river windpump to powering the pump by harnessing water flow – another form of *associative thinking*.
>
> The idea depended on Fraenkel's *engineering knowledge* of fluid dynamics and wind turbines.
>
> A low-cost *prototype* was designed and built to *prove the concept*.
>
> This low-tech concept was developed over some 40 years to produce powerful, technologically advanced marine current turbines involving *large design and engineering teams* and consortia.
>
> Marine current turbines have still to be proven for robustness and cost-effectiveness against better-established, but intermittent, wind power technology. Nevertheless, the marine current turbine example shows that a *creative idea* may be developed over many years into a *radical innovation* in renewable energy technology.

## INDUSTRIAL DESIGN

### *Izhar Gafni – Cardboard bicycle*

Izhar Gafni, an Israeli craftsman and designer, whose hobby is cycling, designed the world's first *cardboard bicycle*. When interviewed for a video (Kariv, 2012) Gafni said, 'It has always excited me to take neglected materials and turn them into something completely different, something useful.'

He explained that the idea came to him when visiting a cycle shop and heard about someone who had made a cardboard canoe, 'this canoe made of cardboard was sitting in the back of my head … And suddenly it just struck my mind; why not make a bicycle out of cardboard?' (Kariv, 2012).

Figure 2.3
Izhar Gafni's
prototype
cardboard bicycle.
'I.G. Cardboard
Technologies
cardboard bicycle
at the Museum
of Science and
Industry' by
Marcus Qwertyus
licensed under CC
BY-SA 3.0. (https://
commons.
wikimedia.org/w/
index.php?
curid=30649522).

He was told by several engineers he consulted that a cardboard bicycle was impossible, but when he told his wife about the idea she said,

> I know you; you've got to try it. Or you're going to drive yourself crazy, then you're going to drive me crazy, then you're going to drive the whole family crazy, so just go ahead and try it (Kariv, 2012).

Gafni spent two years experimenting with and learning about cardboard as a structural material and made a rough prototype. By 2012, after three years work using computer-aided design and origami techniques, he succeeded in making a rideable bicycle from waterproofed and painted cardboard (Figure 2.3). He said,

> I've done a lot of things in my life [tackling different engineering and design problems]. And basically, I took everything I knew and focused on working with that material to accomplish what I wanted to do (Kariv, 2012).

The prototype adult bike weighs about nine kilograms and was intended to cost about £6 per unit to make. Attempts were made through a finance company and a crowdfunding campaign to develop the bicycle for production, but so far it only exists as a high-cost prototype rather than as a commercial innovation (Chalcraft, 2012).

**The *cardboard bicycle* provides several lessons about the invention, design, and development of an innovative product, but which failed to become a commercial innovation on the market.**

A *'big idea'* provided the context – Gafni's idea of using neglected materials like cardboard to make something useful.

A chance *external trigger* initiated the project – Gafni hearing about a cardboard canoe led to his idea of making a cardboard bicycle.

Gafni had *strong motivation* to undertake the project – Gafni's wife said he would 'drive himself and his family crazy' if he did not try to make a cardboard bicycle.

Gafni is a *determined, hard worker* and was undeterred by other engineers saying a cardboard bicycle was impossible.

Gafni had *relevant knowledge, skills, and experience* – he had knowledge of bicycles as a keen cyclist and professional experience of solving a variety of engineering and design problems.

Gafni rapidly acquired *additional specialised knowledge* by learning about the properties of cardboard through research and experimentation.

Gafni developed the cardboard bicycle through *sketching and drawing, computer modelling, practical experimentation* (using origami techniques), and making *prototypes.*

The product potentially offered *unique functions or benefits* as a cardboard bicycle could potentially cost little to make and be recyclable.

An innovation needs to be *affordable, reliable, and durable* to succeed – the prototypes were too expensive and potential customers were unsure how durable a cardboard bicycle would be.

There was a *lack of funding* to continue the development through to innovation, as attempts at commercial financing and crowdfunding did not raise the investment needed to produce a low-cost volume product.

### Jonathan Ive – Consumer electronics

Sir Jonathan (Jony) Ive was head of design at Apple from 1997 to 2019. From childhood Ive was fascinated with drawing, understanding, and making things.

In a radio interview (BBC, 2012) he said,

> What I love to do is draw and make stuff. [From seven years old] I was fascinated by drawing … when I drew it was to an end, to explore ideas, develop them and try to build them.

And when interviewed for a website profile for London's Design Museum (Design Museum, 2014a), Ive said,

> I remember always being interested in made objects … As a kid, I remember taking apart whatever I could get my hands on. Later, this developed into an interest in how they were made, how they worked, their form and material.

Ive and his team's work includes the original *iMac* (Figure 2.4), the *iPod*, the *iPhone*, and the *iPad* (see Chapter 3). Ive says that the brief for the iMac was,

> To try and design the best consumer computer we could … Early on we talked about designing a computer for *The Jetsons* [a 1960s cartoon TV series about an American family living in a future with robots and other high-tech gadgets]. Every detail is there for a reason (Garratt, 2002).

The colourful, partly translucent, egg-shaped plastic casing of the iMac represented a radical break from the grey or beige box design of personal computers and is an example of the so-called 'blobject' aesthetic of brightly coloured, flowing shapes current in design circles in the 1990s. Internally the iMac used electronics from existing Apple computers and was the first to provide USB connections as standard.

Figure 2.4
Apple iMac
G3 all-in-one
personal computer
1998–2003 with its
innovative egg-
shaped translucent
design marked a
break from the grey
boxes of previous
PCs. 'An iMac G3, a
personal computer
produced by Apple
Inc. from 1998 to
2003'. Alterations
by David Fuchs;
original by Rama,
licensed under CC
BY-SA 4.0. (https://
commons.
wikimedia.org/w/
index.php?
curid=98219515).

In the Design Museum (2014a) profile when asked what distinguished the products his team developed, Ive said,

> Perhaps the decisive factor is … the obsessive attention to details … Take the iMac … A detail example is the handle. While its primary function is obviously associated with making the product easy to move … Seeing an object with a handle, you instantly understand … I can touch it, move it, it's not too precious.

For the iMac, and for design more generally, Ive says he gets ideas from new materials and manufacturing processes. In the Design Museum (2014a) profile he said,

> Materials, processes, product architecture and construction are huge drivers in design. Polymer advances mean that we can now create composites to meet very specific functional goals and requirements … moulding different plastics together or co-moulding plastic to metal, gives us a range of functional and formal opportunities that really didn't exist before … Metal forming and … new methods of joining metals with advanced adhesives and laser welding is another exciting area right now.

After being knighted for services to design in 2012, Ive was interviewed for a London newspaper and said about the creative design process at Apple (Prigg, 2012),

> What I love about the creative process … is that one day there is no idea, and no solution, but then the next day there is an idea … which is solitary, fragile and tentative and doesn't have form. What we've found is that it then becomes a conversation, although remains very fragile. When you see the most dramatic shift is when you transition from an abstract idea to a slightly more material conversation. But when you make a 3D model, however crude, you bring form to a nebulous idea, and everything changes … It galvanises and brings focus from a broad group of people.

**What do Ive's statements say about the creative design and innovation process at Apple and more generally?**

*The background of a creative individual* is important – Ive had an interest from childhood in drawing, in designed objects, how they work, what they are made from, and how they are made.

An innovative design, such as the *iMac*, may arise from a combination of several sources. For example, *ideas current in the design community* (e.g., 'blobject' aesthetics), a design that expresses the *look and feel of a product* (e.g., *The Jetsons* cartoon series), and the availability of *new materials, components, and manufacturing processes.*

Sometimes creative ideas come after *incubating* or *sleeping on a problem* – Ive says, 'one day there is no idea, and no solution, but then the next day there is an idea'.

*Enabling knowledge, technologies, materials* (e.g., co-moulded high-performance plastics), *or components* (e.g., USB connections) are available and are known to the innovator. Ive exploits his knowledge of materials, product architectures, and manufacturing processes when designing.

*Great attention to detail design* is crucial to ensure the product functions well, expresses its practical and emotional appeal, and can be economically manufactured.

*Working in a team* within a *creative environment,* such as at Apple, where fragile new ideas can be explored and developed if promising, is vital for innovation.

Embodying a concept as *3D models* (physical and/or computer) allows it to be evaluated and developed individually and in a team.

## ARCHITECTURE

### Richard MacCormac, architect

Richard MacCormac was one of Britain's most eminent architects, having been president of the Royal Institute of British Architects and head of a major architectural practice, MacCormac, Jamieson and Prichard, with many prestigious commissions.

### St John's College, Oxford

One of the projects by MacCormac's practice was a new residential building, the *Garden Quadrangle*, for St John's College, Oxford, built 1991–94. In an interview about where his ideas come from, MacCormac said, 'What architects do ... is they acquire a lot of visual relationships that they have liked' (Parry, 1990). For example, when searching for ideas for the college building, given its postmodernist style, MacCormac had the image of a 'belvedere' (a structure designed to command a view) which he said was 'the crucial idea that stabilised the whole concept' (Parry, 1990). Such ideas that drive a design have been called '*primary generators*' (Darke, 1979). The belvedere idea came from images of places with a view that MacCormac admired, such as the Rialto bridge in Venice. As well as a central belvedere, the Garden Quadrangle has viewing towers at the top level of the building (Figure 2.5).

Figure 2.5
The Garden
Quadrangle,
St John's College,
Oxford, in 2009,
showing the
belvedere and
viewing towers
above the student
accommodation.
'The Garden
Quadrangle (1989–
93) by MacCormac,
Jamieson and
Pritchard' by
Steve Cadman
licensed under CC
BY 2.0. (https://
commons.
wikimedia.org/wiki/
File:St_John%27s_
College_Garden_
Quad.jpg).

### HQ and Training building for Cable and Wireless

Brian Lawson interviewed 11 eminent architects on how they design for his book *Design in Mind* (Lawson, 1994). One of the case studies is on MacCormac's practice and its creation of a HQ and Training building for Cable and Wireless. Lawson (1994, p. 60) quotes MacCormac on how the concept for the building emerged,

> At the beginning … the centre of the scheme was a circular courtyard … then we had this V idea going, in which the building opens in a V shape, rather like the wings of a bird … towards this wonderful landscape. Then suddenly I had this idea that the courtyard should be pulled into an oculus, a sort of eye shape, which would reflect the dynamic of the whole project.

MacCormac's account illustrates how ideas emerge from an individual and through team discussions and that the ideas may be based on *analogies*, such as a bird's wing, or geometrical shapes, such as an oculus or an eye. Such ideas then act as primary generators, helping to narrow the options for the creation of a design. Lawson (1994, p. 64) notes that MacCormac's designs are often driven by *geometry*, 'All our schemes have a geometric basis, whether … the pinwheel … the courtyard system … the tartan grid … or the circle.'

**What do these examples of MacCormac's architecture say about where he got the ideas that shaped his designs?**

Architects (and other designers) often use ideas, images, and forms from existing artefacts, geometrical shapes, etc., that they like or admire, to provide the core idea or concept that drives a design project. They may also make use of *analogies* to provide a core idea.

These ideas, images, forms, and analogies add to the *'repertoire' or store of knowledge and experience* of a creative individual.

Such core ideas and concepts have been called *primary generators.* Turning such ideas into a final design requires much work *usually involving a team.*

### David Marks and Julia Barfield, architects

The next two examples concern two architects whose firm, Marks Barfield, created innovative designs that involved a significant amount of engineering and may conventionally have been considered to be engineering projects.

#### Bridge of the Future

Architects David Marks and Julia Barfield entered an ideas competition to design a *Bridge of the Future* which could potentially span the Grand Canyon, with a brief that specified a link to nature. Their design was inspired by the vertebrae of a dinosaur skeleton they saw on a visit to the Natural History Museum, London (Figure 2.6 (a)) – a *biological analogy.* The bridge was conceived to have its main support on one side of the canyon and built from there to the other side without scaffolding (Figure 2.6 (b)). The design comprised triangular metal 'vertebrae' with forward-facing prongs linked together by tension wires, curved in an arc like the dinosaur's spine with a pedestrian walkway fixed between the triangles and services running where the spinal cord would be (Figure 2.6 (c)). The spine concept, created with structural engineer Jane Wernick, was only the start. Developing the idea involved exploring different configurations of vertebrae and methods of joining them together through sketches, drawings, and models until a workable design had been produced. The design won first prize in the competition with the judges commenting,

> This was the one we felt best expressed the theme of 'an image of the bridge of the future' … The brief referred to the world of nature, and the relationship between nature and the structure are explored well. The bridge would be a joy to walk over (Marks Barfield, 2023).

The design was created for the competition, so it was not implemented as a practical innovation in bridge design and engineering.

Figure 2.6
(a) (b) (c) 1989
competition entries
for a Bridge of the
Future which could
potentially span the
Grand Canyon, with
a structure inspired
by the spine of a
dinosaur (Marks
Barfield, 2023).
Courtesy of Marks
Barfield Architects
and Jane Wernick.

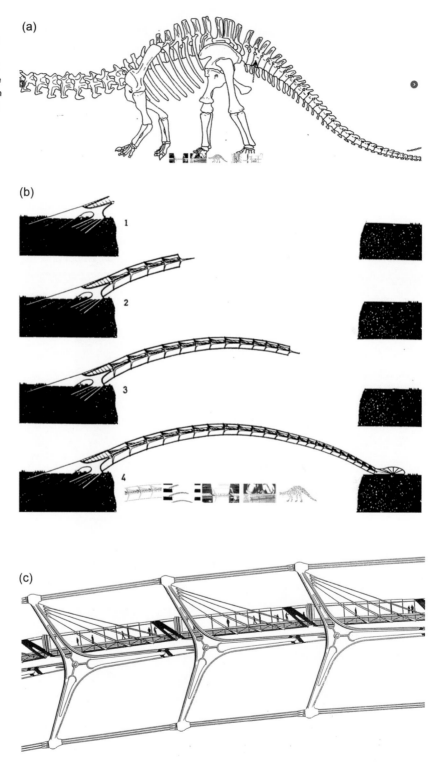

(a)

(b)

(c)

### The London Eye

*The London Eye* is an innovative design, also created by Marks Barfield Architects, that was conceived and built to celebrate the advent of the Year 2000.

In the run up the Millennium the press called for ways to celebrate the event and various landmarks and monuments were proposed. David Marks and Julia Barfield felt that the construction should be symbolic of the transition from the 20th to the 21st century. 'Their vision was to create a beautiful structure that would allow people to see one of the world's greatest cities from a new perspective' with a wheel 'representing the turning of the century and as a universally recognised symbol of time and regeneration' (British Airways, 2023).

Turning the concept into reality took the architects seven years, required the establishment of a dedicated company, and involved many people and organisations, including finance partners, engineering consultants, and construction companies. The London Eye is the world's largest observation wheel and, like the Eiffel Tower, allows people to enter the structure and gain new perspectives of the city below (Figure 2.7 and cover design).

Figure 2.7
The London Eye or Millennium Wheel with its observation capsules. 'London Eye, London, England' by Diego Delso, delso.photo licensed under CC BY-SA 4.0. (https://commons.wikimedia.org/w/index.php?curid=35491680).

**What do the *Bridge of the Future* and *London Eye* projects reveal about creativity, design, and innovation?**

A competition or the celebration of an important event may provide the *starting point and motivation* for the creation of an innovative design.

Architects and designers are always on the lookout for artefacts and images that may provide ideas or inspiration.

The Bridge of the Future is an example of a concept inspired by a *biological analogy* – the vertebrae of a dinosaur.

Developing the concept of a bridge based on the vertebrae of a dinosaur into a design potentially capable of spanning the Grand Canyon involved an extended process of *creative thinking, 2D and 3D modelling, application of structural engineering, and experimentation.*

The London Eye was conceived as a wheel *symbolising the passage of time* from the 20th to the 21st century on which people could ride and get a new perspective on London.

Implementing the concept for the London Eye, including its novel passenger capsules, required a lengthy *organisational, financing, engineering, design, and construction project.*

## PRODUCT AND FASHION DESIGN

Many designers, including product and fashion designers, say they find inspiration by researching, observing, and sometimes modifying existing objects or images of animals, plants, or natural forms.

### *Claire Norcross, lighting designer*

Lighting designer Claire Norcross says that she gets many of her ideas for lamp designs from plants and natural forms. For example, her idea for the *Eight-Fifty* lamp occurred while dyeing a plastic cable tie resulting in an anemone-like design made from 850 ties, which became a bestseller for *Habitat*. Another example is the *Aikiko* lamp which mimics plant berries but greatly enlarged (Figure 2.8). Her ideas are evolved into practical products within the constraints of a commercial brief through sketching and 3D modelling to explore alternative concepts before selecting one for development. Her experience as Design Manager of Lighting at Habitat, as the founder of a lighting company, and through working with manufacturers, has given her an understanding of what can be made using different materials and production processes to satisfy the cost and other requirements in a brief (Norcross, 2023).

Figure 2.8
Claire Norcross's
Aikiko lamp for
Habitat created by
super-sizing plant
berries. Courtesy
of Claire Norcross
and Sainsbury's
Supermarkets Ltd.

**What characterises Claire Norcross's successful creative design process?**

Creative ideas, such as for the *Eight-Fifty* lamp, may occur (sometimes by chance) to an alert designer while *experimenting or playing with materials*.

The *Aikiko* lamp is an example of a design inspired by a *biological analogy* made into a practical product through the creative technique of *scaling up* or '*super-sizing*'.

Norcross's designing follows a typical process of translating ideas into products through *sketching, drawing, and 3D modelling*.

Norcross's concepts are developed to meet the *cost and production requirements* of a commercial brief by making use of her business experience and knowledge of materials and manufacturing processes.

### *Paul Smith, fashion and product designer*

The renowned British fashion designer, Paul Smith, wrote in an article about his work (Smith, 2007),

Figure 2.9
(a) Paul Smith shirt with signature stripe design, 2011. 'A striped shirt designed by the Paul Smith company' by Robert Sheile licenced under CC BY 2.0. (https://commons.wikimedia.org/wiki/File:Paul_Smith_striped_shirt.jpg).
2.9 (b) Paul Smith striped T-shirt, 2023. Photograph by the author.
2.9 (c) Mini car with stripe design for 2013 Design Museum exhibition 'Hello My Name is Paul Smith'. Photograph by the author.

(a)                                      (b)

(c)

> I find inspiration in everything: I just have these magpie eyes … I can pick up on something and it'll go through some obscure mental process and turn into an idea for a suit or shirt or fashion show or shop window.

In an interview for a Design Museum profile Smith said (Design Museum, 2014b),

> Literally anything can spark off an idea. I keep track of the countless images and ideas that come into my head with a digital camera and a notebook … that

reflects how I find inspiration from observing … We are famous for … our stripes which are all developed in our design studio [Figures 2.9 (a)–(c)] …We develop our stripes by winding coloured yarn around cardboard which slowly builds up to create a stripe.

Smith was knighted in 2000 for services to the fashion industry.

**What do Paul Smith's statements illustrate about creative design and new product development?**

*Observing, recording, and making use of anything he sees,* using his 'magpie eyes', a camera, and notebook, inspires him with direct or indirect images and ideas for new designs.

Smith says the mental process he goes through to move from a source of inspiration to a specific idea or concept for a product or display seems mysterious.

*A successful design concept,* such as coloured stripes, may be applied to create *a range or diversity of new products* (Figures 2.9 (a)–(c)).

## FILMMAKING

### Ridley Scott, film director
*The origins of* Alien

The 1979 film *Alien* directed by Ridley Scott is one of the most influential science fiction films ever made. An account of the people, ideas, and influences that eventually resulted in *Alien* is the subject of a documentary film *Memory: The Origins of Alien* (2019).

*Memory* traces the beginnings of the film to a partial science fiction script written in 1971 by Daniel O'Bannon, whose ideas came from his consumption from childhood of science fiction and horror comics and films. He was also fascinated by the hatching of cicadas from nymphs that live underground for years. Other influences include Ridley Scott meeting the Swiss artist H.R. Giger for an unrealised film version of the science fiction story *Dune*.

*Alien's* producer had come up with the idea that an alien creature could enter a spaceship from an unexplored moon by impregnating one of the crew. Giger was then responsible for the design of the impregnating creature and early designs of the baby alien that hatched inside and burst out of the chest of one of the spaceship's crew in the film's most famous scene. This horrific scene was first envisaged in a drawing by O'Bannon in his partial script for the film that became *Alien*.

The director Ridley Scott had pointed Giger to the artist Francis Bacon's *Three Studies for Figures at the Base of a Crucifixion* for inspiration. However, Giger's baby alien had to be redesigned by one of the film's technicians to make the 'chest burster' scene technically feasible. Giger went on to design the slime-dripping adult alien that terrorises the ship.

These are only some of the multiple influences on the finished film identified in the *Memory* documentary and in many reviews and studies of *Alien*. O'Bannon later said, 'I didn't steal *Alien* from anybody. I stole it from everybody!' (McIntee, 2005). Other influences are said to include Egyptian art and architecture and the radical politics of the 1970s. What is apparent is the collective effort, not just of O'Bannon, Scott, and Giger but of many others within and outside of the film's team, which led to its creation and realisation. The key contributors include the studio *20th Century Fox* that financed the film and insisted on many changes to the script before commencing production. *Alien's* commercial and critical suc-cess led to the production of three sequels over the following 18 years.

> **What lessons may be learned about the creative process which resulted in the highly successful film *Alien*?**
>
> Creative individuals, like O'Bannon, are inspired by *childhood and early inter-ests* and say they *'steal' ideas from many sources*.
>
> Making a film like *Alien* involved the bringing together of *multiple influences and inspirations* filtered through many people working individually and col-lectively over a long period.
>
> Translating a *creative concept*, such as the alien chest burster scene, into a practical form may involve *technical design skills* different from a those of an artist.
>
> Such films need many *million dollars of finance* from a studio (investors or other sources) who must be convinced that the film is likely to be a commercial success. If successful, the film may be followed by series of sequels.

### Darren Walsh, advertising

Advertising agency people are sometimes called 'creatives' because of the eye-catching and memorable advertisements they (sometimes) create.

An example is the *Compare the Meerkat* advertising campaign for the com-parethemarket.com price comparison website business, created by the multiple award-winning film director Darren Walsh, first shown on television in 2009. The adverts created and directed by Walsh feature Aleksandr Orlov, a Russian meerkat character, portrayed as the founder of *comparethemeerkat.com* with his family and friends. The campaign originally centred on Orlov's frustration over the confusion between his website and the similar sounding *comparethemarket. com* website. This clever play on words and the amusing meerkat characters arose because market research conducted for the brief indicated consumers did not recall the 'market' part of comparethemarket.com brand. A brainstorming session around the name Compare the Market led to the idea of 'meerkat' characters voiced in a Russian accent (Patterson et al., 2013). Walsh says,

> The original idea came … from the ad agency … 'if you say Compare the Market in a dodgy Russian accent it sounds a bit like meerkat' … I thought 'This has the potential to be completely off the wall and hilarious'. I started coming up with the back story for a Russian meerkat (Walsh, 2015).

The Compare the Meerkat campaign won a silver and three gold awards at the 2010 British Television Advertising Awards. Aleksandr has hundreds of thousands of Facebook followers and his catchphrase 'simples' has entered the language. Following the original advertisements comparethemarket.com became the fourth most visited insurance website in the UK and the site's overall sales doubled. The original adverts were followed by a series, also directed by Walsh, featuring Aleksandr and different meerkat characters.

**What does the *Compare the Meerkat* campaign illustrate about creativity, for example in advertising?**

In advertising *market research* is an important starting point to understand consumers and what might be an effective form of communication.

*Brainstorming* in a group may sometimes result in a worthwhile original idea.

For the advertising campaign Walsh applied his creative skills developed through his *long experience of successful filmmaking*. He transformed the 'meerkat' idea, through humorous use of wordplay, unforgettable characters, images, and names, to create a highly effective and memorable message.

## FINE ART

### Grayson Perry, contemporary artist and broadcaster

In a radio programme about creativity (BBC, 2010) the Turner Prize winning artist Grayson Perry, best known for his fine art ceramics (Figure 2.10), tapestries, and television work emphasised the importance of constantly looking at the world around him for ideas, saying,

> The important thing is to feed yourself – looking, looking, looking … Most of the time creating is drudgery, looking through books, listening to radio, and 'dibbing' [fishing by allowing the bait to bob and dip on the surface].

In another interview, for a television programme (BBC, 2011), Perry also stressed the importance of sketching to artistic creativity by saying, 'One of the most

Figure 2.10
Grayson
Perry's *Idealised*
*Heterosexual*
*Couple* vase for the
National Portrait
Gallery, 'Who Are
You' exhibition,
2014. Photograph
by the author.

important parts of my business is sketchbooks. This is my kind of ideas and doodles and what I work on slightly pissed in front of the telly.'

Perry was knighted for services to the arts in 2023.

### What do the quotes from Grayson Perry say about how to be creative?

Perry stresses the importance for (artistic) creativity of *saturating the mind with images and information* from many sources by constantly *looking, listening, and observing*. (Paul Smith wrote similarly about his 'magpie eyes' to provide material for his product and fashion designs.)

*Sketching* is a key visual medium for artists (as well as for designers and architects) to record, explore, and develop creative ideas.

Notes, doodles, and sketches provide the ideas for current projects as well as providing *a store in the mind or on paper* for projects to come.

### *Barbara Hepworth, sculptor and Ben Nicholson, painter*

Inspiration is, of course, crucial for artists and there are numerous accounts of where such individuals get their ideas from. But sometimes the origin of an important new idea is unclear (or unrecorded) as was the case for a breakthrough made by sculptor Barbara Hepworth in 1931–2.

A biography of Hepworth and other artists, designers, and architects who lived in and around Hampstead, north London in the 1930s describes what happened (McLean, 2020, p. 26),

> [Barbara] decided to pierce a hole in a small abstract sculpture made of pink alabaster now known as Pierced Form [1932]. She described the act of piecing the delicate pink stone as a moment of intense pleasure … A review of Henry Moore's work had somehow given her the idea, and Moore, in turn, was inspired by her pierced form … By opening up sculptural form to involve interior space Hepworth transformed twentieth-century sculpture. She said later that the ten-inch sculpture formed the basis of all her work.

Before 1931, Moore had been carving sculptures of human figures and other objects that Hepworth, who met Moore at art school, would have known about. Perhaps she remembered a 1930 head by Moore in which the eyes were a round hole. Or touring the Yorkshire countryside with her father as child, she would have observed holes in rocks and stones. After Hepworth's *Pierced Form*, Moore and Hepworth began to produce sculptures with holes in them (such as Hepworth's *Makutu* in Figure 2.11). The idea of pierced forms became a *primary generator* for both artists lasting for the rest of their lives.

Figure 2.11
Barbara Hepworth,
*Makutu*, 1969–70,
St Ives. Photograph
by the author.

Barbara's collaborator and future husband Ben Nicholson also had a key moment of inspiration soon after Pierced Form. According to Mclean's research on Hepworth and Nicholson (McLean, 2020, p. 42),

> Ben had the most important breakthrough of his career in Paris in December 1933. He was incising a piece of board covered in some 'kind of plaster preparation' and by accident 'a piece came out where lines crossed'. Instead of feeling frustration, he was interested in the different planes and 'developed this lower idea further'. This became his first 'relief'. He said later that he had been ready for the accident … at that moment.

This account lends support to Pasteur's statement in an 1854 lecture that, 'in the fields of observation chance favours only the prepared mind'. Nicholson's further development of his white abstract reliefs, McLean says, were probably inspired by Le Corbusier's white painted villas in Paris and a visit to Piet Mondrian's studio where he saw Mondrian's geometric abstract paintings.

### What do the examples of Hepworth, Moore, and Nicholson illustrate about creativity?

An idea (a hole in a sculpture) may be *transferred from one work to another*, perhaps subconsciously.

*Chance* may be the source of a new idea (a 2D artwork accidentally becoming a 3D relief). Creative individuals are *open to chance discoveries* to provide new ideas.

A breakthrough idea (holes in sculptures, relief paintings) may become the *primary generator* or *signature style* for further works by the original artist and others that follow.

There are often *multiple influences and sources of inspiration* which combine to lead to important new ideas. *Social groups* of creative individuals, artists, architects, writers, etc. *cross-fertilise and inspire each other*.

## FACTORS, PROCESSES, AND LESSONS FOR SUCCESSFUL CREATIVE DESIGN AND INNOVATION

As I noted at the beginning of Chapter 1 and this chapter, an aim of this book is to identify factors, processes, and lessons associated with the creation of successful products, buildings, and innovations, that when lacking may result in limited success or failure.

Table 2.1 below lists a few of these factors and processes illustrated by the boxed 'lessons' provided by the examples in this chapter. *Only a few of the many possible factors, processes, and lessons and their supporting exam-*

*ples are presented in Table 2.1.* Chapter 8 will provide a full analysis of factors, processes, and lessons for successful and unsuccessful creative design and innovation based on the examples in this chapter and the extended case studies in Chapters 3 to 7.

*Table 2.1* **Some factors, processes, and lessons for successful creative design and innovation illustrated by selected examples from this chapter**

| FACTOR/PROCESS/LESSON | EXAMPLE(S) |
| --- | --- |
| PERSONAL | |
| The *background* of a creative individual is often significant. | *Jony Ive*, designer of Apple products, had an interest from childhood in drawing, designed objects, how they work, and how they are made. <br> *O'Bannon*, author of the original *Alien* script, had a childhood interest in hatching of cicadas, science fiction, and horror comics and films. |
| To innovate creative individuals must be *motivated* and prepared to *work hard* often over long periods. | *Gafni* was highly motivated and determined to make a cardboard bicycle, despite the difficulties. |
| The individual, team, or organisation has a '*repertoire*' of relevant *knowledge, skills, and experience.* | *Fraenkel*, originator of the marine current turbine, had engineering knowledge of fluid dynamics and wind turbines. <br> *Gafni* had knowledge and experience of cycling and solving a variety of engineering and design problems. <br> *MacCormac's* store of knowledge, images, and experience provide him with ideas and forms to inspire his architectural designs. |
| ORGANISATIONAL | |
| If the innovation mainly takes place within an organisation, it has a *culture, people, and management* that supports creativity and innovation. | *Ive* worked at Apple, a company with leadership and management committed to the creation of innovative, elegant, and usable products. |
| Developing an idea or concept into an innovation almost always requires *collaboration and teamwork.* | *Ive* works with his design and engineering teams to develop ideas and concepts into innovative products. <br> *Marks Barfield* established a dedicated company to develop the London Eye which coordinated the work of many people and organisations on the project. |

*Table 2.1* (Continued)

| FACTOR/PROCESS/LESSON | EXAMPLE(S) |
|---|---|
| CONTEXTUAL | |
| Essential *enabling technologies* (technologies or systems that enable an innovation to be developed and adopted) are available and sufficiently developed. | *Ive* has knowledge of materials and manufacturing processes, which enabled Apple products to be designed and made in new ways and in new material combinations. |
| THE CREATIVE DESIGN AND INNOVATION PROCESS | |
| Sometimes the process starts with a *big idea* or *primary generator* that drives the idea or solution based on the creator's or team's philosophy, preferences, images, or preferred materials. | *Gafni* was interested in using neglected materials to make useful things. He had the idea for a cardboard bicycle after hearing about a cardboard canoe. *MacCormac's* architecture is often driven by admired products, buildings, shapes, and analogies. *Marks Barfield's* London Eye was conceived as an observation wheel symbolising the turning of the Millennium and providing a new perspective on the city. |
| Often ideas and solutions are created by *associative thinking*, including – *adapting* or developing existing ideas or solutions, *transferring* ideas and solutions between different fields, using *analogies*, or *combining* ideas or solutions from different fields. | *Fraenkel's* idea for an 'underwater windmill' involved transferring wind pump technology to using water flow to power a pump. *MacCormac's* Cable & Wireless building form was inspired by the geometry of the eye. *Draper's* idea of rotating gates for the Thames Barrier was created by a direct analogy – how a gas stopcock works. *Marks Barfield's* Bridge of the Future was inspired by a biological analogy – a dinosaur spine. |
| Several *forms of representation* are typically involved in the creative design and innovation process. The availability of sufficient *finance* is crucial for innovation. | The design and development of *most of the examples of products, buildings, fashion, media, and art* in this chapter involved sketching, drawing, modelling, and prototyping. The successful products, buildings, and innovations had sufficient funding for development and introduction; those which did not (e.g., Gafni's cardboard bicycle) did not become innovations. |
| THE INNOVATION ITSELF | |
| Innovations that are to be adopted or used by others should offer one or more *unique functions, features, or benefits* not provided by existing artefacts or systems. | *Fraenkel's* tidal turbines are a *non-intermittent* renewable energy system, unlike wind, but for widespread adoption must be proven competitively economic and robust. *Gafni's* cardboard bicycle was conceived as being cheap and recyclable but could not be made sufficiently durable and affordable compared to conventional bicycles. |

*(Continued)*

Table 2.1 (Continued)

| FACTOR/PROCESS/LESSON | EXAMPLE(S) |
|---|---|
| If consumer facing, the innovation is *aesthetically attractive, easy to use*, and designed for both *functional and emotional appeal*. | *Ive's* Apple products, such as the iMac, aim to achieve all these benefits. |
| CONTINUING INNOVATION | |
| *Building on and improving a design or innovation* with further new products or innovations is important for continued success. | *Fraenkel* was involved in developing many generations of increasingly powerful marine current turbines.<br>*Smith* exploits his striped designs in a variety of products.<br>*Ridley Scott's Alien* led to three film sequels.<br>*Hepworth and Nicholson* produced a lifetime work of pierced sculptures and relief paintings that followed their original creative breakthroughs. |

## REFERENCES

BBC (2010) 'Grayson Perry'. *Creativity and Imagination,* BBC Radio 4, 6 July.

BBC (2011) 'Grayson Perry'. *Imagine,* BBC1 TV, 1 November.

BBC (2012) 'Interview with Jonathan Ive'. *Today,* BBC Radio 4, 4 May.

British Airways (2023) *British Airways London Eye.* Available at: http://www.design-technology.info/engineers/Engineering-London-Eye-press_pack.pdf (Accessed: 6 June 2023).

Bruton, E. (2017) 'The Thames barrier'. *Science Museum, London.* Available at: https://blog.sciencemuseum.org.uk/thames-barrier-guardian-river-product-mathematics/ (Accessed: 5 June 2023).

Chalcraft, E. (2012) 'Cardboard Bicycle by Izhar Gafni'. *Dezeen,* 12 November. Available at: https://www.dezeen.com/2012/11/12/cardboard-bicycle-by-izhar-gafni/# (Accessed: 5 June 2023).

Darke, J. (1979) 'The primary generator and the design process', *Design Studies,* 1(1), pp. 36–44.

Design Museum (2014a) *Profile. Jonathan Ive.* Available at: https://designmuseum.org/designers/jonathan-ive (Accessed: 3 July 2023).

Design Museum (2014b) *Profile. Paul Smith.* Available at: https://designmuseum.org/designers/paul-smith (Accessed: 3 July 2023).

Fraenkel, P. (1997) *Water pumping devices.* London: Intermediate Technology Publications.

Fraenkel, P. (2007) 'Marine current turbines: pioneering the development of marine kinetic energy converters', *Proceedings of the Institution of Mechanical Engineers, Part A: Journal of Power and Energy,* 221(2), pp. 159–69.

Garratt, S. (2002) 'The innovator. Jonathan Ive designer of the iMac', *The Observer Magazine,* 31 March, p. 20.

Kariv, G. (2012) *Cardboard bicycle* (Video). Available at: https://www.dezeen.com/2012/11/12/cardboard-bicycle-by-izhar-gafni/# (Accessed: 5 June 2023).

Lawson, B. (1994) *Design in mind.* London: Architectural Press.

Marks Barfield (2023) *Bridge of the Future* (Marks Barfield Architects). Available at: https://marksbarfield.com/projects/bridge-of-the-future/ (Accessed: 5 June 2023).

McIntee, D.A. (2005) Beautiful Monsters: The unofficial and unauthorised guide to the Alien and Predator films. Surrey, UK: Telos.

*Memory: The Origins of Alien* (2019) Directed by A.O Philippe (Documentary film). USA: Exhibit A Pictures.

McLean, C. (2020) Circles and Squares. The lives and art of the Hampstead Modernists. London: Bloomsbury.

Norcross, C. (2023) *Claire Norcross Lighting Designer*. Available at: https://www.clairenorcross.co.uk/claire2 (Accessed: 3 July 2023).

Parry, E. (1990) 'MacCormac Jamieson Pritchard', *Architects' Journal*, 19 and 26 December, pp. 28–9.

Patterson, A., Khogeer, Y. and Hodgson, J: (2013) 'How to create an influential anthropomorphic mascot', *Journal of Marketing Management*, 29(1–2), pp. 69–85.

Prigg, M. (2012) 'Sir Jonathan Ive: The iMan cometh', *Evening Standard*, 9 May.

Rendel Ltd. (2022) *The Thames Barrier*. Available at: https://www.rendel-ltd.com/projects/view/thames-barrier (Accessed: 5 June 2023).

Roy, R. (2016) *Consumer Product Innovation and Sustainable Design. The evolution and impacts of successful products*. Abingdon, Oxfordshire: Routledge.

Smith, P. (2007) 'Sir John Soanes Museum', *The Observer Magazine*, 2 September.

Stoughton, P. (2019) 'The Thames Barrier'. *Ebb & Flow*, 27 October. Available at: https://thetidalthames.com/2019/10/27/the-thames-barrier/ (Accessed: 6 June 2023).

Walsh, D. (2015) 'Aleksandr the meerkat', *The Guardian*, 'Bright Ideas' supplement, November, p. 17.

# 3  Revolutionary innovation

## The smartphone

## INTRODUCTION

This chapter will examine the creation of the smartphone, a revolutionary innovation, which has transformed how people live, work, and communicate. Indeed, a smartphone – a pocket-size mobile telephone and powerful computer offering not only phone calls and text messaging but internet access, email, music player, camera, games, GPS mapping, online entertainment, and hundreds of other applications ('apps') – has become an indispensable tool for living (Figures 3.1 and 3.2). In 2022 smartphones were owned or leased by over 80 per cent of people in industrialised countries, such as the UK and the US, and by 50 to 70 per cent of the population of newly industrialised countries like India, Brazil, and China. In the developing world mobile phones have been widely adopted given

Figure 3.1
User with two smartphones on a train, UK. Photograph by the author.

DOI: 10.4324/9781003354406-3

Figure 3.2
Smartphone user,
India. Photograph
by the author.

the lack of fixed line telephones, while smartphone adoption is increasing fast due to functions such as remote payment systems that they offer. For example, in 2022 nearly 40 per cent of Nigerians and 30 per cent of Bangladeshis had a smartphone (Statista, 2023).

The main case study in this chapter concerns the conception, development, introduction, and evolution of the Apple iPhone. Although the iPhone was not the first smartphone, it was the first to the world with a multitouch screen covering the phone's front face, which set the standard and design for smartphones developed subsequently by other mobile (cell) phone producers.

The iPhone has been described as a convergence product; 'a deeply collective achievement … a containership of inventions' (Merchant, 2017, p. 9). That is, it depends on a myriad of inventions and innovations developed since World War Two. Without these prior innovations (so-called 'enabling technologies') the iPhone could not have been developed and succeeded.

Mazzucato (2013, pp. 87–112) has documented how most of the technologies on which the iPhone depends originated in (mainly US) government-supported military and civil R&D programmes, with some then developed by the private sector, often helped by government procurement. They include the computer, microprocessors, liquid crystal displays, lithium-ion batteries, cellular communications, the internet, and the web. Mazzucato further points out that the technologies that make the iPhone so useful – GPS navigation, its multitouch display, and the virtual assistant Siri – were also originally developed with government support (Figure 3.3).

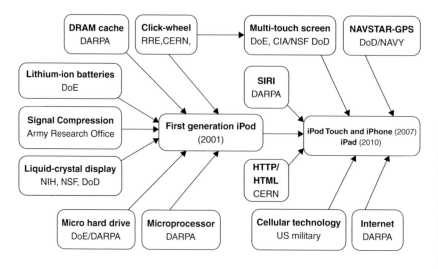

Figure 3.3 Technologies involving government agencies on which the iPod, iPhone, and iPad depend e.g, DARPA (Defense Advanced Research Projects Agency); DoE (Department of Energy); CERN (European Council for Nuclear Research) (Mazzucato, 2013, p. 109). Courtesy of Mariana Mazzucato.

### Structure of this chapter

Before focusing on the iPhone project, and the innovations Apple's teams of engineers, industrial designers, and managers created during its development – driven by Apple's visionary CEO, Steve Jobs – I will briefly discuss four of the many technological and product innovations which eventually led to the iPhone. These innovations – cellular radio communications; integrated circuits; the Motorola DynaTAC portable cell phone; and the IBM Simon smartphone – are the subject of the next two sections in this chapter. The rest of the chapter then discusses the iPhone project and some of the other systems on which its success depends. It is possible to read the iPhone case study alone, but that will miss the lessons of the other innovations.

> **As in Chapter 2 and subsequent chapters – in text boxes like this – I will attempt to draw out factors, processes, and lessons for successful creative design and innovation from the four prior innovations and the iPhone case study.**

## KEY INNOVATIONS LEADING TO THE SMARTPHONE

### Cellular radio communications

The invention, innovation, and continued development of cellular radio communications is one of the key technologies on which mobile and smartphones depend, starting with the first generation (1G) analogue systems and evolving in stages to the latest 5G digital networks.

The first commercial mobile phone call was made in the US in 1946, from a car fitted with a large radio transmitter and receiver. But until the innovation of cellular radio communications only a few users within an area could make calls simultaneously. In 1947, Bell engineers proposed the concept of a cellular network that divided an area into small regions, or cells, containing radio base stations, allowing limited radio frequencies to be reused by different users. However, the technology to implement these ideas only emerged in the 1960s and 1970s. In 1974, the US Federal Communications Commission released part of the radio frequency spectrum allowing cellular communication experiments to take place leading to a ten-cell commercial network in Chicago in 1977. In Europe, cellular communications were led by Scandinavian countries with the Nordic Mobile Telephony 1G analogue cellular system for car and bulky transportable phones introduced from 1981. This was followed in 1983 by the first US analogue cellular system used to make calls from the world's first portable cell phone, the Motorola DynaTAC 8000X (discussed below).

In the 1990s, second generation (2G) mobile phone systems emerged, including GSM (Global System for Mobile communications) in Europe and CDMA in the US, with GSM becoming dominant worldwide. 2G used digital transmission and enabled new services like text messaging and internet access (Agar, 2003). The advent of the smartphone, leading to the original 2G iPhone in 2007, transformed the mobile phone from a device for telephone calls and texts into a powerful handheld computer with multiple functions.

With the widespread use of 2G digital phones, the industry began developing 3G technology to provide the data transmission rates required for browsing the internet and downloading music. This made video calls, fast downloading of audio and video content, GPS location and navigation, and other services possible. Then 4G was developed to handle the growth of applications that required even faster data transmission rates, providing broadband-like speeds for services like video streaming and using social networks. The latest 5G cellular networks, introduced from 2020, provide up to ten times faster download speeds than 4G and can connect to up to a million devices per square kilometre. This 5G technology is suitable for new mobile services like virtual and augmented reality and can used for other applications like autonomous vehicles and remote medicine.

**What is the significance of cellular radio communications for the successful innovation of the mobile (cell) phone and subsequently the smartphone?**

Without the *enabling technologies* of cellular radio systems, the mobile phone and smartphone would not have been practical innovations.

*Radical innovations* in cellular radio technology from *1G analogue* from the 1970s, used by the first portable mobile phone, to *2G digital* from the 1990s enabled the development of the first smartphones with computer capabilities, including the original iPhone 2G.

*Continuing innovation* in cellular communications from *3G to 5G digital* allowed smartphones to offer new and improved functions, such as increasingly fast internet access and GPS navigation, making smartphones increasingly attractive and successful products.

### Integrated circuits

The *integrated circuit*, or *microchip*, was invented almost simultaneously by two American engineers – in 1958 by Jack Kilby of Texas Instruments and in 1959 by Robert Noyce of Fairchild Semiconductor.

Kilby had the typical background of a creative engineer; a teenager who tinkered in his father's workshop and built ham radios. He came to believe in the vital role of radio communications when he used his ham radio to contact customers of his father's utility company when they were cut off in a blizzard. He joined the US Navy and worked on repairing and improving radios. Isaacson (2014, p. 172) says Kilby had 'an insatiable curiosity about inventions and ... patents' and quotes him as saying, 'You read everything ... and hope that maybe a millionth will be useful.'

Kilby joined Texas Instruments (TI) in 1958 after attending a seminar where he learned about the difficulty of connecting components in electronic circuits as their number increased. Alone, while others were on holiday, Kilby started thinking what could be done with semiconductor materials other than making transistors. From his accumulated knowledge he realised that different electronic components could be made from a semiconductordepending on what impurities it had been 'doped' with, leading him to the idea that circuits could be created on a single slice of semiconductor material. He made the first 'solid circuit' from components joined by tiny gold wires arranged on a single piece of germanium and demonstrated that it worked. Although this prototype integrated circuit or 'microchip' with its complicated connections was too costly to mass manufacture, TI patented the invention in 1959 (Isaacson, 2014, pp. 173–4).

Robert Noyce's integrated circuit concept at Fairchild Semiconductor was based on silicon and stemmed from a different problem; silicon transistors could fail if knocked or exposed to dust or gases. A physicist colleague, Jean Hoerni, had the idea of protecting transistors with a layer of silicon oxide. Then in 1959, while showering, Hoerni had a breakthrough idea. If tiny windows could be engraved in the oxide layer and impurities diffused into the exposed silicon many transistors could be created on a single piece of silicon. In discussions with Fairchild's patent agent about commercial applications of Hoerni's idea, Noyce, and another Fairchild engineer, Gordon Moore, invented the first practical integrated circuit on a silicon chip without wired connections. They first had the idea that wires connecting several transistors could be replaced by copper strips printed on the oxide layer, then in further discussions realised (like Kilby) that different electronic components could be produced by diffusing impurities into the silicon windows. Noyce later wrote,

> I don't remember any time when a light bulb went off and the whole thing was there. It was more like ... if I could do this, then maybe I could do that, and that would lead me to do this, and eventually you had the concept (Isaacson, 2014, p. 176).

The almost simultaneous invention of the integrated circuit by Kilby and Noyce led to a protracted patent dispute between TI and Fairchild. But during that time the demand for microchips had grown enormously, there had been a dramatic fall in their cost and increase in the number of components on each chip. So, both parties agreed in 1969 that they would cross-licence their technology to each other while other suppliers would have to make licencing deals with both companies.

In 1968 Moore and Noyce left Fairchild to help found Intel (*Int*egrated *El*ectronics) a company where the next key innovation – a general-purpose microchip that could be programmed to act as a computer processor, the *microprocessor* – was invented. Isaacson (2014, p. 196) observes that, 'Inventions sometimes occur when people are confronted with a problem … At other times they happen when people embrace a visionary goal'.

Isaacson argues that the invention of the microprocessor was triggered by both a problem and a goal. The problem arose when an Intel team led by Ted Hoff was given the task of designing 12 different microchips for a Japanese calculator. This would have been uneconomic for Intel, so Noyce suggested simplifying the design. Hoff then had the idea of creating a general-purpose microchip that could be programmed to provide the calculator's memory, display, etc. Noyce and Stan Mazor went on to design what was the first microprocessor, a computer processor on a chip. In 1972 Intel released the first of a series of microprocessors that by the 1980s were essential to the growing personal computer industry.

Isaacson (2014, pp. 189–95) argues that the importance of Intel lay not only in its technological innovations but in its non-hierarchical organisational culture and management style. Intel aimed, for example, to treat its staff equally and allow them to solve problems collaboratively without always having to refer to senior management. 'The Intel Way' was an organisational innovation that set the pattern for other American technology companies to emulate.

### The ARM RISC microprocessor

A microprocessor for smartphones like the iPhone that was sufficiently powerful yet used little energy to function involved further radical innovation. The technology originated in a British company, Acorn, while its engineers were attempting to develop a business computer to follow its success with the *BBC Microcomputer* series designed in 1981 for a BBC Computer Literacy Project. Two of the BBC Micro's design team, Sophie Wilson (then known as Roger Wilson) and Steve Furber, were in the team working on the proposed business machine.

Sophie Wilson was born to a family of teachers and DIY enthusiasts. Her father built cars, boats, and furniture, her mother made clothes and furnishings. Young Wilson followed their lead, for example building electronic devices from scratch. After entering Cambridge University to study mathematics, Wilson switched to computer science and joined the Microprocessor Society and met Furber and the future founder of Acorn, Herman Hauser.

The Acorn business computer team were unable to source a suitable micro-processor. But while researching existing microprocessors Wilson found papers from Berkley and Stanford Universities on Reduced Instruction Set Computing (RISC). Inspired by a visit to an American chip design centre, Wilson and Furber began designing one of the first *RISC microprocessors* for the Acorn RISC Machine (ARM1), which was delivered in 1985.

Wilson later said in an interview that the ARM1 RISC architecture was largely created in her head and in discussions with Hauser and Steve Furber, who implemented her designs.

> First step is playing fantasy instruction set ... that does what you want ... Then you bounce your ideas off your co-conspirators ... then Steve is trying to com-prehend the instruction set's implementation. It's a dynamic between the two of us (Merchant, 2017, p. 158).

The extremely low power requirement of the RISC microprocessor was not part of its specification and was only discovered by accident while it was being tested. The RISC microprocessor's efficiency turned out to be crucial to its appli-cation in smartphones. By 1992 Acorn introduced a further innovation for its range of computers: a *System on a Chip* (SoC) which integrates most computer components on a single microchip.

As Acorn experienced financial problems, in 1990 it spun off its ARM micro-processor business into a new company, Advanced RISC Machines (ARM), in partnership with Apple. ARM designs microchips, often to a customer's require-ments, and licences the design to the customer and for manufacture. ARM's great success as the creator of microchips for smartphones and other mobile devices was the result of twin innovations: the RISC microprocessor and System on a Chip and its licence-based, collaborative business model. ARM was the UK's most important technology company, but was acquired by a Japanese conglomerate in 2016.

**What lessons about creativity and innovation can be learned from the innovations of *integrated circuits* and ARM's *RISC microprocessor*?**

The *family background* of individuals like Kilby and Wilson led to their early interest in electronic technologies, their degree and career choices, and eventually to creative ideas and radical innovations in their fields.

Such individuals accumulate the *deep (and wide) knowledge of their field* needed to create new ideas through their higher education, job, general curiosity, in-depth research, and experience.

The starting point and motivation needed for creative people to undertake a challenging task may be a *difficult problem and/or a visionary goal*.

Creative ideas may arise in a *'lightbulb moment'* sometimes when some-one is alone to think, or after sleeping on a problem. Or ideas may come through *thinking and working on the problem over time,* or occasionally by *chance.*

Turning radical creative ideas into practical solutions involves *persistence and dedicated work* usually involving other people and often over a long period.

Successful innovation requires strong *intellectual property protection* and may involve *organisational as well as technological change.*

## PRECURSORS TO THE IPHONE

Portable mobile phones, mainly for telephoning on the move, and smartphones that also provide computer functions, were innovations introduced many years before the start of the iPhone project.

### The Motorola DynaTAC portable cell phone

The first commercial portable mobile (cell) phone, the *Motorola DynaTAC 8000X,* was licenced for use and then launched in the US in 1984 following a decade of research, design, and development which occurred in parallel with the development of cellular technology and the first cellular networks. The phone was the result of the vision of Dr Martin Cooper. Cooper had qualified as an electrical engineer and then worked for many years at the US telecommunications company Motorola. Motorola had started making car radio receivers and walkie-talkie radios for the police and military before and during World War Two and then made two-way car radios, walkie-talkies, and televisions.

In 2015 Cooper gave an extended video interview in a series on technology pioneers for an electronic magazine *Scene World.* In the interview Cooper said that he was inspired to create a portable personal communications device by the two-way wrist radio first shown in the cartoon strip detective series *Dick Tracy* in 1946 (Cooper, 2015). By the early 1970s the telecommunications giant AT&T had developed 1G cellular communications technology but envisaged it for radio telephones fixed in cars. Cooper felt that allowing AT&T a monopoly and trapping users in cars was wrong, and the time was right to create a cellular communications device that gave users complete freedom. Cooper said, 'AT&T's vision was to make car telephones. People don't want to talk to cars. They want to talk to people' (Cooper, 2001).

Cooper felt that to compete with AT&T Motorola had to create something 'completely dazzling'. So, unusually for an engineer, Cooper started by asking Motorola's industrial designers to sketch what the device would look like. In December 1972 he said to Rudy Krolopp, head of Motorola's industrial design team, 'We've got to build a portable cell phone', to which Krolopp replied, 'What's a portable cell phone?' (NBC News, 2005). Different designers presented their ideas, which included phones with covers that slid or flipped open. Cooper selected a simple, small design and in 1973 gave his engineers the task of fitting the phone's components inside. However, this was before the availability of suitable integrated circuits and before small lithium-ion batteries, so the phone was built using individual electronic components powered by a nickel-cadmium battery, with the result that it increased in size and weight. A two-kilogram prototype was ready by April 1973 on which Cooper made the first ever call from a portable cell phone to his counterpart in AT&T (Figure 3.4).

Ten years of development through five prototypes followed, including patenting of an improved cellular radio system (Cooper et al., 1975), costing Motorola $100 million. Cooper commented, 'We had to virtually shut down all engineering at our company and have everybody working on the phone and the infrastructure to make the thing work' (Teixeira, 2010). The project resulted in the 1983 DynaTAC 8000X which weighed 800 grams and offered 30 minutes talk and 8 hours standby time. It cost $4000 (about $12,000 or £10,000 in 2023 money), ensuring it only had a limited market. Motorola's and other manufacturers' early portable cell phone designs were called 'brick' phones because of their size and weight dictated by their use of 1G analogue radio communications.

Motorola continued design and development to create some of most desirable mobile phones of the 1990s. These included the 1996 *StarTAC*, the world's first 'clamshell' phone, which echoed the communicator device in the television

Figure 3.4
Dr Martin Cooper demonstrating a 1973 Motorola DynaTAC prototype in 2007. 'Dr. Martin Cooper, the inventor of the cell phone, with DynaTAC prototype from 1973' by Rico Shen licenced under CC BY-SA 3.0. (https://commons.wikimedia.org/wiki/File:2007Computex_e21Forum-MartinCooper.jpg)

series *Star Trek*. In 2004 Motorola's engineers and industrial designers created the ultra-thin 2G *RAZR*. The RAZR became highly desirable and fashionable, selling over 130 million units worldwide and (as discussed later) had an influence on the iPhone project.

### The IBM Simon smartphone

The first mobile phone that combined voice calls with personal digital assistant (PDA) functions, such as address book, calendar, and the ability to receive and send emails and faxes, was the IBM *Simon Personal Communicator* introduced in 1994. The key innovation of the Simon was combining a cellular mobile phone with a computer. It also had a stylus-operated touchscreen and is considered to be the first smartphone.

The Simon was conceived and prototyped by Frank Canova, an IBM engineer. When young Canova liked tinkering with electronic equipment and built his own computers. He later graduated in electrical engineering before joining IBM, ending up in its advanced research team in charge of developing a small laptop computer. Canova recalls, 'One of the goals was to make a computer that could fit into your shirt pocket' (Merchant, 2017, p. 32). But the technologies to create a pocket computer did not exist in the 1980s. However, Motorola, then the largest supplier of mobile phones, was interested in working with IBM to combine their products. Canova argued that such a product should not be a desktop computer with radio communications, favoured by IBM, but be an easy-to-use portable device.

Fictional concepts for smartphone-like devices, such as the 1960s *Star Trek Communicator*, had existed for decades. Canova got support to develop his visionary concept by showing his manager items such as a calculator, GPS radio, and atlas and claiming he would combine them in a single device that was as easy to use as a telephone. Canova and his team worked extremely long hours for several months in 1992 – Canova said later he only managed to see his new baby while at work – to produce a working prototype based on phones provided by Motorola. The prototype had a positive media response which led to IBM providing further development funds and the creation and launch of the Simon (Figure 3.5). The device included early versions of apps such as maps and operated on an analogue cellular network as digital systems were still emerging.

The Simon, however, was not a commercial success. Only 50,000 models were sold before it was discontinued in 1995. The reasons included its price, at nearly $900 ($1800 or about £2200 in 2023); its boxy shape and heavy, bulky design dictated by the technology of the time; and a short-life battery. In addition, it could only send emails via slow dial-up, could not play high-quality music or video, had poor games, and the stylus operated interface was cumbersome to use. Canova later said, 'The technologies ... just barely allowed us to make this kind of phone ... The Simon was ahead of its time in so many ways' (Merchant, 2017, p. 30, p. 34).

Figure 3.5
The IBM Simon
Personal
Communicator,
1994. 'The IBM
Simon Personal
Communicator and
charging base' by
Bcos47. Released
into the public
domain.

**What can be learned from the pioneering innovations of Motorola's portable cell phone and IBM's *Simon* smartphone?**

Both innovations started from *big ideas or visions*. Martin Cooper was determined to realise Motorola's vision of a *portable cellular phone* to free users from AT&T's car-based cell phones. Frank Canova and other IBM engineers had the vision of an innovation that they hoped to achieve one day, 'a computer that would fit into a shirt pocket'. When the opportunity to work with Motorola arose, Canova had another big idea – a *combined computer and mobile phone* that was portable and as easy to use as a telephone.

Both innovations were, or might have been, *inspired by fictional depictions of futuristic technologies*. For Cooper, Dick Tracy's two-way wrist radio and perhaps for Canova, *Star Trek*-type communication devices.

Both innovations were limited by the *enabling technologies* available at the time. It was before the general availability of suitable integrated circuits, before the development of lithium-ion batteries, and cellular systems were 1G analogue. This meant that Motorola's prototype phone had to be larger and heavier than envisaged, although its size and weight was reduced using newer components before launch. The technologies needed to make the IBM Simon fully portable, functionable, and easy to use also did not exist when it was being developed.

Both Cooper and Canova were able to convince their company's management to devote *substantial resources* to developing their proposed innovations. To develop the portable phone and a related cellular system involved Motorola dedicating much of its engineering and financial resources to the project over many years. Canova was able to convince IBM management, through ingenious presentation of the idea, to provide resources to pursue his vision of a combined computer and mobile phone.

Both innovations were expensive, with limited functionality and an unattractive design when introduced. Consequently, the first Motorola portable cell phone only had a limited market, while the IBM Simon smartphone was a *premature innovation* that was discontinued soon after launch.

Motorola built on its portable cell phone innovation by going on to develop highly fashionable and successful phones through its application of *engineering and industrial design* expertise. IBM with an engineering-oriented design approach and a premature innovation failed to exploit its development of the first smartphone, which was left to other companies.

The Simon of 1994 was introduced too soon to inspire the iPhone. However, a product which combined a mobile phone and a PDA with stylus-operated touchscreen that was first described as a 'smartphone' was the Ericsson R380 released in 2000. This and other early smartphones – notably the Blackberry with its physical keyboard, that became very popular among business users, and Nokia camera smartphones, both introduced in 2002 – provided the technological and market context which eventually led to the iPhone. Both Blackberry and Nokia, which dominated the mobile phone market into the 2000s, continued to produce smartphones for many years after the launch of the iPhone series. But ultimately, they could not compete with the user experience, functionality, and fashionableness that iPhones and similar touchscreen smartphones offered.

## CASE STUDY: THE IPHONE

The Apple *iPhone* was not the first smartphone, but it was the product that started the mass adoption of smartphones leading to the revolutionary impacts of this technological and design innovation. The iPhone is also one of the world's most successful products. By 2023 it is estimated that 2.24 billion iPhones had been sold – 240 million units in 2021 alone – with more than 1.5 billion iPhone users in the world and 28 per cent of the global smartphone market (Ruby, 2023).

There are many accounts of the origins and development of the iPhone. Partly due to the great secrecy surrounding Apple's innovation projects, the accounts differ from each other. This case study draws especially on the book *The One Device* by Brian Merchant (2017). But so as not to rely on one source, I checked Merchant's account against other sources – Vogelstein (2008); Murtazin (2010); Isaacson (2011); Mazzucato (2013); Vogelstein (2017); Pierce and Goode (2018); Jones (2022); and Fadell (2022a) – and attempted to reconcile any differences. As I noted in Chapter 1, Merchant spent ten years researching the iPhone project. He interviewed managers, engineers, and designers involved in creating the iPhone inside and outside Apple as well as consulting publications and patents, historians, and journalists, and visiting museums, mines, and Chinese iPhone factories. Merchant found that even within Apple there were many accounts of how the iPhone project began and evolved, hence there is probably no definitive version. But that is not the main point of this case study as, whatever happened, the iPhone case provides many lessons about successful innovation.

To keep the subject within bounds, the case study focuses on the invention, design, and innovation process that helped make the iPhone such a success. It will include little about Apple's business strategy and management, and only briefly discuss the production and marketing of the iPhone at the end of the study, as there are many other publications on these topics (e.g., West and Mace, 2010; Galloway, 2017; Podolny and Hansen, 2020; Patel, 2020). Neither does it discuss the social, economic, cultural, and environmental impacts of the smartphone revolution begun by the iPhone, as this is also covered elsewhere (e.g., Plant, 2001; Goggin, 2009; Goggin, 2012; Rodriguez et al., 2015; Arndt and Ewe, 2017; Hackford, 2018; Antonia, 2020; Apple, 2022) and in the author's previous book (Roy, 2016).

### The iPhone innovation process
### The multitouch interface

Merchant argues that the real beginning of the iPhone project was the attempt in the early 2000s by an unofficial group of engineers and designers to create less cumbersome methods than mice and keyboards of interacting with computers. The group brainstormed many ideas. By chance one of Apple's engineers was testing a trackpad designed by a company called FingerWorks that allowed users with hand injuries to use finger tracking to operate a Macintosh computer. She suggested that the group should consider FingerWorks' innovative multitouch technology, which used capacitive sensing (in which the conductivity of human fingers changes the capacitance of the screen where touched) and software to simultaneously process multiple finger touches.

The team obtained a FingerWorks trackpad and focused on its key gestures to make them easier to use. However, the opaque trackpad could not provide a computer with a transparent *touchscreen*. The team explored the internet for ideas resulting in a mock-up, which projected a Macintosh computer's screen on to the trackpad covered with white paper, to simulate a computer touchscreen.

With improved software the mock-up could demonstrate many multitouch functions, such as zooming in on maps. When shown the mock-up, Apple's industrial designers including their head Jony Ive were enthusiastic, but felt it was too crude to show to Apple's notoriously critical CEO, Steve Jobs.

However, by 2003 Jobs had seen and was also enthusiastic about the multitouch demonstration and authorised its development into a touchscreen tablet computer. Jobs's vision for the tablet was 'a piece of glass he could write his emails on, while on the toilet' (Merchant, 2017, p. 94). Apple licenced FingerWorks' patents and in 2005 acquired the company and its founders. But the problem remained of how to convert the simulation into a transparent touchscreen. One of the original team, Josh Strickon, conducted intensive research into touch technology and came across a Sony portable music player whose capacitive sensing system he used to mock up a glass touchscreen. Strickon considered that discovery of the Sony device was crucial to the innovation of the multitouch screen. He said, 'I came from a research background where you look what is in the field … I am not sure how you innovate without an understanding of what was done before' (Merchant, 2017, p. 96).

**What lessons can be learned from the early stages of the project that led to the *iPhone*?**

*Constructive discontent* is often the starting point for creativity and innovation. That is individuals or groups being dissatisfied with what exists (e.g., computer mice and keyboards for human-computer interaction) and determining to create something better.

At the early stages the need for a creative team to explore the *search space* for alternative solutions, for example through group brainstorming, group discussions, and information searching.

Sometimes there is a *fortuitous or chance* discovery of a possible solution: the FingerWorks tablet with its multitouch interface.

A *rough mock-up* is often required to test the feasibility and demonstrate a novel concept: the multitouch simulation.

A *big idea* or *vision* is often required to drive the innovation process: Jobs's vision of a touchscreen tablet computer as 'a piece of glass he could write his emails on, while on the toilet'.

Further exploration of the search space may be needed through *'immersion' in existing knowledge* to find ways of improving an existing solution: developing an opaque touchpad into a transparent touchscreen.

Solutions (e.g., a usable touchscreen) often derive from *adapting and developing existing products or technology*: the Sony music player's touchscreen.

*The iPod*

As well as the external enabling technologies mentioned earlier, the iPhone builds on products developed within Apple over many years, especially Macintosh computers and their operating systems and the *iPod* music player. Tony Fadell, who led the team that developed the iPod, claimed 'There would be no iPhone without the iPod' (Merchant, 2017, p. 200).

What got the iPhone project fully started was Steve Jobs being convinced that, as mobile phones began to incorporate digital music players, the demand for Apple's most successful product, the iPod, would fall. The first iPod was launched in 2001 with the slogan 'a thousand songs in your pocket' (Fadell, 2022a, p. 92). By 2004, with the addition of the iTunes music store to download audio-visual material via Apple iTunes software using both Windows and Macintosh computers, iPods accounted for nearly half of Apple's revenue. By the time it was discontinued in 2022, it is estimated that 450 million of the iPod series (Figure 3.6) had been sold.

When interviewed for BBC radio in 2022 about the critical insight that made the iPod so desirable, Tony Fadell said, 'Everyone loves music … and usually everybody wants a lot more music than they could carry with them, that was "a thousand songs in your pocket"' (Fadell, 2022b). Being able to carry much more music than rival digital music players was made technically possible by Toshiba's development of a miniature hard disc drive that could store many music files.

Figure 3.6
Various iPod models, left to right: fifth generation, fourth generation, Mini, Nano, Shuffle. 'iPods I now own' by Chris Harrison from Augusta, GA, USA licenced under CC BY-SA 2.0. (https://commons.wikimedia.org/wiki/File:Various_iPods.jpg)

In his 2022 BBC interview Fadell also said he had a principle for successful innovative design,

> The principle for design is solve for people's pain … how do you bring technology and service … that meets a real need … something that I can't live without. So, it's beautiful, it's something you feel proud of … and takes away the pain.

In other words, a successful product must satisfy a genuine unmet need with a solution that not only provides unique functions but meets emotional and aesthetic needs too.

### The Motorola ROKR 'iTunes phone'

Apple's initial strategy to counter the threat to iPod sales was to partner with the Cingular cellular network and Motorola, which made a highly fashionable camera phone, the RAZR (mentioned earlier). Partnering was not something Jobs normally agreed to but accepted as he knew the head of Motorola and admired the RAZR's design. The result of the collaboration was the Motorola *ROKR* launched in 2005 (Figure 3.7). However, the original ROKR with Apple iTunes was not a success. It was a compromised design created by three different organisations. It could store far fewer tracks than an iPod and Apple did not want it to compete directly with the iPod, so accepted a design that was unattractive and difficult to use (Isaacson, 2011, p. 466; Merchant, 2017, p. 203). Apple discontinued its relationship with Motorola in 2006.

Figure 3.7
First generation
Motorola ROKR.
'Motorola ROKR
EM30' by Ged
Carroll licenced
under CC BY
2.0. (https://
commons.
wikimedia.org/wiki/
File:The_Motorola_
ROKR.jpg)

**What can be learned from Apple's development of the *iPod* and the *ROKR*?**

The iPod was a highly successful product series because it offered a *function valued by users* ('a thousand songs in your pocket') not provided, at least initially, by rival products. In addition, the iPod's elegant, user-friendly design satisfied *emotional and aesthetic as well as functional needs*. It set the standard for digital music players that ensured that the iPod series continued to be successful.

The original iPod was made possible by an *enabling technology* developed outside Apple: Toshiba's miniature disc drive that could store many music files.

The iPod's success also depended on Apple's introduction of a *service innovation*: an online music store (the iTunes Store) from which music could be downloaded on to the iPod using iTunes software compatible with both Macintosh and the more widely owned Windows computers.

The market for the iPod was threatened by competition from mobile phones with digital music players, leading Apple to partner with Motorola and the Cingular network to develop a phone that could play music downloaded from iTunes.

The original Motorola ROKR 'iTunes phone' was not a success because of its limited music storage capacity and its clumsy user interface and design compared to the iPod.

### Rival Apple phone projects

The ROKR experience reinforced the view within Apple that existing mobile phones were very badly designed. Apple had created the elegant, user-friendly iPod and so believed it could create a smartphone as good as the iPod and so capture a share of the huge mobile phone market.

The initial attempt in 2004 was to modify an iPod as a phone. But it became clear that the trackwheel interface that was so effective on the iPod (Figure 3.6) was difficult to use for a phone.

At noted earlier, in 2003 Jobs had a team trying to apply multitouch technology to a tablet computer (what was to become the iPad in 2010). But at the time the demand and uses for an expensive touchscreen tablet were uncertain and so Jobs decided in 2004–5 to apply multitouch instead to a smartphone. He said to the head of the tablet team, 'We're gonna do a phone. There's gonna be no buttons. Just a touchscreen.' Another member of the team observed, 'Steve had to give us that vision' (Merchant, 2017, p. 105).

Rather than abandoning the iPod phone Jobs decided to create two rival teams; P1 to work on converting the iPod into a usable mobile phone, and P2 to develop a revolutionary smartphone – essentially a miniature touchscreen computer operated by Macintosh OS X software adapted for a phone-size device. P2 was an extremely challenging and costly project, but Jobs felt the high risk was worthwhile for its high rewards if successful (Isaacson, 2011, p. 469). It took over two years for secret teams of Apple hardware and software engineers and industrial designers to realise Jobs's vision. The iPhone teams worked under relentless pressure with inputs from other technology companies who were not told what they were contributing to.

Much of the pressure on the project leaders and team members came from Jobs, who was an extreme perfectionist and believed seemingly impossible technological goals and deadlines were possible. Isaacson (2011, pp. 118–9) called these characteristics Jobs's 'reality distortion field', arguing that it came from a belief that he was a 'special' or 'chosen' individual to whom normal rules did not apply.

### Project Purple

When it became clear that an iPod phone was not going to be the revolutionary product he envisaged, Jobs and his senior managers decided to focus on the multitouch smartphone project, codenamed Purple. Tony Fadell, who had headed the iPod phone team, was made responsible for hardware development. The phone's software was developed by engineers experienced in the Mac OS X operating system (based on NeXTSTEP software developed by Jobs's computer company NEXT between him being forced out of Apple in 1985 and returning in 1997). These teams of about 40 engineers and designers, mainly men, managed over two years first to make the multitouch simulation operate as a fluid and intuitive interface, and then develop a multitouch screen for the iPhone.

Merchant (2017, p. 338) claims that the multitouch user experience was inspired by the gesture controls in the 2002 science fiction film *Minority Report*. The interface, including its screen icons, was designed through many brainstorming and software coding sessions to be intuitive and not to require a user manual. As Jobs set the vision of a smartphone operated entirely via a touchscreen, designing a virtual keyboard was another challenge. A standard layout of touch buttons would not fit the screen, so the team were given free rein to create new keyboard designs. Many designs were created but Jobs insisted that the phone had to be immediately comprehensible to users. So, the team had to develop software that enlarged QWERTY buttons when touched. This was the only element of the iPhone that was consumer tested outside the core team. Developing all the interface software, Merchant (2017, p. 337) notes, was 'a colossal amount of work'.

Developing the hardware, including the multitouch screen, radio, antennas, and wi-fi, was another immense task involving 40 to 50 engineers and designers and external suppliers of sensors and other components. The cost of developing the original iPhone is reported to be about $150 million (Vogelstein, 2008), an investment that only a company as profitable as Apple could risk and afford before getting any revenue from its innovation.

A major decision was taken to prioritise battery life by designing the first iPhone to be 2G rather than 3G compatible, as 3G communications would require larger, more energy-hungry microchips. Jobs and the industrial design team also wanted the phone to be as thin as possible, which meant that it could not easily be serviced or repaired. Despite these compromises, unlike other smartphones, the 2G iPhone could access the full internet (negotiated with its exclusive carrier AT&T) and had wi-fi connectivity.

An ARM RISC microprocessor with its low power requirements and the adapted OS X software enabled the original iPhone to function as a powerful touchscreen computer with a good battery life. The microprocessor was custom designed by Samsung working with Apple engineers. Samsung made micro-chips for the iPod and already had an ARM processor in one of its products (Merchant, 2017, p. 359). Since then, a succession of increasingly powerful RISC microprocessors have been used on later iPhone models.

### Industrial design

The industrial design group, under Jony Ive, had been involved from the start of the iPhone project as Steve Jobs believed that design was crucial to the success of Apple products. Jobs absorbed an interest in design from his father and Zen-like, minimalist design became one of his obsessions. But Jobs believed products created with this aesthetic had also to be usable, intuitive, and perfect in every detail, both inside and out (Isaacson, 2011, pp. 126–7).

Ive, who became head of Apple industrial design in 1996, shared Jobs's views on design. On the form of the iPhone he said, 'some of our early discussions about the iPhone centred on the idea of this infinity pool ... where the display would magically appear ... everything should defer to the display' (Merchant, 2017, p. 352).

The ID team sketched many design concepts, modelled many design variants, and tested a few working prototypes for usability. But eventually, at Jobs's insistence, the team produced a design dominated by the display screen like the product that was launched (Figures 3.8 and 3.9).

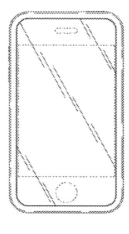

Figure 3.8 Drawing from the iPhone Design Patent (Andre et al., 2012). Courtesy of United States Patent and Trademark Office.

Figure 3.9
Original iPhone 2G,
2007. 'iPhone First
Generation 8GB'
by Carl Berkeley
licenced under CC
BY-SA 2.0. (https://
fr.wikipedia.
org/wiki/
Fichier:IPhone_First_
Generation_8GB_
(3677961514).jpg)

*Materials*

Both Jobs and Ive had long been keenly interested in the materials, such as plastics and aluminium, used in Apple products for their appearance, texture, and quality, and had accumulated in-depth knowledge about materials and their manufacture (Isaacson, 2011, p. 470).

Between announcing the iPhone in January 2007 and its public release in June, Jobs found that the plastic screen of his iPhone prototype had become scratched and decided the screen had to be glass. Following a last-minute request by Jobs to the head of the US glass company Corning, the strong, thin glass for the iPhone's screen was created in a few hectic months, using a chemical strengthening process Corning had originally developed in the 1960s (Isaacson, 2011, pp. 470–2). The phone's Chinese manufacturer then had to rapidly adapt its processes to accommodate the change (Cheng, 2015). By 2008 Corning's product had been named *Gorilla Glass* and is now used on most smartphones. Another last-minute change was to the iPhone's design, involving a switch from an aluminium to a stainless steel case to allow the glass screen to cover most of the phone's face, which also required changes to its electronics (Isaacson, 2011, p. 472–3).

Making last-minute design and manufacturing changes, such as switching from plastic to glass and aluminium to steel, is not recommended in product development projects but was achieved through Jobs setting others 'impossible' tasks and deadlines in his pursuit of product perfection.

### *Leadership and teamwork*

Steve Jobs has been mentioned many times in this case study and much has been written (e.g., by Isaacson, 2011) about his charismatic, extremely demanding (combining inspiration and fear), and visionary leadership of Apple, especially since he returned to the company in 1997.

One of Jobs's greatest talents was to conceive a big idea for a product and then relentlessly drive a project to develop it, via his senior managers and their teams and overseen by himself, until his vision was achieved. Jobs's vision for the iPhone was a smartphone operated entirely through a touchscreen. It was achieved involving enormous technical and design challenges and workloads, which Jobs with his 'reality distortion field' refused to believe were impossible. Nevertheless, the original iPhone and some of its successor models required a physical 'Home' button indicating that even Jobs was willing to compromise to make the phone usable.

Although Jobs is sometimes given the credit for the iPhone, it could not have been created without the dedicated individuals and teams inside Apple, and by outside suppliers like Samsung, that worked on the project. Merchant (2017, p. 378) observes,

> Steve Jobs will forever be associated with the iPhone ... But he did not invent it. ... Proving the lone inventor myth inadequate does not diminish Jobs's role as curator, editor, bar-setter – it elevates the role of everyone else to show he was not alone in making it possible.

Isaacson (2014, p. 480, pp. 486–7) comments more generally that the best technology innovators, like Jobs, are those 'who understood the trajectory of technological change and took the baton from innovators that preceded them', and that Jobs was especially creative due to 'his ability to bring together the arts and sciences when conceiving revolutionary new products'. Similarly, Mazzucato (2013, p. 93) argues that,

> Apple concentrates its ingenuity not on developing new technologies and components, but on *integrating* them into an innovative architecture ... its innovative product designs are based on technologies ... that are mostly invented somewhere else, often backed by tax dollars.

**What can be learned from the *iPhone* project, starting with Jobs's decision that Apple could develop a mobile phone as successful as the *iPod* to the product's launch?**

Jobs provided his teams with the *big idea* or *vision* of a smartphone operated entirely via a touchscreen. He considered that the multitouch technology being developed for a tablet computer (a previous big idea) could be used for a smartphone instead.

The iPhone depended on many *enabling technologies* developed over decades inside and outside Apple, the latter often with government support.

The attempt to create a touchscreen phone based on the iPod's trackwheel interface was eventually abandoned as unusable.

The touchscreen smartphone was a challenging, costly, *high-risk*, project. Jobs was willing to take the *risk for the potential rewards*.

The iPhone's interface and form were *inspired by several sources*: probably the gesture controls in the science fiction film, *Minority Report*, and definitely Jobs's and Ives's love of minimalist, intuitive, user-friendly designs.

To create the *form design* of the iPhone, the industrial design team produced many concepts and tested prototypes for usability, but finally decided on a design dominated by the screen to realise Jobs's original vision.

To create the desired *user-friendly, intuitive interface,* software engineers generated many design concepts for a virtual keyboard before Jobs chose a conventional QWERTY layout that he believed users could immediately understand. The virtual keyboard was one of the very few elements of the iPhone that was *consumer tested*.

Like most products the original iPhone involved *design compromises*, e.g., choosing 2G rather than faster 3G cellular communications for longer battery life, and choosing thinness over repairability.

A highly complex product such as the iPhone, requires *knowledge of materials and manufacturing* for implementation.

Making *significant design changes* to an innovative product at the last minute is likely to be risky and problematic and was only achieved for the iPhone through enormous drive and effort.

Jobs conceived and drove the iPhone project to completion through self-belief and force of personality. But developing the product involved *large teams* of hardware and software engineers and designers. They worked in secret for long periods under relentless pressure with essential inputs from companies outside Apple.

### Systems to make the iPhone into a successful innovation

The iPhone is not just a revolutionary product it depends on many other organisations and systems, what Teece (1986) called 'complementary assets', to succeed as an innovation in widespread use.

*Networks*

A mobile phone cannot function without a network carrier, so the introduction of the iPhone depended on at least one of the carriers agreeing to allow it to use their network. Apple negotiated with two US networks and eventually came to an exclusive agreement with Cingular (later taken over by AT&T) for users of the original 2G iPhone to access its network on two-year contracts and not to restrict the volume and speed of data transmission. This enabled the iPhone to access the full internet rather than the simplified version then available on other smartphones. From the introduction of the iPhone 3G in 2008 the product became available in many more countries and useable on different networks around the world (Jones, 2022). This had the effect of removing the restrictions held by the carriers on smartphone specification and design, network choice, and data use. As Vogelstein (2008) expressed it, 'the iPhone blew up the wireless industry', which previously had made their revenues by subsidising phone handsets to tie users to their networks.

### Apps

One element of the iPhone that Jobs initially failed to appreciate was the importance to smartphone users of third-party apps (software applications). The first 2G iPhone had 16 built-in apps (including Phone, Mail, Safari internet browser, Music player, Camera, and Google Maps). Jobs refused to allow the phone to include any apps not developed by or with Apple. However, he soon discovered that users demanded that the iPhone could run the growing number of apps available on other smartphones. Thus, for the launch of the 3G iPhone in 2008, Jobs approved the creation of an App Store enabling third-party apps approved by Apple to be downloaded on to the phone. Sales of the iPhone then really took off as users were able to use it not mainly as a phone, music player, and internet communicator as originally envisaged by Jobs, but for social media, entertainment, games, and navigation, as well as for almost every possible human interest or activity. For example, on my iPhone as well as the built-in apps, I have several health, travel, weather, entertainment, social media, navigation, and many other apps, including specialist ones for electric car charging and plant identification (see Figure 3.12). There are many activities that would be impossible without my iPhone, so having it with me most of the time has become essential.

The App Store, in which Apple took a cut of 'paid for' third-party apps, became a multibillion-dollar business, in the so-called 'app economy' (Merchant, 2017, pp. 166–8).

### Manufacture

The ability to manufacture a product as complex as an iPhone to high levels of quality and reliability in sufficient volume and at an economic cost is as important to its success as its technology and design.

There is not space in this case study to discuss the sophisticated supply chains that Apple began to establish in China and elsewhere under the direction of Tim Cook for the launch of the iPhone 2G, accelerating when Cook became CEO after Jobs's death in 2011. In 2022 over 95 per cent of iPhones were assembled in China (McGee, 2023), although companies in many other, mainly Asian, countries are involved in supplying components (Cheng, 2015).

To establish the system to manufacture the iPhone and other devices Apple sent product designers and manufacturing engineers to China to co-design production processes and spent billions of dollars on obtaining custom machinery to build the products. China offered Apple not just low-cost, plentiful labour but labour with specialised skills willing to work hard for long hours (McGee, 2023).

This can be seen as an example of a shift in emphasis, proposed by Abernathy and Utterback (1978), from product to process innovation as a product matures. Although the iPhone has evolved through many generations (see below), cost-effective operations assumed an importance in Apple relative to design and innovation that is said to have resulted in the company's head of design, Jony Ive, resigning in 2019 and working for Apple as a consultant before prematurely leaving the role in 2022.

The dependence on production in China has raised problems for Apple. By 2010 the Taiwanese contract manufacturer Foxconn's factories in Shenzhen, China alone had some half a million workers working under high pressure to make Apple products. When it emerged that several employees had taken their own lives, Apple suffered significant damage to its reputation to which it responded by attempting to make its suppliers more accountable for workplace conditions and helping to train workers on their rights (Merchant, 2017, p. 292). Apple's dependence on China has also made it vulnerable to geopolitical tensions as, under President Xi Jinping, China has grown increasingly authoritarian and estranged from the West resulting in pressure on the company to move production elsewhere, resulting for instance in a major planned expansion in India (McGee, 2023).

### Marketing

Apple's marketing and sales capability is another key element in the success of the iPhone, which has been discussed in detail elsewhere (e.g., Mickalowski et al., 2008; Patel, 2020; Fadell, 2022a, pp. 208–12) and so is only noted here. This capability is based on several aspects, including: the secrecy in which products are developed, thus creating consumer anticipation and pent-up demand; exciting product launches, at which Steve Jobs excelled and his successor attempts to emulate; and the immaculate design of the Apple stores.

Merchant (2017, p. 297) sums up what makes Apple's marketing and sales exceptional: 'the iPhone would not be what it is today were it not for Apple's extraordinary marketing and retail strategies. It is a league of its own in creating want, fostering demand, and broadcasting technological cool.'

### *Continuous evolution of the iPhone*

From the launch of the original 2G iPhone in 2007 to 2023, there have been 12 generations (iPhone 3 to iPhone 15) including 24 different models and 37 model variants with different, case materials, screen sizes and cameras, excluding variants with different memory capacities (Jones, 2022; Montgomery and Mingis, 2022) (Figures 3.10 to 3.13).

The iPhone is a prime example of continuous development to take advantage of fast-changing technology, respond to competition, and maintain sales. The evolution of the iPhone over 16 years has involved the whole spectrum of technical and design changes. These range from radical technological innovations, such as the Siri voice-operated virtual assistant and face recognition, to major innovations such as video calling, new operating systems, multi-lens cameras, faster processors, and high-resolution displays. Other improvements include incremental technical changes, such as tougher screens, water resistance, and improved batteries, and design variants such as redesigned casings and different colours. There are also lower-priced models to target markets dominated by rival manufacturers.

Figure 3.10
iPhone 3G,
2008. Photograph
by the author.

Figure 3.11
iPhone 6 Plus,
2014. Photograph
by the author.

Figure 3.12
iPhone 12 Pro, 2020,
showing some of its
apps. Photograph
by the author

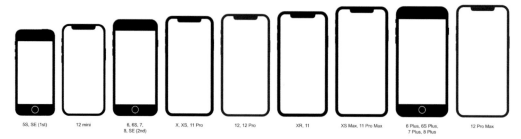

| 5S, SE (1st) | 12 mini | 6, 6S, 7, 8, SE (2nd) | X, XS, 11 Pro | 12, 12 Pro | XR, 11 | XS Max, 11 Pro Max | 6 Plus, 6S Plus, 7 Plus, 8 Plus | 12 Pro Max |

What might Apple do next? It is facing increasing competition from other smartphone manufacturers using Google's Android operating system, notably Samsung which in 2022 launched premium smartphones with folding or flip open screens, and from several lower cost suppliers. iPhones are beautifully designed, powerful, and reliable, have a highly prestigious brand image, and their customers are extremely loyal, but they sell at high prices and Apple lost its largest share of the smartphone market to Android phones from around 2010 (Edwards, 2014). Apple is therefore developing and introducing further innovations for its smartphones. At the same time Apple is developing radical and major innovations for its ecosystem of related products and services to continue competing successfully at the top end of the market, ranging from new generations of the Apple Watch to augmented reality systems and a 'spatial computing' headset to be available in 2024.

Figure 3.13 iPhone screen sizes from iPhone 5S (4 inch) to iPhone 12 Pro Max (6.7 inch). 'A comparison of iPhone sizes from the iPhone 5S to the iPhone 12' by Tboa licenced under CC BY-SA 4.0 (https://commons.wikimedia.org/wiki/File:IPhone_size_comparison.svg)

**What further lessons can be learned from what happened after the launch of the original *iPhone*?**

For an innovation such as the iPhone to succeed commercially and diffuse into widespread use, many other organisations and systems, or *complementary assets*, are involved to supply components; to manufacture, distribute, and sell the product; and to enable it to function.

Consumers may discover or create new uses for an innovation not anticipated by its originators. They may demand that the innovation supports those new uses, such as the functions offered by third-party apps, before they are willing to adopt it.

*Continuous innovation and development*, from radical new technology to incremental design improvements, is required to ensure the continued success of an innovation such as the iPhone and to respond to competition from products which followed the original innovation.

## REFERENCES

Abernathy, W.J. and Utterback, J.M. (1978) 'Patterns of industrial innovation', *Technology Review*, 80(7), June/July.

Agar, J. (2003) *Constant Touch. A global history of the mobile phone.* Cambridge: Icon Books.

Andre, B.K. et al. (2012) *Electronic device*. US Patent Office Design Patent D672,769S. Available at: https://www.freepatentsonline.com/D672769.pdf (Accessed: 20 June 2023).

Antonia (2020) 'iPhone Lifecycle: What Is the Carbon Footprint of an iPhone'. *Compare and Recycle*, 27 April. Available at: https://www.compareandrecycle.co.uk/blog/iphone-lifecycle-what-is-the-carbon-footprint-of-an-iphone (Accessed: 20 June 2023).

Arndt, H-K. and Ewe, C. (2017) 'Analysis of Product Lifecycle Data to Determine the Environmental Impact of the Apple iPhone', in V. Wohlgemuth et al. *Advances and New Trends in Environmental Informatics*. Springer Cham, pp. 3–13.

Apple Inc. (2022) *Product Environmental Report iPhone 14 Pro*. Available at: https://www.apple.com/environment/pdf/products/iphone/iPhone_14_Pro_PER_Sept2022.pdf (Accessed: 20 June 2023).

Cheng, L. (2015) *Making of the iPhone*. Available at: https://u.osu.edu/iphone/3-the-manufacture-of-the-iphone/ (Accessed: 20 June 2023).

Cooper, M. et al. (1975) *Radio Telephone System*. US Patent Office Patent 3,906,166. Available at: https://patents.google.com/patent/US3906166A/en (Accessed: 5 July 2023).

Cooper, M. (2001) 'Everyone is wrong', *MIT Technology Review*, June. Available at: https://www.technologyreview.com/2001/06/01/235752/everyone-is-wrong/ (Accessed: 19 June 2023).

Cooper, M. (2015) 'Marty Cooper inventor of the mobile phone'. Interview by Joerg Droege of *Scene World* Magazine. Available at: https://www.youtube.com/watch?v=B6OKTJMavtw&list=PLE3A053CEEE38AE81&index=6 (Accessed: 5 July 2023).

Edwards, J. (2014) 'Apple Is losing the war to Android', *Business Insider*, 31 May. Available at: https://www.businessinsider.com/iphone-v-android-market-share-2014-5?r=US&IR=T (Accessed: 20 June 2023).

Fadell, T. (2022a) *Build. An unorthodox guide to making things worth making*. London: Bantam Press.

Fadell, T. (2022b) 'Tony Fadell interviewed by Amul Rajan', *Today,* BBC Radio 4, 12 May.

Galloway, S. (2017) *The Four: The hidden DNA of Amazon, Apple, Facebook and Google*. London: Bantam Press.

Goggin, G. (2009) 'Adapting the mobile phone: The iPhone and its consumption', *Continuum. Journal of Media and Cultural Studies*, 23(2), pp. 231–44.

Goggin, G. (2012) 'The iPhone and Communication', in L. Hjorth et al. (eds.) *Studying mobile media: Cultural technologies, mobile communication and the iPhone*. New York: Routledge, pp. 11–27.

Hackford, H. (2018) 'Not just for calling anymore: The social impact of the iPhone revolution'. *CHM Blog*, Computer History Museum, 25 January. Available at: https://computerhistory.org/blog/not-just-for-calling-anymore-the-social-impact-of-the-iphone-revolution/ (Accessed: 5 July 2023).

Isaacson, W. (2011*) Steve Jobs*. London: Little Brown.

Isaacson, W. (2014) *The Innovators. How a group of hackers, geniuses and geeks created the digital revolution*. London: Simon and Schuster.

Jones, M. (2022) 'iPhone History: Every Generation in Timeline Order 2007–2022'. *History Cooperative*, 14 September. Available at: https://historycooperative.org/the-history-of-the-iphone/ (Accessed: 20 June 2023).

Mazzucato, M. (2013) *The Entrepreneurial State. Debunking public vs. private sector myths*. London: Anthem Press.

McGee P. (2023) 'How Apple tied its fortunes to China', *Financial Times,* 17 January. Available at: https://www.ft.com/content/d5a80891-b27d-4110-90c9-561b7836f11b (Accessed: 20 June 2023).

Merchant, B. (2017) *The One Device. The secret history of the iPhone*. London: Bantam Press.

Mickalowski, K., Mickelson, M. and Keltgen, J. (2008) *Apple's iPhone Launch: A case study in effective marketing.* Available at: https://www.augie.edu/sites/default/files/u57/pdf/jaciel_subdocs/iPhone.pdf (Accessed: 20 June 2023).

Montgomery, A. and Mingis, K. (2022) 'The evolution of Apple's iPhone', *Computerworld*, 14 September. Available at: https://www.computerworld.com/article/2604020/the-evolution-of-apples-iphone.html#slide1 (Accessed: 5 July 2023).

Murtazin, E. (2010) 'Apple's Phone: From 1980s' Sketches to iPhone', *mobile-review*. (In 3 parts. Trans. M. Antonenko). Available at: https://mobile-review.com/articles/2010/iphone-history3-en.shtml (Accessed: 20 June 2023).

NBC News (2005) *First cell phone a true 'brick'*, 11 April. Available at: https://www.nbcnews.com/id/wbna7432915 (Accessed: 5 July 2023).

Patel, N. (2020) 'How Apple Changed the World – 4 Core Marketing Strategies of the Tech Icon'. *Blog.* Available at: https://neilpatel.com/blog/how-apple-changed-the-world/ (Accessed: 5 July 2023).

Pierce, D. and Goode, L. (2018) 'The WIRED Guide to the iPhone', *WIRED*, 7 December. Available at: https://www.wired.com/story/guide-iphone/ (Accessed: 6 July 2023).

Plant, S. (2001) *On the Mobile: The effects of mobile telephones on social and individual life.* London: Motorola.

Podolny, J.M. and Hansen, M.T. (2020) 'How Apple Is organized for innovation', *Harvard Business Review*, November–December. Available at: https://hbr.org/2020/11/how-apple-is-organized-for-innovation (Accessed: 5 July 2023).

Rodriguez, E., Carrasquillo, O., Lee, C., Lee, J. and Zhou, A. (2015). 'iGo Green: A Life Cycle Assessment of Apple's iPhone', in *iConference 2015 Proceedings*. Available at: https://www.ideals.illinois.edu/items/73967 (Accessed: 5 July 2023).

Roy, R. (2016) *Consumer Product Innovation and Sustainable Design. The evolution and impacts of successful products.* Abingdon, Oxfordshire: Routledge.

Ruby, D. (2023) *iPhone User & Sales Statistics.* Demand Sage, 3 February. Available at: https://www.demandsage.com/iphone-user-statistics/#:~:text=Although%20it's%20been%2015%20years, have%20an%2018%25%20market%20share (Accessed: 20 June 2023).

Statista (2023) *Penetration rate of smartphones in selected countries 2022.* Available at: https://www.statista.com/statistics/539395/smartphone-penetration-worldwide-by-country/ (Accessed: 19 June 2023).

Teece, D. J. (1986) 'Profiting from technological innovation: Implications for integration, collaboration, licensing and public policy', *Research Policy*, 15(6), pp. 285–305.

Teixeira, T. (2010) *Meet Marty Cooper – the inventor of the mobile phone.* BBC Click, 23 April. Available at: http://news.bbc.co.uk/1/hi/programmes/click_online/8639590.stm (Accessed: 5 July 2023).

Vogelstein, F. (2008) 'The Untold Story: How the iPhone blew up the wireless industry', *WIRED*, 9 January. Available at: https://www.wired.com/2008/01/ff-iphone/?currentPage=1 (Accessed: 20 June 2023).

Vogelstein, F. (2017) 'Inside Apple's 6-Month Race to Make the First iPhone a Reality', *WIRED*, 28 June. Available at: https://www.wired.com/story/iphone-history-dogfight/?mbid=GuidesLearnMore (Accessed: 3 July 2023).

West, J. and Mace, M. (2010) 'Browsing as the killer app: Explaining the rapid success of Apple's iPhone', *Telecommunications Policy*, 34, pp. 270–86.

# 4    Radical product and building innovations

## INTRODUCTION

In this chapter I will discuss three cases of radical or disruptive innovations through which to examine the factors, processes, and lessons associated with their success, or lack of it. Two cases are of innovations that are not only radically different from what existed previously, but which have been widely adopted and have contributed to creating new industries or disrupted the established industries into which they were introduced. The third case concerns radically innovative eco-designs which have yet to be adopted.

The first case is of the cyclone vacuum cleaner invented and developed into a highly successful innovation by the British designer-entrepreneur Sir James Dyson. The second is a historical case; the invention, design, and innovation of the Rover Safety bicycle, which established the classic chain-driven, diamond-frame bicycle which is still dominant today. The third case, however, is of radical designs of vertical axis wind turbines and zero and positive carbon buildings which remain as one-offs, prototypes, or concepts.

## CASE STUDY: JAMES DYSON – CYCLONE VACUUM CLEANERS

This case study of the *cyclone vacuum cleaner*, which turned out to be a disruptive radical innovation that changed the vacuum cleaner market and made James Dyson into a billionaire, draws on several sources. The main source for the period up to 2001 is James Dyson's autobiography written with Giles Coren (Coren and Dyson, 2001) and online material summarising chapters from his second autobiography (Dyson, 2021). Other sources include a filmed interview I conducted with Dyson for an Open University design course (Roy, 1995) while he was still developing his first mass-produced cyclone cleaner, the DC01. This was followed by Open University videos of Dyson demonstrating how he developed the DC01 and talking about his approach to design and innovation (Roy, 2009). There are also materials produced by others that provided additional information, including Utterback et al. (2006, pp. 72–5); Bessant (2020); and James Dyson Foundation (undated).

### Background

James Dyson was born in 1947 and attended Gresham's public (i.e., private) school in Norfolk where, according to his autobiography, he was highly competitive,

DOI: 10.4324/9781003354406-4

determined, and something of a rebel. After a year at art school, James Dyson was accepted to study furniture, product, and interior design at the Royal College of Art, London. There he was introduced to the ideas of the visionary American architect and engineer, Buckminster Fuller, best known for his geodesic domes. In a BBC interview (BBC, 2019) Dyson recalled, 'Here was an engineer creating this engineering structure, which was incredibly beautiful, without even trying to be beautiful. Its elegance came not from its styling but from its engineering and I latched on to that.'

Dyson was also greatly influenced by the life and work of the Victorian engineer Isambard Kingdom Brunel. So, as well as learning to design, Dyson became excited by the possibilities of innovative engineering and technology. Fuller and Brunel also inspired Dyson, like Steve Jobs, to believe in dreaming the apparently technically impossible combined with a self-belief and determination to achieve the impossible against all obstacles. In his autobiography Dyson writes,

> I have tried … to draw on Brunel's dream of applying emerging technology in ways yet unimagined … he had to overcome the most incredible resistance to his ideas … so I have sought originality for its own sake … even if only to redefine a stale market (Coren and Dyson, 2001, pp. 39–40).

**From this brief account of Dyson's background, what factors are likely to enable him to produce creative ideas, inventions, and innovative products?**

Dyson's *personality*; determined, competitive, driven, and somewhat rebellious.

Dyson's formal and informal *education*; trained in art and product design.

*Inspired by visionary engineers*, notably Brunel and Buckminster Fuller, to dream up new ideas and solve apparently impossible problems using new technologies.

### The Ballbarrow

Before he had the idea for a cyclone vacuum cleaner Dyson invented and developed a novel design of wheelbarrow with a ball-shaped wheel, which he named the *Ballbarrow* (Figure 4.1). The idea arose from Dyson's experience of using a conventional wheelbarrow, which he found had many faults, such as being unstable when full and having a narrow wheel that sank into soft ground. Determined to improve the design, Dyson turned over the problem in his mind for over a year and then drew on his previous experience of designing, developing, and selling a fibreglass boat called the *Sea Truck* for a company called Rotork. The boat project had taught him how to mould tough pneumatic plastic spheres from low density polyethylene. This knowledge inspired Dyson with the idea that a ball-shaped wheel would solve one of the conventional wheelbarrow's major faults – sinking into soft ground – while redesigning the shallow body as a deep plastic bin would solve many of its other faults.

After testing a rough prototype using a fibreglass wheel moulded around a football, Dyson developed and patented the design. He felt there would be a relatively uncompetitive market for a better wheelbarrow given that their design had not fundamentally changed for centuries. So, after failing to interest a major plastics manufacturer in the product, he established a business to assemble and sell the Ballbarrow, eventually managing to raise funding through family contacts and finding component suppliers. Initially this product innovation was marketed by mail order because retailers did not think it would succeed, but it sold well, even at about three times the price of conventional wheelbarrows. The Ballbarrow was launched in 1974, but after four years the business was sold by its outside investors resulting in Dyson being forced out of the company. The Ballbarrow continued in production for at least a further 12 years. This experience made Dyson realise the importance for an inventor of personally retaining their patent rights.

Figure 4.1
The author interviewing James Dyson with the Ballbarrow in 1991 (Roy, 2009, p. 49). Courtesy of the Open University.

**What creative design and innovation processes resulted in the invention and design of the *Ballbarrow* and it becoming a relatively successful innovation?**

Dyson's *'constructive discontent'*; critical of an existing design and a strong *motivation* to improve it.

*Preparation*; a lengthy period considering the problem.

*User-centred design* based on Dyson's personal experience.

Dyson's *knowledge and experience* from his previous work provided the *inspiration* and *technology* for the ball-shaped wheel.

Dyson recognised a *potential market opportunity* for a better wheelbarrow.

*Rough prototyping* to test the basic concept followed by detailed technical and aesthetic design of the product.

Dyson *obtaining funding* and *collaboration with others* to establish a business to make and market the product.

*Patenting* to protect Dyson's intellectual property, but learning he should have retained his personal patent rights after being forced out of the company he founded.

### The cyclone vacuum cleaner
*Invention*

The cyclone vacuum cleaner project began in 1978 when Dyson had been using a Hoover upright vacuum cleaner. Annoyed by its inefficiency, he replaced it with a powerful cylinder cleaner. He was also struck by the deficiencies of the cylinder cleaner because its suction rapidly reduced in use. It took Dyson days of investigation and thought before he discovered the reason; the collection bag's pores became clogged by dust before it was full.

At the same time Dyson was having 'suction' problems at the Ballbarrow factory. The powder paint used to coat the Ballbarrow's metal parts kept clogging the factory's filtration system. Dyson was advised to install an industrial cyclone to separate the powder from the air like the cyclones used to remove dust from the air in sawmills. In such a device a rotating air flow is created within a conical container called a cyclone. The air rotates so fast that any particles in the air are forced to the cyclone's walls from where they spiral down and can be collected, whilst clean air moves to the centre and exits.

While constructing a cyclone for the factory, and thinking about how it worked, Dyson suddenly got the idea that the cyclone principle could be used instead of a bag to trap the dust collected by a vacuum cleaner. He rapidly tested his idea by fitting a miniature cardboard cyclone to his old Hoover upright and found that the cyclone principle did work (Coren and Dyson, 2001, pp. 106–7).

For an Open University video interview (Roy, 2009) Dyson explained how he got the cyclone idea and immediately tested it in his home workshop,

> I thought this is what the vacuum cleaner needs but the one in my factory is 35-foot high, would it work if I miniaturised it down to vacuum cleaner size? So, I raced home and got one of these [Hoover upright] vacuum cleaners … and replace the bag with a cardboard and gaffer tape cyclone … I've got a bit of swimming pool hose … connected it so the dirty air comes up here, enters the cyclone spirals round, the dust collects in this pot at the bottom and the clean air comes out of this chimney at the top. I fired it up and vacuumed the home … it was doing a fantastic cleaning job. So, I thought this is a wonderful solution to the problem of vacuuming.

Although Dyson says that the cyclone cleaner idea arose as a 'stroke of fortune' (Coren and Dyson, 2001, p. 104), it is significant that he is always on the lookout for how to improve existing products. Dyson's cyclone cleaner involved a mental transfer of technology from one application to another; 'We're never original' he observed, 'there are always connections somewhere' (Roy, 1993, p. 427).

**What important factors enabled Dyson to create and test the idea of a cyclone vacuum cleaner?**

Once again Dyson's *constructive discontent,* this time from his experience of using conventional vacuum cleaners.

Rigorous *investigation and thought* to identify the cause of the deficiencies of existing vacuum cleaners.

Dyson *making a mental connection* between the clogged paint filtration system in the *Ballbarrow* factory and the clogging of vacuum cleaner bags with dust.

The *creative idea* of making a *transfer* of industrial cyclone technology to vacuum cleaners.

A *critical experiment* using a cardboard *mock-up* to test whether a miniature cyclone could work on a vacuum cleaner.

*Original innovation*

It took another four years, which involved Dyson raising business finance and making and testing over 5000 brass, aluminium, and Perspex model cyclones and much tinkering with mock-ups and prototypes, before he was ready to show his cleaner to potential licensees. Determining the shape of the cyclone to efficiently separate coarse particles and fine dust entailed Dyson testing those thousands of different cyclones in his workshop (Figure 4.2 right). He argues that this very laborious approach was necessary because none of the mathematical models on how cyclones worked could tell him how to design a cyclone that could separate particles of many different sizes. Dyson observed, 'That is what development is all about. Empirical testing demands that you make only one change at a time. It is the Edisonian principle, and it is bloody slow' (Coren and Dyson, 2001, p. 124). Dyson also argued that a person without prior knowledge can, through in-depth study, quickly become sufficiently expert in any subject, such as cyclones, if required to do so to solve a problem. In an interview with me (Roy, 1995) Dyson commented,

> you don't have to be expert at the early stages … But to really make it work you have to become an expert … once you're focussed in on a finite area of engineering there isn't an awful lot to learn from textbooks and, once you've learned that, your experience of empirical tests will render you an expert quite quickly.

Dyson's efforts first went into developing a cyclone that could extract fine dust particles. By 1980 Dyson had embodied his invention in the design of a prototype cleaner, with a telescopic hose and two cyclones that could be quickly converted from upright to cylinder mode (Figure 4.2 centre). In 1981 Dyson applied for a patent for a vacuum cleaner of this type. However, this prototype could not cope with both coarse and fine particles, so Dyson continued development work until by 1982 he had a concentric dual cyclone system that filtered out all dirt and dust particles without a bag, which he built into a demonstration tank cleaner.

Dyson then demonstrated his prototype upright and demonstration tank bagless cyclone cleaners to almost every UK and continental European appliance manufacturer. However, they all declined to licence Dyson's invention. In a classic case of 'not-invented-here' they remained wedded to existing vacuum cleaner designs and were unconvinced by Dyson's cyclone technology telling him that if there was a better type of vacuum cleaner Hoover or Electrolux would have invented it already (Coren and Dyson, 2001, pp. 132–5). When I asked him to comment on this experience Dyson said,

> it's very difficult to walk into a company and expect them to take on a new idea … because don't forget the company is out selling the existing technology … and here you are coming along as a jumped-up inventor telling them what they are selling isn't any good (Roy, 1995).

Dyson continued to develop his dual cyclone cleaner, using both his engineering and industrial design skills, and through various business deals succeeded getting a design called the *Cyclon* manufactured by Zanussi and launched on the market in 1984. The Cyclon was therefore the original cyclone cleaner innovation, even though only about 550 were sold.

Figure 4.2
Left: G-Force pink cyclone cleaner, 1986; Centre: blue and red prototype dual cyclone cleaner, 1981; Right: some of the cyclone models used to test their effectiveness in collecting course and fine dust (Roy, 2009, p. 48). Photograph by the author.

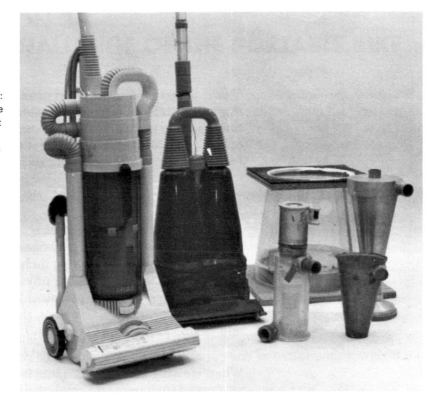

**What lessons can be learned from Dyson's development of his initial idea to the market launch of the world's first cyclone vacuum cleaner, the *Cyclon*, as a product innovation?**

Dyson's *immersion* in and *research* into existing knowledge of cyclone technology.

Dyson's belief in exhaustive *empirical testing* and *modification* to develop an effective cyclone configuration.

*Iterative design and development* of the cyclone vacuum cleaner from prototypes to product innovation.

Dyson's application of *engineering and industrial design* skills to produce attractive and functional prototypes and product.

*Patenting* to protect Dyson's intellectual property.

Dyson's use of his *business and interpersonal skills* to raise finance, demonstrate prototypes, and attempt to licence his invention to existing manufacturers.

Dyson's *dedicated hard work* for six years to progress the project from idea to original innovation.

*Collaboration* with others as necessary to progress the project.

Dyson's *persistence* in the face of rejection by, or problems with, manufacturers, financiers, and component suppliers, driven by his belief that was a *latent market* for a radically innovative vacuum cleaner.

### International licencing and the G-Force

After further abortive deals in the US and UK, Dyson finally succeeded in licensing his dual cyclone cleaner to a Japanese company, Apex. Someone in the company had seen a picture of the Cyclon in a design magazine and contacted Dyson. Dyson spent time in Japan working with Apex, where he found a culture where innovative design and technology was appreciated and a company with the necessary skills and resources to perfect and redesign the Cyclon for production. Renamed the *G-Force* the cleaner looked quite different from conventional upright vacuum cleaners (Figure 4.3). Dyson deliberately kept the Cyclon's lavender and pink colour scheme – inspired, Dyson says, by visits to the lavender fields of Provence – to emphasis its innovativeness. He also made the cyclone enclosure transparent so that customers could see the swirling dust particles. 'From a market standpoint', Dyson argues, 'if the product contains any new ideas, then it is essential that the product be visually different' (Roy, 1993, p. 429).

Following its launch in 1986 the G-Force sold to Japanese design-conscious consumers for the equivalent of £1200 (about £3600 in 2023). Thus, Dyson's invention had through design and eight years of effort finally become a successful, if niche, product innovation (Coren and Dyson, 2001, p. 165).

Now he had a successful innovation, Dyson thought he could make a deal to export the G-Force to the US, but again met with legal and business obstacles. Another idea, a dry powder carpet cleaner, came again from a transfer of technology, inspired by Dyson remembering a friend who used dry powder shampoo. This idea allowed Dyson, and the small design team he had recruited, to develop and licence another innovative product, a cyclone dry powder carpet cleaner called *Drytech* launched in 1986 by a Canadian firm, Iona.

Dyson also agreed to licence his patented technology to Johnson Wax which then developed and launched cyclonic cleaners for the commercial market in 1991. Meanwhile Dyson became embroiled in protracted patent litigation with another US company Amway which had developed and launched their own cyclone vacuum cleaner. The legal costs of the Amway case were threatening Dyson's business survival, but fortunately it was eventually settled giving him a share of the licence fees (Coren and Dyson, 2001, p. 182, p. 187).

Figure 4.3
G-Force cyclone
lavender and pink
vacuum cleaner
made in Japan,
1986. Photograph
by the author.

### The UK mass-market DC01

The royalties from sales of the G-Force, and from the Canadian and US licences, allowed Dyson's company to design, develop, and manufacture a bagless upright cyclone vacuum cleaner aimed at the UK mass market. For this project Dyson assembled a design team, negotiated a promise of finance for tooling, and began the task of developing a mass market dual cyclone cleaner. Dyson wanted the product to look like a piece of space technology, such as he saw as a child reading the *Eagle* comic. The team put great effort into considering how people would use the product, as well as making it function as efficiently as possible and be economical to manufacture. For example, its handle doubled as a telescopic hose and tool for cleaning stairs and above floor level, the transparent outer cyclone allowed the user to see the collected dust swirling around, and it was to be largely made from moulded plastics, coloured yellow and silver-grey. Developing the cleaner involved significant changes to the G-Force's design and numerous detailed improvements modelled on computer then in physical models and prototypes. In his autobiography Dyson waxes lyrical about the pleasure and excitement of working with his team of four young graduate design engineers to develop the best possible product without the constraints imposed by marketing and salespeople (Coren and Dyson, 2001, pp. 192–200). The first *Dyson Dual*

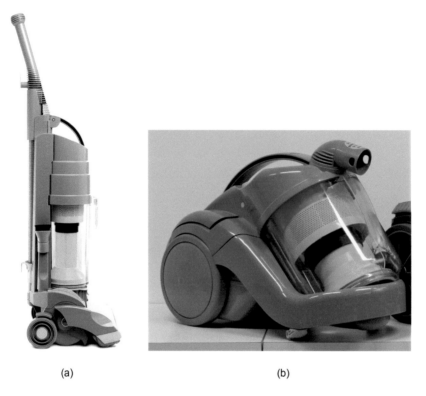

Figure 4.4
(a) Dyson DC01 Dual
Cyclone upright
cleaner, made in the
UK, 1993. Courtesy
of Dyson.
4.4 (b) Dyson
DC02 cyclone
cylinder cleaner,
1996. Courtesy of
Dyson.

(a)                                               (b)

*Cyclone* cleaner, the *DC01* (Figure 4.4 (a)), was made and launched in the UK in 1993. This was 15 years after Dyson's initial creative idea, clearly showing how long it can take to get ideas and inventions into mass production.

The (UK) Consumers' Association tested the DC01 in 1994. Its magazine *Which?* reported that, unlike vacuum cleaners with bags, the DC01 met its claims of not losing suction as it filled and produced little exhaust dust. However, the Dyson was heavy, noisy, and expensive, so although it performed well the DC01 did not rate as a 'Best Buy' (Consumers' Association, 1994). Despite selling for £200 (about double the price of most other vacuums at the time, and about £450 in 2023) Dyson's innovation proved to be very successful and quickly gained nearly a fifth of the British market. A cylinder version, the *DC02* (Figure 4.4 (b)), and an improved version of the DC01 followed, both of which performed well in Consumers' Association tests, resulting in the DC01 becoming a Best Buy (Which? Ltd, 1996).

**What additional lessons may be learned from the development from the *Cyclon,* to the niche-market *G-Force,* then to the mass-market *Dual Cyclone DC01*?**

Dyson's willingness to risk great effort and resources to *defend his patents* against imitators.

Dyson's *business and interpersonal skills* which enabled him to agree licencing deals and raise funds.

Dyson licencing his cyclone patents to a Japanese company with a *corporate culture* that appreciated innovative design and technology.

The Japanese company had the *engineering and design skills and resources* that enabled the Cyclon to be developed into the G-Force cleaner.

The success of the G-Force in Japan depended on its *innovative design* and *visual appearance* and its *unusual colours*, inspired by Dyson's visit to France.

Dyson's effectiveness in *collaborating with others* in creative design and engineering teams in Japan and the UK free from marketing constraints.

The Dyson team's integrated application of *industrial design and engineering* for the DC01 to provide unique functions, be easy to use, look innovative, and be designed for economic manufacture.

### Continuous innovation and creative design

Dyson bagless cyclone cleaners had by 1997 captured nearly half of the UK market by value, while versions developed under licence by Iona/Fantom were selling well in America. This stimulated other vacuum cleaner manufacturers to develop new products, including their own bagless designs. The *disruptive* effect of Dyson's innovation thus set off a divergent phase of vacuum cleaner design. As the Consumers' Association commented in its magazine (Which? Ltd., 2001, p. 50),

> it was undoubtedly the launch of Dyson's bagless ... cleaner in 1993 that injected new life into the market. It set new standards for continuous dust pickup ... such technological change combined with Dyson's fresh approach to design has prompted many rival manufacturers to reassess their own products.

Dyson had the patents on cleaners with multiple cyclones. This did not stop other companies trying to copy Dyson's innovation. Hoover, for example, lost a court case against Dyson in 2000 when it launched a bagless cleaner with three cyclone stages. But when Dyson's original patents expired from 2001, other manufacturers were able to develop and launch their own multi-cyclone cleaners.

To compete, Dyson's company has invested heavily in the research, design, and development of a whole series of bagless cyclone cleaners and applying the company's R&D to other innovative air movement products, such as commercial hand dryers, hair dryers, and fans.

### Mains-powered vacuum cleaners

Significant innovations and improvements have been made in successive gen-erations of Dyson mains-powered vacuum cleaners, especially to their cyclone designs, electric motor technologies, and usability (Which? Ltd., 2000). The prod-ucts now include upright and cylinder cleaners that have multiple 'root cyclones', powered floor heads to collect the finest particles and detangle hairs, and retract-able wands for cleaning above floor level. Since 2005 upright models run on a ball instead of wheels, an adaptation from the Ballbarrow, to provide better manoeuvrability (Figure 4.5).

### Cordless vacuum cleaners

Dyson was one of the first companies to develop cordless cleaners. This required two innovations in technology: a compact, powerful motor and improved batter-ies. Improvements in lithium-ion batteries came from a *transfer of technology* from the many other fields that used such batteries. Dyson's engineers spent many years developing powerful motors small enough to fit into the head of a cordless cleaner such as the Dyson *V10*. The motor of the subsequent range, the *V11*, revolves on a carbon fibre composite shaft at extremely high speed and has an impeller with overlapping vanes to create a much more powerful suc-tion than in previous models. These innovations are marketed as 'digital motors' since such brushless DC motors are controlled by a microprocessor generating

Figure 4.5
Dyson Ball™
Multi-floor upright
vacuum cleaner.
Courtesy of Dyson.

a rotating magnetic field. The company says that given the improvements in its cordless machines (such as the model shown in Figure 4.6) it will devote its research, design, and development (RD&D) resources to developing cordless rather than mains cyclone cleaners.

### Robot vacuum cleaners

In 2001 Dyson designed and trialled a prototype robot vacuum cleaner but did not put it into production because of its weight, complexity, and cost. A year later the first production robot cleaners, the *Trilobite* from Electrolux and the *Roomba* from iRobot, a US robotics company, were launched. In response Dyson developed its *360 Eye*™ robot vacuum cleaner, first launched in Japan in 2014. A panoramic camera and infrared sensors allowed the cleaner to visualise the room, work out its location, and use landmarks in the room to navigate. The cleaner could be controlled via a mobile app which allowed users to set it to clean at specific times. The 360 Eye™ was replaced in 2020 by a more powerful model, the *360 Heurist*™, that learns where it has cleaned previously to improve efficiency. A new design, the Dyson *360 Vis Nav*™, with an even more powerful motor and sensors for avoiding or climbing small obstacles, creating dust maps of the home, and knowing where to clean, is being launched in 2023 (Figure 4.7).

Figure 4.6
Dyson Gen5detect™ cordless vacuum cleaner with a more powerful motor and battery and a dust detection system, 2023. Courtesy of Dyson.

Figure 4.7
Dyson 360 Vis
Nav™ robot
vacuum cleaner,
2023. Courtesy of
Dyson.

**What lessons can be learned from the Dyson company's strategy to keep ahead of its competitors after the market success of the *DC01* and *DC02* vacuum cleaners and expiry of its cyclone patents?**

The company's vigorous continued *defence of its patents* before they expired.

*Major investment in RD&D staff and other resources* to develop generations of new and improved cyclone vacuum cleaners, and to exploit the company's expertise and technology in further innovations, such as cordless and robot vacuum cleaners, and other air movement products such as hand and hair dryers and fans.

*Adaptation* of ideas and components from earlier Dyson products, such as the *Ballbarrow*, into new products and *transfer* of technologies and materials, such as batteries, developed by other researchers and manufacturers into new and improved products.

### The Contrarotator washing machine

In 2000 Dyson's company launched another radical appliance innovation, the *Contrarotator* washing machine. The machine had two drums rotating in opposite directions to provide an action similar to, but more effective than, hand washing. The innovation functioned well in independent tests and was updated once, but production of Dyson washing machines was discontinued in 2005 because the company could not charge enough for them to be both profitable and sell at a price acceptable to many consumers (Bessant, 2020).

### Moving to the Far East and an abandoned innovation

From 2002, after attempts to keep manufacture in the UK, the company decided to make Dyson cleaners in Malaysia to reduce costs and to bring component suppliers closer to the factory. In 2019 the company announced it was establishing a new headquarters in Singapore while expanding its UK RD&D workforce. Dyson said the new HQ's location was because its largest markets and manufacturing operations were all in Asia (Pooler et al., 2019). Singapore was also the site for Dyson's planned, but later abandoned, project to build an electric car. An innovative large-wheel, seven-seat prototype of the car with a claimed 1000 km range, had already been developed. The abandonment of the electric car project Dyson said was commercial rather than technical. It was due to the cost of developing and manufacturing the car which would have made its price uncompetitive compared to electric cars from major car producers (Cropley, 2020). This was a lesson that Dyson had learned from the Contrarotator washing machine and the early prototype robot cleaner. The washing machine, the prototype robot cleaner, and the electric car were Dyson's few unsuccessful or unrealised innovations.

### Educational initiatives

As well as being a successful innovator Dyson has a mission to increase the employment and status of engineering, design, and manufacturing in UK industry. Hence his company supports educational initiatives, such as the James Dyson Foundation, which produces educational resources for schools and universities, and the establishment of the Dyson Institute of Engineering and Technology where young engineers and designers can gain a UK degree while working on real-life Dyson projects.

An example of the Foundation's work is a teacher's pack about how the *DC22* 'Baby' cylinder model was designed and developed, which illustrates how a typical new product development team works at Dyson (James Dyson Foundation, undated). The development process is summarised in Box 4.1.

---

**BOX 4.1 THE DYSON DC22 RESEARCH, DESIGN, AND DEVELOPMENT PROCESS**

The design process begins with a *brief*. For the *DC22* team the brief was to develop a new vacuum cleaner that was very compact because of the lack of storage space in modern homes. This took two years and a team of 25 design engineers before the product was launched in 2008.

First design engineers create a *vision specification*; diagrams, sketches, and drawings of what they imagine the machine will look like and what features it will have. The next step is to develop a detailed engineering specification, establishing the product's size, weight, power, and noise.

---

This is followed by *research and idea development*, during which 'eureka moments' are rare. Instead, ideas come from design engineers working together in *research, design, and development teams*. They analyse problems with existing products, carry out research into new technologies, discuss, experiment, and sketch their ideas.

Once the design engineers have identified an idea and sketched it out, the next step is to build a *3D prototype*. In the early stages, cardboard, glue, and tape are used to construct layouts and demonstrate basic functions quickly and cheaply. As the design develops, computer-aided design (CAD) software is used for the details and to create realistic prototypes that can be used for testing and modification. When the design is finalised, tooling for the plastics mouldings for making the product can be designed and ordered.

During the process the team has always to keep in mind the people who will use the product, for example by the *detailed design* of an easy-to-use release mechanism for the waste bin. The team also consider how to minimise the environmental impacts of the product throughout its lifecycle, especially by designing for energy efficiency in use, and to design its components for rapid and fool-proof assembly.

After the product has gone into mass production, reliability and durability testing and consumer feedback is used to identify any problems and to address them with improved designs.

**What lessons might be learned from the typical new product development process in Dyson's company?**

New product development projects usually start with a *brief* informed by consumer feedback.

Projects go through *a systematic research, design, and development process* with defined phases.

Sketches, drawings, and computer and physical *models,* which become more detailed and realistic are created as the project develops.

*New technologies and materials* are adopted and developed as required.

*End user requirements, lifecycle environmental impacts, and manufacturing* are kept in mind throughout the process.

*Testing and consumer feedback* are used to improve existing products and provide information for new ones.

### Global investment in research, design, and innovation

From 2000 Dyson began an expansion of RD&D focusing on creating new products and technologies, as well as continuing with existing product innovation. The company announced in 2020 that it planned to invest £2.75 billion over five years in Singapore, the UK, and the Philippines for innovation in robotics, electric motor technology, intelligent products, machine learning, new materials, and the commercialisation of Dyson's solid state battery technology (Dyson, 2023). At the same time Dyson is introducing new consumer products to its portfolio, such as noise cancelling headphones launched in 2023, featuring a detachable air purifying visor that fans clean air into the user's nose and mouth when in an area of high air pollution.

Dyson's history, the growth of his business, and the development of its products represents an outstanding example of success through disruptive innovation and competing through major investments in research and development, creative design, and continuous innovation.

## CASE STUDY: THE ROVER SAFETY BICYCLE

The second case study is of a historical innovation which led to new industries and had significant social impacts.

The rear chain-driven bicycle with similar size wheels and a diamond-shaped frame is one of the most important 19th century innovations. This classic bicycle configuration still dominates today as the design used for transport, sport, and leisure.

The *Rover Safety* bicycle designed by John Kemp Starley in 1885 (Figures 4.8 and 4.10 (b)) is considered to be the key step in the development of the modern bicycle. In this case study I examine how the Rover Safety bicycle came about as an innovation, and why it proved to be so successful.

### Background

John Kemp Starley, whose uncle was the inventor James Starley, was born in 1854. At the time James Starley had established a company to design and manufacture sewing machines and by 1868 the company started to design and make bicycles to meet a growing demand. James Starley with William Hillman went on in 1870 to patent and then make one of the early *Ordinary* or high-wheel ('penny-farthing') bicycles, the *Aerial*, which was much faster and lighter than existing 'boneshaker' bicycles. The Aerial had a metal frame, a large front wheel with pedals attached, and a small rear wheel. Both wheels had the recently invented wire rather than rigid wooden spokes and solid rubber tyres. James Starley subsequently invented and incorporated further innovations into his bicycles, notably tangential wire-spoked wheels, which he patented in 1874 and are still standard today.

As a young man John Kemp Starley joined his uncle's cycle company. He spent several years working in this innovative company which developed a variety of bicycle and tricycle designs. Then in 1877 he established his own cycle company, Starley & Sutton Co. The company set about developing cycles that

Figure 4.8
The Rover Safety
bicycle, 1885. The
prototype of the
standard modern
rear chain-driven
bicycle. Photograph
by the author.

were *safer* than high-wheel bicycles. The business started by designing and making tricycles branded Rover. J.K. Starley's most important innovation, however, was the *Rover Safety* bicycle of 1885 (Sharp, 1896).

### What lessons can be learned from John Kemp Starley's background?

By joining his uncle's cycle company, John Kemp became *immersed* in the design, technology, and manufacturing of bicycles.

While working there he would have acquired a 'repertoire' of relevant *domain-specific knowledge, skills, and experience.*

He would have had to work with others in an *organisation* that supported innovation.

John Kemp's goal when started his own company was to develop *safer* cycles.

### *Predecessors of the Rover Safety*

Like many radical innovations, the Rover Safety arose from an accumulation of ideas developed earlier, so it is worth considering its technical predecessors.

The first proper bicycle, the *Velocipede*, which had pedals fixed to the front wheel was invented in France around 1860. Similar bicycles with iron-rimmed, wooden carriage wheels, aptly called boneshakers, were produced in England by 1868. Such bicycles were a popular innovation despite being heavy, slow, and uncomfortable to ride. These drawbacks stimulated inventors to make improvements in cycle components and designs. Important component innovations included wire-spoked wheels with solid or cushion rubber tyres, ball bearings, and solid or tubular metal frames which were incorporated in high-wheel bicycles. In these bicycles the front wheel was increased in size until it reached the maximum diameter allowed by the rider's leg length to produce higher speeds from a direct pedal drive. High-wheel bicycles were popular among sporting young men but were highly dangerous as the rider could be thrown over the handlebars if the large front wheel hit an obstacle. This led to a search for safer designs of pedal cycle and huge variety of configurations were created by inventors and designers in the 1870s and 1880s. They included *Safety Ordinaries* with a smaller front wheel driven by various mechanisms such as levers or chains; many designs of cycle with three or more wheels; and so-called 'dwarf' safety bicycles with a chain drive to the rear wheel. However, early rear chain-driven bicycles did not become successful innovations. This was partly because their inventors seemed unable to completely break away from a design 'fixation' on a larger front than rear wheel, even though with gearing this was not necessary, and partly because cycle purists ridiculed their inelegant appearance. It required a creative inventor and designer to develop the rear drive concept into a bicycle that was safe, speedy, and comfortable.

**What can be learned from the evolution of cycles from 'boneshakers' to early chain-driven safety bicycles?**

*Various, sometimes conflicting, objectives* (improved comfort, lighter weight, higher speeds, and improved safety) drove inventors and designers to improve pedal cycles. This led to a *huge diversity of designs* of varying practicality before cycle design converged on a few types.

Cycle inventors' unnecessary *'fixation'* on large front wheels and smaller rear wheels hampered development of an efficient and attractive rear chain-driven bicycle.

### Invention and design of the *Rover Safety*

I noted the predecessors of the Rover Safety to show that it did not emerge in a giant leap 'out of the blue', but that it was the outcome of nearly 20 years of continuous cycle design evolution and component innovation. In creating the Rover Safety John Kemp Starley produced a design that overcame the drawbacks of previous cycles in a simple, elegant, and efficient configuration.

What was the thinking process that led Starley to design the Rover Safety? For this I will quote directly from a lecture that he gave to the Society of Arts (Starley, 1898, p. 608),

> I felt the time had arrived for solving the problem of the cycle … I therefore turned my attention solely to the perfection and manufacture of the Rover bicycle. The main principles which guided me in making this machine were to place the rider at the proper distance from the ground; to connect the cranks with the driving wheel in such a way that the gearing could be varied as desired; to place the seat in the right position in relation to the pedals, and constructed so that the saddle could be either laterally or vertically adjusted; to place the handles in such a position in relation to the seat that the rider could exert the greatest force upon the pedals with the least amount of fatigue; and to make them adjustable also. In the Rover, these, my cardinal principles, were all carried out, and although many alterations and improvements have been since effected in detail, it is a fact that there is not more than two- or three-inches difference today in any of the points first embodied in the Rover.

Starley went on in his lecture to explain how he achieved his design objectives (Starley, 1898, p. 610),

> The illustration which I now give [Figure 4.9] will show what was running in my mind at this time. I had been considering what a man could be compared to pedalling a bicycle, and the conclusion I had formed was, it largely resembled walking up a ladder, but … whereas the pedals went down in the former, the man went up in the latter. I therefore had to determine where the handles should be placed to enable him to bring the whole of his weight on to the pedals, and, I think, the illustration will show my selection was correct. It was … the handlebar which compelled me to adopt the present form of machine, as I could not get it sufficiently forward by the other type. It will be seen by the position of the handlebar on the Ordinary bicycle, that it was utterly useless and imperfect for this purpose.

The first prototype of the Rover Safety was built and tested in 1884. It had indirect steering and a 36-inch front wheel (Figure 4.10 (a)). This was not the elegant and efficient design that Starley wanted, and it was not until the third prototype of 1885 (Figure 4.10 (b)) that a diamond-shaped frame and direct steering to sloping front forks appeared. These were ideas originally developed by Humber in a tricycle and safety bicycle of 1884. Like many creative individuals, Starley was willing to transfer and adapt solutions produced by others in his own designs.

By 1885, therefore, the essential form and most of the component parts of the modern bicycle had been established. It remained to develop a triangulated frame structure by adopting straight tubes and adding a seat tube, and to curve the front forks at their ends to lighten the steering. By the mid-1890s most cycles being made were of this standard design configuration (Figure 4.11) and

Figure 4.9
Ladder analogy
used by J.K. Starley
to establish the
configuration of
the Rover Safety
(outlined in blue
compared with a
high-wheel bicycle
in grey) to permit
optimum use of
the rider's muscle
power (Roy, 2013, p.
37). Courtesy of the
Open University.

further improvements were incorporated such as the free-wheel mechanism, which allowed the rider to coast without taking their feet off the pedals.

**What does J. K. Starley's account of his thinking tell us about the creative design process?**

Starley was *dissatisfied* with what already existed and was *motivated* to create a better design, i.e., *constructive discontent*.

Starley had clear *objectives* or *primary generators* on which to base an improved design; namely, a safer bicycle that would make best use of the rider's effort and cater for users with different leg lengths.

He created an ergonomically improved design by thinking of a man climbing a ladder as an *analogy* with cycling.

He put together *available technologies, materials, and components* (e.g., tangent-spoked wheels, roller chains, hollow metal frames) to create a greatly improved design.

He *evolved the design iteratively* through several prototypes.

(a)

(b)

Figure 4.10
(a) First prototype of the Rover Safety bicycle with a single backbone frame, 1884 (Roy, 2013, p. 38). Courtesy of the Open University. 4.10 (b) Third Rover prototype, 1885. This design is considered as the basis of the modern bicycle. Note the diamond-shaped frame, but with no seat tube it is not a triangulated structure (Roy, 2013, p. 38). Courtesy of the Open University.

### Innovation and diffusion of the diamond-frame bicycle

Inventiveness and clever design are, however, not enough to succeed in innovation. What made the rear chain-driven, diamond-frame safety bicycle such a highly successful innovation when earlier safety bicycles had only short-lived success? The answer is that this design configuration quickly proved itself to be superior to all the other types of cycle then prevalent: in speed, comfort, convenience of use, and frame strength and stiffness. And, after some of the strange machines that preceded it, the Rover's design almost matched the high-wheel bicycle's elegance and simplicity. Nevertheless, as Starley comments, the Rover

Figure 4.11
Fully evolved Rover
Safety bicycle of
the mid-1890s
(Roy, 2013, p. 38).
Courtesy of the
Open University.

Safety had first to overcome the reaction of many cyclists against anything new (Starley, 1898, p. 608),

> At the time this machine was introduced, it created a certain amount of ridicule. It was so different in design from anything else made. It was not long, however, before we determined to prove that it possessed qualities which had never before been embodied in a cycle. In September 1885, we broke the world's [cycle] record for one hundred miles on the road. From that day to this we have had with it uninterrupted and ever-increasing success; while we have the satisfaction of seeing that all cycles … have slowly but surely had to give way before it.

The rapidity with which the diamond-frame safety bicycle was adopted by manufacturers in Britain, Europe, and America and the large numbers of safety bicycles that were sold in the period after 1885, depended not only on the superiority of the design but also on the social and commercial conditions towards the end of the 19th century.

The safety bicycle, especially after 1890 when it began to be equipped with pneumatic tyres (discussed in Chapter 5), became a very efficient and comfortable machine which led to a cycling boom. In the mid-1890s a craze for cycling spread through the middle and upper classes and to both men and women. To meet the demand, the number of cycle firms grew rapidly until by 1897 there were over 830 manufacturers in Britain alone.

The cycling boom also led to important innovations in *manufacturing* technology a shift from *product* to *process* innovation. As Saul (1970, p. 163) notes,

> The arrival of the safety bicycle and the pneumatic tyre created such a boom that big makers in Coventry and Nottingham were forced to reorganise their methods completely to meet the demand … Vast capacity was created by the large cycle makers and rows of the best machinery installed as a result of the heavy investment of the 1890s.

By 1898, however, the cycling craze was over, and the industry was left with production over-capacity. The result was that prices slumped, many British manufacturers were forced into liquidation, and many mergers took place. Major firms like Raleigh survived by adopting further manufacturing innovations to reduce costs while maintaining quality. The Rover Cycle Company founded by J. K. Starley also survived but, like many other famous cycle manufacturers, such as Humber, Hillman, Singer, and BSA, diversified into developing and making motorcycles and motor cars.

The first vehicles with internal combustion engines were motorised bicycles and tricycles which appeared in Germany in the same year, 1885, that the bicycle had evolved to the stage of the Rover Safety. The cycle industry and many of the components and manufacturing innovations it produced thus provided the basis for the newly emerging motor industry.

**What made the evolved *Rover Safety* bicycle such a successful and important innovation?**

The Rover Safety, as well as being *safe* to ride, proved itself to be *superior (or relative advantage)* in speed, comfort, and convenience to other types of cycle then being made.

It was *aesthetically simple and attractive* to consumers, despite initial ridicule by adherents of high-wheel bicycles.

It stimulated *manufacturing innovations* that allowed the product to be afforded by more people.

It came at a time when *changes in society*, including the role of women, created a demand for a personal form of transport and a fashion for cycling.

It provided the *businesses, design skills, manufacturing processes,* and some of the components for the fledgling *motor industry*.

### CASE STUDY: DEREK TAYLOR – THE COP26 BUILDING-INTEGRATED RENEWABLES HOUSE

This case study is of radical ideas and designs for renewable energy and sustainable buildings created by inventor, architect, and engineer Derek Taylor. He brought together several of his ideas in a series of concept designs for building-integrated renewable energy houses shown at the 'Images of Climate Innovation' exhibition during the United Nations COP26 Climate Change Conference held in Glasgow, Scotland in November 2021 (Figure 4.12). (Another less innovative COP26 house was built in Glasgow for the conference. This was a small, prefabricated timber frame house, using local renewable materials, designed for affordable rural housing.)

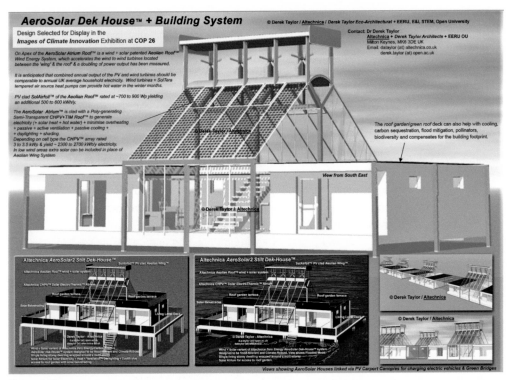

Figure 4.12
Concept designs for the AeroSolar Dek House™ + Building System exhibited at COP26 (Taylor, 2021). Copyright © 2021 Derek Taylor/Altechnica. Courtesy of Derek Taylor.

The COP26 designs evolved from Derek's 50 years of invention, research, design, and development and teaching on renewable energy, especially on solar and wind power, and on homes that combine very high energy efficiency with building-integrated renewable energy. To understand how these designs emerged I interviewed Derek three times in 2022 and 2023 and drew on documents and lectures about his life and career, including a short biography and details of the COP26 house designs (Taylor, 2021; 2022a; 2022b; 2023).

### Background

Derek grew up in an English market town with a tradition of local building construction. According to Derek's biography (Taylor, 2022a) his paternal grandfather was a master carpenter, and his maternal grandfather is said to have patented a bicycle for use by injured servicemen. As a child Derek, like Dyson, read the *Eagle* comic with its detailed drawings of futuristic technologies. He also made models from Meccano and 'Brickplayer', a miniature bricks and mortar building system. Derek also constructed model aircraft and learned how to make furniture from his father, who was a keen woodworker. At school his woodwork teacher taught Derek furniture making, building construction, and technical drawing.

### Early career and higher education

After school Derek got a job as an architectural technician and draughts-man with a local practice where he learnt much about the architect's trade and worked on architectural drawings of buildings, including innovative tim-ber buildings. He later worked in the architectural office at the Ministry of Public Buildings & Works in Bristol, preparing drawings of government build-ings. During his early career Derek obtained qualifications in Construction Technology which enabled him in 1970 to begin undergraduate architectural studies at the Polytechnic of Central London (PCL), now the University of Westminster (Taylor, 2022a).

At PCL Derek worked on a range of projects, including the design of a geo-desic structure that resembled the Eden Project's domes but predated them by several decades. Amongst the PCL staff were Chris Day and Steven Szokolay who were influential in raising awareness of environmental and energy issues related to buildings. For example, Szokolay worked on a project that later became the UK's first active solar house in Milton Keynes (see the Oxley Woods case study in Chapter 5).

By the time Derek joined PCL, the anti-establishment, countercultural movement that emerged in the US in the 1960s was well established in the UK. A major strand of this movement was deep environmentalism which developed from the increasing awareness during the 1960s and 1970s of environmental threats to the planet, wildlife, and health. In 1968 the first *Whole Earth Catalog* was published in the US, with a NASA image of the earth from space on the cover emphasising the finite nature of the planet. The *Catalog* series to 1975 became a source of information and tools for individu-als and groups wanting to establish alternative lifestyles and self-governing communities, usually with a strong ecological ethos. An influential philosopher on global environmental issues at the time was the inventor, architect, engi-neer, and futurist Buckminster Fuller. With his radically innovative solutions to environmental and many other problems, notably the geodesic dome as an efficient form of shelter, Fuller's ideas were especially influential among archi-tects, designers, and engineers including the producers of the *Whole Earth Catalog* and, in the UK, what became known as the Alternative Technology (AT) movement.

Like many other architecture students, Derek was influenced by Fuller's ideas and the countercultural *Whole Earth Catalog* and became an active mem-ber of the AT movement. In joining friends such as Peter Harper and Godfrey Boyle who started the movement in the UK, Derek was mainly concerned with alternative energy sources, solar design, building energy conservation, low-impact building materials, and vernacular building methods (Taylor, 2022a; 2022b). Whilst he was also interested in self-building, co-housing, alternative farming, and self-sufficiency, Derek was less involved with the movement's radi-cal visions for an alternative society with a decentralised economy, and a 'new age' culture. At PCL Derek worked on the design of a solar house for the UK climate and was attempting to find solutions for domestic energy provision in winter. After considering and discussing different energy options, Derek realised that wind power could complement solar energy in winter and seemed to have substantial potential in the UK. Yet in the early 1970s few were researching wind resources or technology.

After being discouraged from working on eco-architecture at PCL, in 1972 Derek switched to the more receptive Architectural Association (AA) School of Architecture. At the AA students and some staff were interested in AT ideas and projects. A Rational Technology Unit was set up, co-founded by Derek, and Buckminster Fuller came to speak at the AA. Throughout the 1970s, Derek worked on a variety of solar building projects and wind power technologies and wrote a guide to designing wind turbines. While at the AA, Derek also worked in several small architectural practices.

After graduating from the AA, to develop his engineering knowledge, Derek took a master's degree in Industrial Design Engineering at the Royal College of Art where from 1976 he conducted an in-depth study of wind power engineering and for his dissertation wrote a two-volume *Wind Power Primer* (Taylor, 1978).

**What lessons may be drawn from this brief account of Derek's background, early career, and higher education?**

Derek grew up in a culture of *creating and making things* such as furniture and buildings.

His *background* and the *skills* learned in his childhood and at school helped to equip Derek for *practical and creative* career in architecture.

The context of *growing environmental consciousness* during the 1960s and 1970s got Derek interested in environmental issues, especially concerning energy and buildings.

Derek's thinking and work was *influenced by individuals, groups, and publications* with radically alternative ideas for society, technology, and design.

Moving from PCL to the more *creative and innovative environment* of the AA was important in encouraging and supporting Derek's interest and work in eco-architecture.

*Collaboration with people* with similar ideas in the AA's Rational Technology Unit was important in developing Derek's ideas and designs.

Derek took an MSc degree to study wind power engineering to the level of *domain-specific knowledge* needed to develop wind turbines to power buildings.

## Wind power invention, research, and development

In 1979 Derek joined ATG (the Alternative Technology Group) and the Design Discipline at the Open University (OU), groups with many likeminded members, including renewable energy pioneer Godfrey Boyle. As well as producing teaching materials on renewable energy (e.g., Taylor, 2018), Derek invented, patented, researched, and tested several innovative wind turbines. For his PhD he developed the Taylor *Sailfoil*™ turbine (Figure 4.13 (a)). This was followed by the Taylor *V-VAWT*™ family of vertical axis wind turbines (Figure 4.13 (b)) for which he collaborated with David Sharpe, an aeronautical engineer at Queen Mary College and with Jim Platts and others at Gifford Technology Ltd., designers and makers of wind turbine blades (now part of the Danish wind energy com-

(a)

(b)

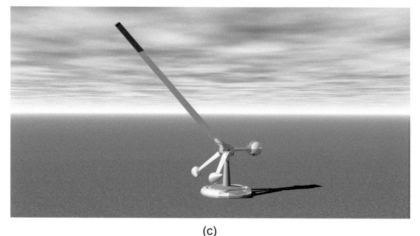

(c)

Figure 4.13
(a) 4m diameter Taylor Sailfoil™ turbine built and tested at the Open University, Milton Keynes, early 1980s (Taylor, 2022b). Courtesy of Derek Taylor.
4.13 (b) Taylor V-VAWT™ (V-Type Vertical Axis Wind Turbine) prototype with 5.5m blades developed and tested at the Open University, Milton Keynes, 1980s (Taylor, 2018, p. 366). Courtesy of Derek Taylor.
4.13 (c) Visualisation of single-blade counterbalanced Taylor Sycamore Rotor™ turbine. A wind tunnel model was built and successfully tested, late 1990s. Copyright Derek Taylor/Altechnica. Courtesy of Derek Taylor.

pany Vestas). Later in the OU Energy and Environment Research Unit (EERU) he researched and tested the innovative Taylor *Sycamore Rotor*™ turbine (Figure 4.13 (c)), helped by ATG/EERU technicians and another EERU researcher for the mathematical modelling required.

Key drivers for Derek's wind power inventions were the high cost of turbine towers and of propellor-type turbine blades and the technical skills required to make such blades. Derek addressed these problems by using fabric-covered blades and/or vertical axis designs. The *V-Turbine* (Figure 4.13 (b)) was self-starting, unlike other aerofoil type vertical axis turbines, while the Sycamore Rotor™ vertical axis turbine saved costs further by using a single counterbalanced, carbon fibre blade (Figure 4.13 (c)). The Sycamore was a complex design that offered many potential advantages, which Derek regarded as a 'blue skies thinking' challenge (Taylor, 2022b).

However, the cost of propellor-type blades and towers for horizontal axis turbines gradually reduced with innovations and serial production in Denmark and elsewhere and such turbines began to be produced in increasing sizes and outputs. So, despite Derek obtaining research funding and some industrial collaboration to develop his innovative designs, none went beyond the prototype stage. It became too difficult to fund the extensive development and testing programme needed to commercialise Derek's designs in competition with an increasingly successful horizontal axis wind turbine technology. A fast-growing wind energy industry began to produce such turbines with progressively higher outputs; from 10 to 55 kW at the beginning of the 1980s to megawatt turbines in the 2000s. Also, UK R&D policy under the 1980s Conservative government restricted wind turbine research funding. A further barrier was the damaged reputation of *all* vertical axis turbines in the 1980s and early 1990s due to blade failures on a 500kW experimental vertical axis turbine in the UK and on vertical axis wind farms in the US.

How did Derek create and develop his inventions and designs? The conception, design, and development of the Sailfoil™ turbine developed for Derek's PhD is described in his thesis (Taylor, 1986). The process involved a review of existing wind turbines, focusing on small and medium sized designs that did not involve the aerospace technology of large-scale machines. The aim was to design an efficient, low-cost turbine that could be made by small engineering companies across the world. Derek concluded that sail type designs, and especially the D-spar Sailwing developed at Princeton University in the 1970s, offered the most aerodynamic promise. Derek's design addressed its disadvantages by simplifying and stiffening the trailing edge of the sail and using a more durable fabric cover. This design was developed involving engineering and aerodynamic analyses, successfully built and tested, and then patented at the Open University. In 2022 Derek returned to working on the Sailfoil™ design with blades using materials and manufacturing methods unavailable when it was originally developed.

**What lessons about creative design and innovation can be learned from Derek's invention, research, design, and development of wind turbines?**

Joining a *supportive group* at the OU whose members had similar environmental ideas enabled Derek to work on designing innovative wind turbines.

Derek was *dissatisfied* with existing small and medium sized wind turbines and was strongly *motivated* to create improved designs.

Before creating the *Sailfoil™* and vertical axis wind turbines Derek had accumulated *in-depth knowledge of and skills* in wind power technology and had designed and built early prototypes of these turbines.

Derek was *determined* and prepared to dedicate himself to the difficult task of developing his innovative ideas and concepts, including the technical challenge of designing the *Sycamore Rotor™*.

Derek's initial idea, *goal*, or *primary generator* was to create turbines that avoided the high cost and complexity of turbine blades and towers. This led to his improvement of low-cost fabric-covered blades and invention of a family of vertical axis turbines which did not need an expensive, tall steel lattice or concrete tower.

Another likely motivation for Derek as an inventor and designer was to create designs that were *original*. He was awarded a PhD for the design, development, and testing of the Sailfoil™ turbine, and took out *patents and trademarks* on his inventions to protect his intellectual property.

Derek's process of researching, inventing, designing, and developing the Sailfoil™ turbine involved typical creative design approaches. These included: *immersion* in information about the problem to be addressed; reviewing *existing inventions, designs, and solutions* to identify a promising concept; *adapting* an existing design to address its disadvantages; and developing and testing the design by employing *engineering science, sketches, drawings, models, and prototypes*.

Derek keeps up with the development of relevant *new materials and components*, e.g., he used a more durable fabric for the Sailfoil™ blades. He is still improving the design to make use of the latest materials and manufacturing methods, i.e., *continous innovation*.

Derek's turbines were not developed beyond prototypes given several *barriers to innovation*, including *competition* from established horizontal axis designs; the *cost of development and testing* for commercialisation; the *damaged reputation* of all vertical axis turbines due to technical failures in other projects; and lack of *government support*.

### The Altechnica eco-innovation and design consultancy

In 1989, given the difficulty of obtaining renewable energy research funding under the Conservative government, Derek returned to commercial architectural practice. Then in 1990 he founded a consultancy called *Altechnica* to continue his work on zero- and positive-energy buildings, wind and solar technology, and renewable energy feasibility studies.

### The Energy Showcase

Through Altechnica Derek collaborated with a personal client, energy consultant David Olivier, to design an almost zero heating house, *The Energy Showcase*. The house achieved its performance mainly through a combination of passive solar gain, triple glazing, and a high thermal mass concrete shell wrapped with super-insulation (Olivier, 2015; Olivier and Taylor, 2016). The house also has solar photovoltaic (PV) panels built into the south-facing roof to provide some of its electricity (Figure 4.14). This project built on and adapted ultra-low energy building methods already demonstrated in Europe and North America and, whilst based on a different approach, shared many attributes of the work of other British eco-architects that Derek knew, including Sue Roaf's *Oxford Solar House*, Robert and Brenda Vale's *Autonomous Urban House*, and the Hockerton earth-sheltered terraced housing, both in Nottinghamshire, UK.

The poured unreinforced concrete construction used to build The Energy Showcase was innovative, but in this site-built demonstration project it proved to be a time-consuming method. Also, the difficulties experienced in obtaining commercial reusable formwork necessitated using custom-made formwork, which further slowed the build.

### The Aeolian Roof™

In the 1990s through Altechnica Derek invented and patented a family of planar concentrator devices which accelerate wind speed as it interacts with a wind turbine. He called these inventions *Aeolian Wing Concentrators*™ due to their similarities to wings (Taylor, 1998).

Many wind concentrator devices had already been invented and some built and tested. Derek's invention arose from him thinking about the many drawbacks of cylindrical ducted wind turbine concentrators and mentally 'unrolling' the duct to form a flat inverted aerofoil, like that on the wings that provide the downforce for a Formula 1 car. Derek considered that if small turbines were placed in the space between an upper inverted aerofoil and a lower surface, the wind speed should be accelerated and the turbine output increased. Derek had long been attempting to find a viable way to utilise wind energy for buildings and wondered whether the shape of a building could also contribute to augmenting wind power. He did some computer modelling and wind tunnel testing at the UK Building Research Establishment (BRE) to see if his idea would work, with promising results.

Derek's Aeolian Wing Concentrators™ can be freestanding or attached to buildings. The *Aeolian Roof*™ variant is designed to be located above the ridge

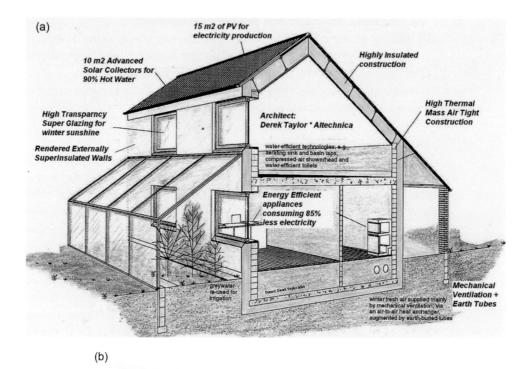

(a)

15 m2 of PV for
electricity production

10 m2 Advanced
Solar Collectors for
90% Hot Water

Highly insulated
construction

High Transparncy
Super Glazing for
winter sunshine

Architect:
Derek Taylor * Altechnica

High Thermal
Mass Air Tight
Construction

Rendered Externally
Superinsulated Walls

water-efficient technologies; e.g.,
aerating sink and basin taps,
compressed-air showerhead and
water-efficient toilets

Energy Efficient
appliances
consuming 85%
less electricity

greywater
re-used for
irrigation

winter fresh air supplied mainly
by mechanical ventilation, via
an air-to-air heat exchanger,
augmented by earth-buried tubes

Mechanical
Ventilation +
Earth Tubes

(b)

Figure 4.14
(a) 3D section of The Energy Showcase, 1994. Copyright Derek Taylor/Altechnica. Courtesy of Derek Taylor.
4.14  (b) Completed Energy Showcase house, Herefordshire, UK. Construction started in the late 1990s and the house was ready for occupation from 2012 (Olivier and Taylor, 2016). Courtesy of Derek Taylor and David Olivier.

of a building's pitched or curved roof and small wind turbines placed between the underside of the wing and the ridge.

In the mid-2000s, at the Open University, Derek and a PhD student, Antonio Aguiló-Rullàn, collaborated with the BRE, mainly with Dr Robin Wiltshire, and the Silsoe Research Institute, mainly with Dr Adam Robertson, to design, install, and test an Aeolian Roof™ incorporating small commercial horizontal axis turbines on the ridge of a large agricultural building at Silsoe (Aguiló-Rullàn et al., 2004). After experimenting with the height of the space, and much testing and refining of the design, a 60 per cent increase in power output was measured (Aguiló-Rullán, 2009) with a doubling of output after further development. The device was also able to 'bend' the wind from different directions and seems able to 'pull' winds down from higher altitudes, acting somewhat like a tall tower.

According to Derek, if appropriately designed, the Aeolian Roof™ should avoid many of the problems experienced when installing wind turbines on or near buildings. When solar PV cells are incorporated into its upper surface the Aeolian Roof™ could produce solar- and wind-powered electricity from the same device, taking advantage of the complementary seasonal availability of these resources in many countries (Figure 4.15).

However, progressing this highly innovative system further has proved challenging as opportunities to fund innovative projects of this type in the UK beyond initial prototypes has been difficult. Another barrier is the cost of worldwide patents and the impossibility of defending them if, as had happened before, Derek's ideas are copied by potential collaborators. As a way forward, Derek has begun to explore the scope for incorporating the Aeolian Roof™ into his own building designs, such as the *AeroSolar Dek House*™ project, or through open licencing (Taylor, 2023).

**What can be learned about creative design and innovation from the conception, design, development and construction of *The Energy Showcase* and the prototype *Aeolian Roof*™?**

### *The Energy Showcase*

To design The Energy Showcase Derek drew upon the technical principles and designs of *existing ultra-low energy houses* in Europe, the US, and Canada, and in the UK by a group of eco-architects of which he was a member.

Derek and his client put together *available technologies, designs, materials, and components* of ultra-low energy houses to create a new design.

The construction method chosen for the house was unsuited to widespread adoption but accepted for this experimental prototype building.

### *The Aeolian Roof*™

It is possible that Derek had a *'lightbulb moment'* that gave him the idea of a planar wind concentrator by 'unrolling' a ducted concentrator, configured like a 'bi-plane' or a 'wing' attached to a building's roof.

The *goals* or *primary generators* for the Aeolian Roof™ was to find a practical system to increase the output of small wind turbines and complement solar energy, avoid the need for tall turbine towers, and contribute to the renewable energy requirement of buildings.

Developing and evaluating the concept required *research funding and collaboration* between the Open University and other organisations. The projects involved research and development, detailed monitoring, and *iterative design* of a prototype.

Derek *patented* and *trademarked* the Aeolian Roof™ to protect his intellectual property.

Despite demonstration of its effectiveness, progressing the Aeolian Roof™ beyond experimental prototypes has been challenging, given the *lack of funding* for radically innovative projects and the *costs of worldwide patent protection*.

Derek can be wary of collaboration if there is a risk of his *ideas being copied* or his *patents being infringed* as the cost of defending his IP would be prohibitive.

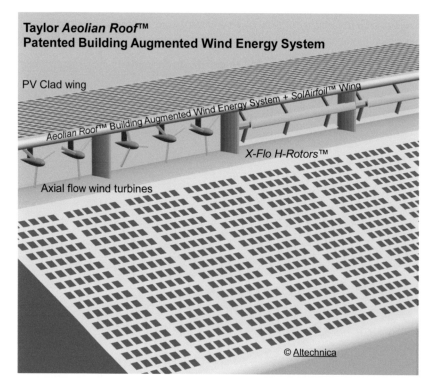

Figure 4.15
Aeolian Roof™ with horizontal axial flow and crossflow wind turbines and solar PV panels (Taylor, 2018, p. 495). Copyright Derek Taylor/Altechnica. Courtesy of Derek Taylor.

### The AeroSolar Dek House™ + Building System

The *AeroSolar Dek House™+ Building System* is the innovative concept design, illustrated at the beginning of this case study (Figure 4.12), that Derek was invited to display at the 'Images of Climate Innovation' exhibition at the 2021 UN COP26 Climate Change Conference. Derek's invitation to show his work is significant given that COP26 was widely seen as one of the international community's last chances to agree on policies and actions to avoid catastrophic climate change.

This concept design brings together many of Derek's ideas, inventions, and designs to explore the potential for combining passive solar design with building-integrated wind and solar energy to substantially reduce the carbon footprint of buildings. Derek had previously demonstrated some of the House's principles and components with The Energy Showcase and the Aeolian Roof™. But a key difference from The Energy Showcase is the innovative construction system. Derek wanted to avoid using concrete, which has high embodied carbon, and imported timber. In response he invented a prefabricated, interlocking double-panel building system, comprising an internal wall panel filled with unbaked earth or other materials to provide thermal mass, clad with a super-insulated and weatherproof panel.

The living areas of the AeroSolar Dek House™ wrap around a large thermally isolated central atrium with a roof (either semi-transparent or opaque) clad in solar panels and high-performance glazing to provide light, passive ventilation, electricity, and optional solar water heating. In areas with suitable wind, the Aeolian Roof™ sits on the atrium's roof ridge to generate additional wind and solar electricity. Derek has proposed several other environmental features to the house such as a green roof, food growing space, energy storage, and solar wall cladding. The aim is a building that helps tackle both the climate and biodiversity crises (Taylor, 2021). Whilst Derek has included many innovative features and options, he does not think that all of them would be implemented, rather he envisages a prototype used as a research test bed and to develop a hierarchy of AeroSolar options and features for climate resilient homes and communities.

Of course, the AeroSolar Dek House™ + Building System is only a concept design at present. It includes numerous novel ideas and highly innovative components and looks completely different from conventional homes. Critics might argue that trying to innovate in so many directions at once is risky (see the Oxley Park eco-housing case in Chapter 5). However, Derek argues that elements such as the Building System could be developed independently. He hopes to build a demonstration scale model or prototype, or an experimental case study house, given sufficient collaboration and/or funding, including from crowdsourcing or open-source licencing (Taylor, 2023). At this point it is an inspiring innovative concept, which Derek hopes will encourage a more holistic, ecologically driven paradigm and toolkit for, and route map to, the design of buildings that combine very high energy efficiency with building-integrated renewable energy innovations. Indeed, radical concept designs can stimulate other architects also to think radically, as Buckminster Fuller and the *Archigram* group at the AA did in the 1960s and 1970s with their futuristic designs that influenced a generation of young architects (Cook, 1999).

**What additional lessons can be learned about creative design and innovation from the *AeroSolar Dek House™ + Building System*?**

Derek Talyor is clearly someone with the *visionary imagination* and *creativity* needed to create such a radically innovative concept.

Whether such innovative concepts, or elements of them, can be adopted in a conservative construction industry and housing market remains to be seen, but it is a highly imaginative and radically different approach.

This futuristic concept could *inspire*, and *provide ideas* to, other architects to enable them to create more innovative and effective sustainable buildings.

Given the existential threat to humanity posed by the climate emergency, radically reducing the environmental impacts of buildings and enabling a rapid transition to carbon-free energy supplies is crucial. The AeroSolar Dek House™ + Building System is an attempt to create an integrated concept design to radically reduce the impact of new housing and increase its climate resilience, showcased at a very prestigious international event. Elements of the building system may also provide an alternative approach to the low carbon retrofitting of existing buildings, a task of equal importance as designing zero and positive carbon new buildings.

## REFERENCES

Aguiló-Rullàn, A., Taylor, D., Wiltshire, R. and Quinn, A. (2004) 'Computational Fluid Dynamic Modelling of wind speed enhancement through a building-augmented wind concentration system'. *European Wind Energy Conference 2004*. London, 22–25 November.

Aguiló-Rullàn, A. (2009) *The Aeolian Roof: a building integrated wind and solar energy system in order to supply the electricity needs of a building* (PhD thesis). The Open University. Available at: https://oro.open.ac.uk/65559/1/850908.pdf (Accessed: 20 June 2023).

BBC (2019) *Sir James Dyson: From barrows to billions*. Available at: https://www.bbc.co.uk/news/business-46149743 (Accessed: 28 June 2023).

Bessant, J. (2020) *Dyson. Managing Innovation case studies*. Available at: https://www.johnbessant.org/_files/ugd/6ba33a_9e2711303e874edcbba8f4f7ca804470.pdf (Accessed: 28 June 2023).

Consumers' Association (1994) 'Cleaning up', *Which?* April, pp. 52–6.

Cook, P. (ed.) (1999) *Archigram*. New York: Princeton Architectural Press.

Coren, G. and Dyson, J. (2001) *Against the odds: An autobiography* (2nd edition). London: Texere Publishing.

Cropley, S. (2020) *The inside story of the Dyson EV*. Available at: https://www.autocar.co.uk/car-news/features/exclusive-inside-story-dyson-ev (Accessed: 6 July 2023).

Dyson, J. (2021) *Invention: A life*. London: Simon & Schuster. Videos of chapters from the book available at: https://www.dyson.co.uk/james-dyson/invention-a-life (Accessed: 6 July 2023).

Dyson (2023) *Technology investment*. Available at: https://www.dyson.co.uk/newsroom/overview/features/november-2020/technology-investment (Accessed: 8 July 2023).

James Dyson Foundation (undated) 'Design Build Test. Teachers Pack'. *James Dyson Foundation*. Available at: http://media.dyson.com/downloads/JDF/JDF_Teachers_Pack.pdf (Accessed: 6 July 2023).

Olivier, D. (2015) *The Energy Showcase. A Pioneering Solar House*. Available at: http://energyshowcase.org.uk/ (Accessed: 20 June 2023).

Olivier, D. and Taylor, D. A. (2016) 'The Energy Showcase: A Pioneering Solar House', in L. Jankovic (ed.) *Zero Carbon Buildings Today and in the Future 2016*. Proceedings of a conference, Birmingham City University, 8–9 September. Birmingham: Birmingham City University.

Pooler, M., Campbell, P. and Palma, S. (2019) 'Why Dyson is shifting its HQ to Singapore', *Financial Times*, 23 January. Available at: https://www.ft.com/content/02a636d8-1f2f-11e9-b2f7-97e4dbd3580d (Accessed: 6 July 2023).

Roy, R. (1993) 'Case studies of creativity in innovative product development', *Design Studies*, 14(4), pp. 423–43. Available at: https://oro.open.ac.uk/28441/ (Accessed: 28 June2023).

Roy, R. (1995) 'Creativity and innovation', Video 3. T204 *Design: Principles and Practice*. Milton Keynes: The Open University.

Roy, R. (2009) 'Creativity and concept design', T211 *Design and designing*, Block 3 (2nd edition) and video 'James Dyson: designer and innovator'. Milton Keynes: The Open University.

Roy, R. (2013) 'Creative design', T217 *Design essentials,* Book 3. Milton Keynes: The Open University.

Sharp, A. (1896) *Bicycles & tricycles. An Elementary Treatise on their Design and Construction*. London: Longmans Green. (1977 Reprint, Cambridge, Mass: MIT Press.)

Starley, W.K. (1898) 'The evolution of the bicycle', *Journal of the Society of Arts*, 46, May, pp. 601–16.

Saul, S.B. (1970) *Technological change: the United States and Britain in the nineteenth century*. London: Methuen.

Taylor, D.A. (1978) *Wind Power Primer* (2 volumes). London: School of Industrial Design (Engineering), Royal College of Art.

Taylor, D.A. (1986) *The design and testing of a horizontal axis wind turbine with sailfoil blades* (PhD thesis). The Open University. Available at: https://oro.open.ac.uk/54193/1/372170.pdf (Accessed: 20 June 2023).

Taylor, D.A. (1998) 'Using buildings to harness wind energy', *Building Research and Information*, 26(3), pp.199–202.

Taylor, D.A. (2018) 'Wind Energy', in S. Peake (ed.) *Renewable Energy: Power for a sustainable future* (4th edition). Oxford: Oxford University Press.

Taylor, D.A. (2021) *AeroSolar Dek House™ + Building System* (Poster, 'Images of Climate Innovation' exhibition, UN COP26 Climate Change conference). Glasgow, 1–12 November.

Taylor, D. A. (2022a) *Dr Derek Taylor – Brief Bio*. For 45+ years of Energy Research at The Open University conference, Milton Keynes, 21 June. Unpublished.

**■ Radical product and building innovations**

Taylor, D.A. (2022b) *OU Renewable Energy Education. The First 25 Years + Some Wind Energy Activities*. For 45+ years of Energy Research at The Open University conference, Milton Keynes, 21 June. Unpublished.

Taylor, D.A. (2023) *Riding the wind and sun for 50 years and other stories* (Lecture). Buckinghamshire Society of Architects, Milton Keynes Gallery, 26 April.

Utterback, J. et al. (2006) *Design-inspired innovation*. Singapore: World Scientific Publishing.

Which? Ltd. (1996) 'Vacuum cleaners', *Which?* April, pp. 38–43.

Which? Ltd. (2000) 'Eight cyclones better than two', *Which?* September, p. 11.

Which? Ltd. (2001) 'Design of the times', *Which?* April, pp. 51–4.

# 5     Major product and building innovations

## INTRODUCTION

In this chapter I examine two case studies of innovations which represent major improvements on what existed previously. The first is a 19th century product innovation, the pneumatic cycle tyre, which has gained almost universal acceptance and led to a major vehicle tyre industry. The second case concerns a significant innovation in prefabricated eco-housing which, even after further development, has so far only gained limited further adoption. As before, I will attempt to identify the factors and processes involved in their creation, development, and introduction to provide lessons for successful, and less successful, innovation.

## CASE STUDY: THE DUNLOP PNEUMATIC TYRE

Dunlop's *pneumatic tyre* of 1888 was probably the most significant of the technical innovations to be applied to the standard diamond-frame bicycle (pioneered by the Rover Safety discussed in Chapter 4), displacing solid rubber and cushion tyres. The pneumatic tyre not only increased the rider's comfort by absorbing road bumps, but also reduced effort and increased speed by minimising the jarring of the cycle and the rider.

### The Thompson pneumatic tyre
The pneumatic tyre had already been invented and patented in 1845 by a Scottish civil engineer, Robert Thompson. He failed, however, to make a commercial success of his invention and consequently his name is almost unknown. The reasons for Thompson's failure to achieve an innovation are instructive. Neither the bicycle nor vulcanised rubber were developed at the time of Thompson's pneumatic tyre, so he had to think in terms of the vehicles and materials available to him. He envisaged that his 'aerial wheels' would be used on horse-drawn carriages, steam vehicles, and even railway carriages. He constructed his tyres from a tube of rubberised canvas with a leather cover that was bolted to the wheel rim, making them difficult to service. Thompson demonstrated that tractive effort on rough roads was considerably reduced with his aerial wheels, and he eventually managed to get his tyres fitted to a few royal carriages. But the cost of making these pneumatic tyres was prohibitive and there was never a sufficiently large market in tyres for horse-drawn and heavy vehicles of the time for his invention to be commercially viable.

DOI: 10.4324/9781003354406-5

**What were the reasons for the failure of Thompson's *pneumatic tyre* to become a commercial innovation?**

Essential *enabling technologies*, suitable materials to make a durable pneumatic tyre, and *complementary assets*, suitable vehicles to apply the tyre to, were not available at the time of the invention.

The design had *technical deficiencies*; for example, it could not easily be removed for replacement or repair.

But the main problem was that there was an *insufficient market* for a costly pneumatic tyre to make it a commercial proposition. That had to wait for the safety bicycle and motor car.

### *Invention of the Dunlop pneumatic cycle tyre*

John Boyd Dunlop, a Scottish veterinary surgeon working in Dublin, was the second and successful inventor of the pneumatic tyre. How did his idea of the pneumatic cycle tyre arise? Arthur du Cros, whose father co-founded what would become the Dunlop Pneumatic Tyre Company, provides an account in his book *Wheels of Fortune* of how he understood Dunlop eventually came up with the idea in 1887, after considering various anti-vibration devices such as spring wheels:

> Dunlop's mind, like Thompson's ... had been revolving for years around the problem of [vehicle] anti-vibration. ... At length it dawned ... that the problem might be solved by means of a triple tube of rubber, canvas and rubber distended with compressed air (du Cros, 1938, p. 32, p. 38).

But why an air-filled rubber tyre? Although Dunlop does not say how he got the idea, according to du Cros it is likely that the idea stemmed from Dunlop's experience of using rubber appliances during his work as a veterinary surgeon (du Cros, 1938, p. 36).

Dunlop quickly tested his basic idea by conducting an experiment using a solid disc of wood to which he nailed a pocket of linen that enclosed an inflated rubber tube. Dunlop compared the rolling properties of this wheel with a solid rubber-tyred wheel, with promising results. In a book about his invention, *The History of the Pneumatic Tyre*, he wrote,

> I first threw the solid tyred wheel along the yard, but it did not go the full length of it. Then I threw the air-tyred disc. It went the whole length of the yard and rebounded with considerable force off the gate (Dunlop, 1922, p. 11).

Dunlop's motivation to develop an air tyre came originally from his son. The boy wanted to beat his friends in cycle races and complained of the difficulty of cycling on the Belfast streets, which were surfaced partly with granite setts. For a proper test of his air tyre Dunlop fitted an improved version to the boy's tricycle. This comprised wooden-rimmed rear wheels with a rubber tube, with a valve for inflation, glued to the rim and contained in a canvas pocket which was protected by an outer wrapping of sheet rubber.

The prototype tricycle trial showed that Dunlop's air tyres provided a much smoother ride on rough surfaces than solid rubber tyres. Arthur du Cros, who knew Dunlop, then tried a pneumatic-tyred tricycle, and was struck by the smooth running and speed of the machine (du Cross, 1938, p. 36). He encouraged Dunlop to exploit his invention and the first bicycle fitted with a pneumatic tyre (like that shown in Figure 5.1) was built. In 1888 Dunlop applied for a patent on his invention.

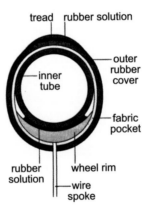

Figure 5.1
Dunlop's original pneumatic cycle tyre of 1888 (Roy, 2013, p. 40). Courtesy of the Open University.

**What does the case of Dunlop's *pneumatic cycle tyre* illustrate about creativity, invention, design, and development?**

Dunlop's creative process shows that attempts to understand and solve a problem may be needed over many years before the idea for its solution occurs. This is sometimes described as the *preparation phase*, in which creators *immerse* themselves in a task and *explore* the problem and think of *alternative solutions*, which may lead to one or more practical ideas.

If du Cros's interpretation is correct, Dunlop's creative idea involved the *transfer* or *bisociation* of ideas or objects from one field (veterinary appliances) to another (vehicle wheels). Another view is that Dunlop got the idea from seeing animal intestines during his work. This would have meant he used a *biological analogy* (intestines looking like an inflated tyre) as inspiration for his idea.

Dunlop's trial air tyre for his son's tricycle shows that experimenting with a mock-up or a *principle-proving model* (like Dyson's cardboard cyclone on a conventional vacuum cleaner) is often required to establish basic feasibility. Once Dunlop had conceived the idea of an air-filled tyre, he performed a series of experiments develop it into a practical design. In the creative process he undertook what has been called *verification*.

To protect his intellectual property Dunlop *patented* his invention that included a design example that embodied the inventive idea in practical form.

### Innovation and diffusion of the pneumatic cycle tyre

Among the earliest converts to pneumatic tyres was Arthur du Cros's father, Harvey du Cros, president of the Irish Cycling Association, with Arthur a member of the Irish racing team. Harvey attempted to interest manufacturers in Dunlop's invention by introducing pneumatic-tyred bicycles into cycle racing. However, the sausage-like pneumatic tyre was at first greeted with scepticism among cyclists, and with outright ridicule from the public. It eventually gained acceptance when Irish cyclists using pneumatic-tyred machines began to win races against English riders of solid- and cushion-tyred bicycles. Convinced of their commercial potential, in 1889 Harvey du Cros founded in Dublin the world's first company for manufacturing pneumatic cycle tyres. This was the beginnings of a business that became the Dunlop multinational rubber and vehicle tyre company. Despite the early racing successes, the pneumatic tyre still met with considerable opposition from cyclists and manufacturers. English manufacturers were not willing to modify their cycle frames to accommodate the fatter pneumatic tyres and cyclists preferred the slimmer and more elegant looking solid and cushion tyres. This led to heated discussions throughout the cycling world, which by publicising the sporting successes of the pneumatic tyre helped to generate public demand.

The Dunlop tyre of 1888, however, suffered from several technical deficiencies; especially that it punctured easily and was permanently fixed to the wheel making its repair or replacement a complex and skilled operation. The tyre therefore required the attention of other inventors before it was developed sufficiently to make its widespread adoption possible. Several inventors devised methods for attaching the outer covers of pneumatic tyres to the rims of cycle wheels so that the tyre could be easily removed. These methods included C.K. Welch's patent for 'wired-on' tyres and W.E. Bartlett's patent, both of 1890, that led to the 'beaded edge' tyre. In France, Edouard Michelin patented his detachable pneumatic tyre in 1891.

With the appearance of the detachable pneumatic tyre, plus other improvements in tyre design, construction, and manufacture, the pneumatic cycle tyre rapidly gained acceptance after 1892 and from the mid-1890s the innovation was in general use. The pneumatic cycle tyre then provided the technical basis for the development and manufacture of pneumatic tyres for other vehicles, including motorcycles and motor cars, which (as was discussed in Chapter 4) were being developed by cycle companies around the same time.

**What lessons can be learned from the successful innovation of the *pneumatic cycle tyre*?**

Developing a promising invention into a commercial product innovation requires *entrepreneurship, finance, and the establishment of a business* to manufacture and market the new product.

Innovations when first introduced may receive considerable *opposition to their adoption* and even ridicule.

Innovations often need *further development* and the incorporation of *further inventions and innovations* before their deficiencies are resolved and they can gain widespread adoption.

Widespread adoption (or diffusion) usually only occurs when an innovation clearly *demonstrates its superiority* (or relative advantage) *over existing designs and technologies.*

## CASE STUDY: OXLEY WOODS PREFABRICATED ECO-HOMES

### The context

In the 1970s and 1980s several low energy homes and housing developments, were designed and built in the new town (now city) of Milton Keynes. The projects started with the design and completion from 1972–4 of the UK's first active solar house. It had a large rooftop solar collector on a standard terraced house and an inter-seasonal water heat store to provide central heating and hot water. This innovation arose in the global context of the first United Nations Environment Conference in 1972 and the energy crisis caused by the 1973 OPEC embargo on oil exports. Low energy housing projects were encouraged by Milton Keynes Development Corporation (MKDC) as a planning authority which employed teams of young modernist architects (such as Robert de Grey whose work is discussed in chapter 6) committed to making the new town a model for the future. Architects and engineers from MKDC worked with energy specialists at the Department of Energy and the Open University to design, build, and monitor several of these low energy homes. The projects employed different energy saving technologies from super-insulation, passive and active solar heating, to the use of heat pumps, and even some houses heated by efficient coal-fired boilers.

In 1979, with the election of a Conservative government under Margaret Thatcher committed to private development, most new Milton Keynes housing became conventional, designed by mass house builders with basic energy-saving features such as good insulation and efficient heating systems. Nevertheless, until MKDC was wound up in 1992 some low energy housing projects continued, including three major developments – *Home World* in 1981, *Energy World* in 1986, and *Future World* in 1994 – which exhibited housing innovations to the public and professionals who came from all over the world to see what was new. For example, Energy World exhibited a variety of low energy house designs including a few experimental homes which for a time had their electricity generated using solar photovoltaics and a wind turbine. As a result of the energy rating system developed for Energy World, conventional homes in the town were designed to meet standards better than those required by national building regulations. John Doggart, an architect involved in several of these low energy housing developments, reviewed them in a retrospective lecture titled *Milton Keynes – Energy Capital UK* (Doggart et al., 2017).

In the 21$^{st}$ century, as the pressures to respond to the climate emergency and the shortage and cost of housing increased, a few Milton Keynes developments again became more innovative in design. One of these innovative projects was the development of 122 new low energy 'eco-homes' at *Oxley Woods* (Figures 5.2 and 5.3) within the Oxley Park area of Milton Keynes.

> ### What can be learned from this account of the evolution of low energy housing projects in Milton Keynes?
>
> The importance of the *environmental, economic, and political context*, including the 1973 oil crisis, Conservative government housing policies, and the climate emergency, in stimulating or hampering innovation.
>
> Vital to the success of the low energy projects were *creative teams* of architects, engineers, energy researchers, and contractors working in and with an *innovative organisation* (MKDC) to design, build, and monitor the low energy housing projects.

### The Design for Manufacture competition

The Oxley Woods development was one of ten winners of an English Partnerships 2005 competition called *Design for Manufacture* (DfM) to design homes which could be built for £60,000 or less, excluding land. I have personal knowledge of this development because a relative has lived in one of the houses since it was completed in 2008.

### The brief for Oxley Woods

As well as a maximum £60,000 construction cost for a proportion of the homes, the Oxley Woods development, like the other winners of the Competition, had

Figure 5.2
Entrance to the
Oxley Woods
development, 2014.
Photograph by the
author.

Figure 5.3
Typical Oxley
Woods living and
kitchen area with
large windows for
natural daylighting.
Photograph by the
author.

to satisfy construction efficiency, environmental, and social sustainability requirements set in the brief and suit the way that housing is financed in Britain. These
requirements, set out in a Homes and Community Agency report on the DfM
projects (HCA, 2010), are listed in Box 5.1.

> **BOX 5.1 REQUIREMENTS OF THE DESIGN FOR MANUFACTURE
> COMPETITION BRIEF (HCA, 2010, p. 8).**
>
> **ECONOMY**
>
> *Designed for manufacture;* at least 30% of homes constructed for £60,000
> or less.

*Construction efficiency;* use of modern methods of construction (MMC) or other methods that achieve significant efficiencies in speed of construction, use of materials, and quality. Examples include factory production of flat wall, floor, or roof panels for assembly on site to make a three-dimensional structure and factory production of three-dimensional 'volumetric' modules ready for site installation (MHCLG, 2019).

*Mortgageable and insurable;* the houses must be innovative but should also use sufficiently trusted and tested solutions to allow them to be mortgaged and insured.

## ENVIRONMENT

*EcoHomes 'Very Good' or Excellent';* at the time of the Oxley Woods project Ecohomes was a scheme that rated new housing developments on environmental and other measures. The measures included: energy (e.g., low $CO_2$ emissions; efficient lights and appliances); transport (e.g., cycling and walking routes; local facilities to reduce car use); materials (e.g., low-impact construction materials); water use (e.g., water-saving toilets); site ecology (e.g., minimal damage to the site); health and wellbeing (e.g., gardens, security).

*Green building materials;* all with a better than 'C' rating on a scale from A+ to E in the BRE *Green Guide to Specification.*

*Car parking;* maximum permitted car parking to the minimum standard acceptable to the local authority; limited on-street parking to supplement on-plot provision.

## SOCIETY AND COMMUNITY

*Secured by design;* design of housing developments to reduce crime and provide safer environments (e.g., by natural surveillance, public lighting).

*Building for Life: Silver;* to achieve this standard, developers had to meet 70% of criteria concerning well-designed housing and neighbourhoods, including: character, environment, and community.

*Inclusive design* to address as many users' needs as possible, including those with different abilities.

*Lifetime homes;* housing that is adaptable to meet the needs of changing lifestyles, households, and generations.

*Minimum space requirement;* floor area for the £60,000 homes to be not less than 76.5m² to appeal to a wide population and future housing markets.

## REPLICABILITY

Competition entries had to provide evidence to show that their approach could be *replicated on other sites.*

### From concept to detailed design and construction

The *concept* design for the Oxley Woods homes to the spatial coordination stage was created by the internationally renowned architectural practice, Rogers Stirk Harbour + Partners (RSHP, formerly Richard Rogers Partnership) working with the developer Taylor Wimpey (then known as George Wimpey). Taylor Wimpey then developed the detailed technical design for manufacture and construction with Wood Newton, a specialised joinery company which designed and supplied the structural timber panels, insulation, cladding, and other components from which the houses were constructed. Building of 122 of the originally planned 145 Oxley Woods houses began in 2007 and was completed in 2008.

The following sections discuss how the RSHP design team responded to the many requirements of the competition.

### The Design for Manufacture concept

The Oxley Woods concept arose from the architects' idea of designing low-cost housing from a standard kit of prefabricated parts. This idea is not new, for example, over 150,000 'prefabs' were built in Britain after World War Two (Baldwin, 2015). The idea was embodied in a concept design using factory-built flat timber panels that could be rapidly assembled and clad in a variety of materials.

The late Lord Richard Rogers – then a senior member of the nine-person project team, although not the project architect – had already worked on prefabricated housing and was well-known for using new technologies in buildings such as the Pompidou Centre in Paris. Among his influences were the French engineer Jean Prouvé who had designed prefabricated housing intended for mass factory production. In 1967, with his then wife Su, Rogers had created the *Zip-up House* designed to be built from available components produced off-site, including walls of neoprene panels originally made for refrigerated trucks. In 1968–70 he and Su designed and built an improved version of the Zip-up House for Rogers' parents (Baldwin, 2015, p. 20, pp. 23–4). The house is Grade II listed by Historic England as a milestone in 'Hi-Tech' design and construction. It comprised a house and separate studio with frames made from yellow painted standard steel sections, sliding windows front and back, and side walls made from prefabricated

PVC-coated aluminium panels linked together with a neoprene zip jointing system (Historic England, 2013). It might be argued that the prefabricated construction and Hi-Tech style of Oxley Woods arose from the design team's immersion in the culture of Rogers' work at RSHP.

Another source of the concept came from an analysis of what RSHP team considered to be the inefficient and inflexible use of space in existing homes. This generated the idea of a standard service core (bathroom, utility room, WC, hall, and stairs) which could be attached to a variety of house types and sizes each with a 'living zone' comprising living/dining room(s), bedrooms, and kitchen (Figures 5.4 (a) and (b)). The team also intended that this concept meant that the living zone could be adapted to changing user needs by moving or adding non-structural internal walls, thus satisfying the Lifetime homes adaptability standard (second drawing from left in Figure 5.4 (a)).

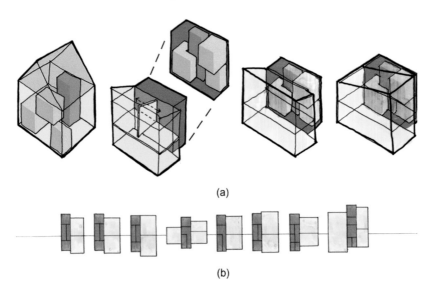

(a)

(b)

Figure 5.4 (a) Design for Manufacture drawings from analysis and reconfiguration of spaces in existing homes by rearranging stairs and services to create the Oxley Woods concept. Stairs (orange), bathroom, utility room, and WC (blue) in a conventional house (left) compared to the same services in a standard core with different living area forms (RSHP, 2014, p. 18). Copyright RSHP. Courtesy of RSHP. Figure 5.4 (b) Different detached and semi-detached living area (yellow) house plans attached to a standard core (red) (RSHP, 2014, p. 18). Copyright RSHP. Courtesy of RSHP.

### What lessons can be learned from the concept design phase of the *Oxley Woods* project?

The DfM Competition provided RSHP's architects with a *strong motivation* to succeed with this project.

An *innovative culture* within RSHP – and probably the legacy of Richard Rogers' ideas – enabled new architectural ideas and concepts to be generated.

The competition brief included many design and planning *requirements and constraints* which provided a *creative challenge* for the design team to meet and resolve.

*Primary generators* that drove the concept design were: houses constructed from a prefabricated kit of parts that could be rapidly assembled on site, and standardised service zones separated from living areas to allow the design of a variety of house types that could be adapted to changing needs.

### Design, development, and construction

Taylor Wimpey invested in a research and development phase with RSHP, leading to the choice of a structural timber panel system for the main components of the houses. This was followed by construction in 2006 of a prototype house near Wood Newton's offices to test and develop the concept. This resulted in significant changes to the design, such as increasing the panel sizes from single story to full height to reduce assembly time and allow the roof to be installed sooner (HCA, 2010, p. 20). Subsequently 30 different two- and three-storey houses with two to five bedrooms were designed by RSHP from concept to the pre-technical stage (that is up to Stage 3 Spatial Coordination in the RIBA *Plan of Work* outlined in Chapter 1, see Figures 5.5 and 5.6).

Figure 5.5
Oxley Woods house
concept drawing
(RSHP, 2009).
Copyright RSHP.
Courtesy of RSHP.

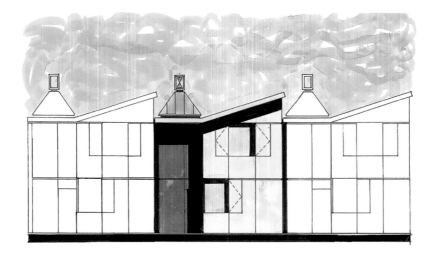

Figure 5.6. Oxley Woods housing early development sketch. Copyright RSHP. Courtesy of RSHP.

Figure 5.7 Oxley Woods homes under construction from prefabricated flat timber panels, roofs, windows, and doors. The full height panels were insulated with recycled newspaper. Photograph by the author.

The prefabricated panel construction with 'Trespa' resin-bound wood fibre rain cladding enabled a range of house types to be built more quickly and efficiently than by traditional methods (Figure 5.7). Other prefabricated components included windows, doors, and floors and the *'EcoHat'* ventilation system. The aim was to build a house in a day, but this this speed of construction was not generally achieved in practice. The construction and cladding (white for living,

Figure 5.8
A completed street
with the Trespa-
clad timber panels,
white for the living
and coloured for
the service zones.
Photograph by the
author.

other colours for service zones) and the red Ecohats gave the homes a novel,
futuristic appearance (Figures 5.2 and 5.8).

*The EcoHat*

An innovative component, the EcoHat, to provide controlled ventilation needed
in such airtight homes, was developed for Oxley Woods to satisfy the *Ecohomes*
energy standard. The EcoHat is a fan-assisted passive ventilation system placed
on top of the service core that uses solar energy when available to pre-warm
cold air entering the building. A version of the EcoHat could also provide solar
heated domestic hot water. The EcoHat concept was developed from an existing Nuaire *Sunwarm* mechanical ventilation system that used solar air panels
to preheat incoming air on cold sunny days (Figure 5.9 (left)). The panels could
also cool the air on hot nights by losing heat to the sky. Oxley Woods homes do
not have lofts and so the Sunwarm's use of the loft space was not possible. The
EcoHat was conceived as a device which could be pointed in any direction, so
avoiding having to orientate the houses towards the sun (Figure 5.9 (right)), as
well as providing a distinctive design feature.

The Ecohat was a major innovation requiring significant design work and
prototype development requiring input from Nuaire and consultant engineers.
The HCA noted, 'Perfecting the technology required time and effort from the
project team, with the successful end-product emerging after a number of
prototypes' (HCA, 2010, p. 21). Further improvements were required after the
first Ecohats were installed and tested. 'The results from the tests prompted
design improvements in future houses to give even better performance. This
aligns with the Competition philosophy of continuous improvement' (HCA,
2010, p. 86).

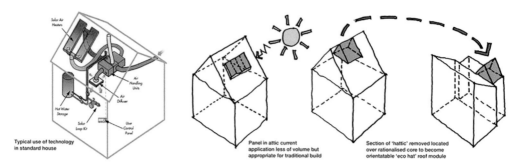

**Figure 5.9**
Left: The existing Nuaire Sunwarm system; Right: The EcoHat concept derived from the Sunwarm. Copyright RSHP. Courtesy of RSHP.

### What can be learned from the design, development, and construction process of *Oxley Woods*?

The need for *research and development* to choose and specify the prefabricated construction system.

The importance of making *prototypes* of the house and *Ecohat* to test and further develop these innovative designs and components.

The use of *associative thinking* to create the Ecohat, involving *transfer from*, and *adaptation of*, an existing product and technology.

The need for *continuous improvement* of the Ecohat in response to experience of the innovation in practice.

### *Meeting constraints and requirements*

Apart from creating the basic concept of the houses and developing the EcoHat, many more decisions were needed by the architects, the developer, and other project partners to meet the requirements of the DfM competition brief.

The basis was a master plan designed to meet the *Building for Life (now Building for a Healthy Life)* standard for new urban developments as places where people would want to live and form a community. The plan, for example, was designed to create a distinctive neighbourhood identity, provide private gardens and public green spaces, be easy to navigate, and reduce reliance on private cars. Oxley Woods is residential but is part of the Oxley Park 'grid square' which has a local centre with shops and a school to provide services and foster community cohesion.

Other requirements of the DfM brief were met through planning and design decisions, including:

> *Design for Manufacture*; 56 (38%) of the homes on the site were built for the £60,000 target. Larger houses on the site were built to the same cost per square metre.

*EcoHomes 'Very Good' or Excellent' standard*; achieved through measures such as airtight construction and insulation, the EcoHat, energy-efficient lamps and appliances, and water-saving toilets and showers. However, standard condensing gas boilers for heating and hot water were chosen for cost and simplicity.

*Green building materials and components*; extensive use of timber from certified managed forests, recycled newspaper insulation.

*Car parking*; on-site parking for one car, no garages, limited on-street parking, and cycle storage.

*Inclusive design;* level thresholds and extra wide doors for wheelchair users; stairs wide enough for a stairlift.

*Secured by design*; high security doors, good views of neighbouring homes from corner windows.

*Lifetime homes*; living areas separated from services and to be adaptable.

## Project management and teamwork

For the prototype and construction phases Wood Newton worked with the developer, architects, suppliers, and other partners. The company was wound up in 2011 (despite having supplied components for the 2012 Olympic velodrome) and its work was taken over by a new company, Coxbench, founded by Wood Newton's directors.

The HCA report on the lessons learnt from the DfM competition stressed the importance of integrated collaborative teams in ensuring the success of the projects (HCA, 2010, p. 14),

> Having an integrated consortium of designers, builders, suppliers and delivery teams engaged … throughout the development … increases the likelihood of success. Integrated teams were characterised by …clear roles and responsibilities, frequent discussions on points of detail and planning, agreed resolution of problems … and a shared desire to make the scheme successful. … Innovations such as EcoHats were implemented successfully where teams … allocated specific areas of responsibility, therefore minimising the need for costly design changes.

A project management company was engaged to facilitate regular progress meetings between Taylor Wimpey, RSHP, and Wood Newton which according to the HCA had worked well. 'Frequent progress meetings allowed … whole team thinking, product innovation and continual learning' (HCA, 2010, p. 21).

The report noted that other DfM projects where integrated collaborative teams had not continued from design to construction led to problems. 'The architect was not retained at some sites and a lot of knowledge and potential efficiencies were lost while construction teams attempted to interpret the plans initially drawn up by the architects' (HCA, 2010, p. 66).

However, while the collaborative team effort created a major innovation in housing, it did not prevent quality problems that emerged later. These are discussed below.

### *Evaluation of Oxley Woods as an innovation*

Environmentally, due to their insulation, airtight construction, and controlled ventilation, the houses are more energy efficient than required under the Building Regulations in force at the time, fully meeting the more stringent Milton Keynes housing energy standards. EcoHomes (now superseded) rated Oxley Woods overall 'Very Good' on seven sustainability measures (HCA, 2010, p. 21). But although residents have shops, schools, open spaces, and woodland within walking distance, the objective of reduced car use seems not to have been achieved. This is due to Milton Keynes's car-based transport system and many households owning two or more cars resulting in more street parking than was planned for. Economically, Oxley Woods had the highest construction costs of the DfM projects due to it being the most innovative with the greatest variety of designs (HCA, 2010, p. 22). Because of their novel architecture and low running costs, the houses originally commanded higher prices than equivalent conventional homes, despite their relatively low cost of construction.

The futuristic appearance of the houses, with their white cladding and coloured service cores, gives a visual identity and unity to the estate, although the homes are not to everyone's taste. Nevertheless, surveys showed that the original residents were delighted with their homes and appreciated the community spirit that the development fostered (Cahalan, 2013; Baldwin, 2015, p. 20). For example, community events have been organised by residents and when the developer wanted to build 23 conventional houses adjacent to their homes, the plan was opposed by residents and originally rejected by the planning authority.

The Oxley Woods development was recognised as an important innovation in housing by gaining 12 innovation, architecture, and sustainability awards, including the prestigious RIBA Manser Medal for Housing in 2008 (RSHP, 2009). The Manser Medal jury stated (Archello, 2009),

> Oxley Woods achieves something which should have happened sixty years ago. This is mass factory-produced housing, erected in three days, incorporating top technology, top energy performance, varied house designs, a choice of cladding materials and a wide variety of estate layouts. It is a radical, innovative and an outstanding step away from the traditional mud and mess of the domestic building site. The project represents a thorough-going attempt at innovation within the all-too risk-averse conventional housebuilders' market.

Thus, Oxley Woods may be considered as a highly successful innovation recognised by its many industry awards and by its original residents.

### *Problems affecting the Oxley Woods homes*

Due to the homes' highly innovative design and construction and, despite the early integrated team approach, given a division of responsibility for concept design and for detail design and construction, problems began to emerge soon after the original development was completed.

Although they had been approved and guaranteed by the National Housebuilding Council (NHBC), it became increasingly apparent that the Oxley Woods homes suffered from a variety of problems associated with rainwater penetration and damp. Such problems were identified on a few properties from 2008 and the number of complaints increased over time. A consultancy appointed by the developer in 2013 reported that, due to poor detailed technical design by the main component supplier (e.g., of the junction between the roof and the cladding) and faulty workmanship in construction, rainwater was entering the gap behind the cladding, causing damage and wet and dry rot in the buildings' timber components. Other problems included poor rooflight and window design and construction, loose cladding, missing damp-proof membranes, and an inadequate ventilation gap behind the cladding (GHCP/Taylor Wimpey, 2014).

The HCA evaluation report on the DFM competition had anticipated such problems by noting that, 'developers quite often experienced problems from too much innovation' (HCA, 2010, p. 66), while the Oxley Woods project architect commented, 'There were lessons to be learnt ... but you are bound to get this with pioneering technology' (Cahalan, 2013).

During 2014 the residents' association, the developer, and the NHBC were engaged in vigorous discussions concerning how best to remedy the problems. It was agreed that a major rectification programme was required that would involve solving damp, decay, and condensation problems, rectifying faulty cladding, stopping water leakage, and resolving double glazing failures. Ultimately, correcting the problems required partial reconstruction of the whole development from 2014 to 2018 reportedly costing the developer an estimated £12 million (Hopkins, 2015). The remedial works included building a prototype of a refurbished house, then removing cladding from the homes to replace unsound timber and insulation, redesigning and replacing roofs, rooflights, windows, doors, and cladding fixings (GHCP/Taylor Wimpey, 2017) and wrapping the buildings in a damp-proof membrane (Figure 5.10 (a)). The problems associated with this innovative project, which received considerable media coverage, were very unfortunate given that Oxley Woods had achieved so many architectural and industry awards. The awards were for the innovative design and modern methods of construction, but the problems experienced in practice highlight the risks involved in major innovation and the crucial importance of detailed technical design and quality of construction to make an innovation succeed.

An NHBC report on *Modern methods of construction* said regarding Oxley Woods, 'eschewing traditional methods raised the risk of untried methods ... A [refurbishment consultant's] report highlighted both poor detailing and poor construction' (NHBC, 2021, p. 37). Amongst its general conclusions the report said, 'Rigorous detailed design, beyond what is required for conventional construction, resolving construction details and specifying all components, known as "early design freeze", is essential before manufacture can commence' (p. 43).

(a)

(b)

Figure 5.10 (a)
Oxley Woods
homes undergoing
refurbishment after
the cladding has
been removed,
2015. Photograph
by the author.
Figure 5.10 (b)
Three-bedroom
house after
refurbishment,
2016. Photograph
by the author.

Following the refurbishment (Figure 5.10 (b)) the homes now seem to be free of problems and the development is again seen as a desirable place to live. However, there remain some issues, such as a lack of storage space leading to a few residents building extensions, arguably out of keeping with the original architecture (Figure 5.11). The houses still have conventional gas central heating

Figure 5.11
Oxley Woods house
with new garage
and extension,
2022. Photograph
by the author.

Figure 5.11
Oxley Woods house with new garage and extension, 2022. Photograph by the author.

which will eventually need to be replaced with low carbon heating and hot water systems such as heat pumps.

### Impact of Oxley Woods on housing design and construction

Following the problems that affected the original Oxley Woods homes, applications by developers to build new conventional homes adjacent to the development eventually led to planning approval and construction (Figure 5.12).

Although the preference for conventional housing demonstrates that the UK house building industry is generally resistant to innovation, RSHP has continued to design and develop innovative prefabricated housing schemes. The practice demonstrated an improved version of the Oxley Woods design, called *Homeshell*, in a prototype house erected in 2013 outside the Royal Academy in London (RSHP, 2013) (Figure 5.13). Homeshell is constructed using a structural panel system called 'Insulshell' developed by Sheffield Insulations Group (SIG) and Coxbench.

RSHP have also evolved Homeshell to create a stackable modular building system called *Y:Cube* used for YMCA low-rent housing units completed in 2015 (RSHP, 2016) (Figure 5.14). A further scheme, *PLACE/Ladywell*, using modular units, was designed by RSHP and completed for Lewisham Council, London in 2015. Together with Aecom, the modular concept was further developed, and a new system (*INNU*) was used for the YMCA in Romford Essex in 2021 and for low carbon council townhouses in Cardiff. Using factory-built 'volumetric' mod-

(a)

(b)

Figure 5.12
(a) and (b)
Conventional brick
and tile housing
built 2020 to 2021
adjacent to the
Oxley Woods
development.
Photographs by the
author.

ules in these projects reduces the amount of work on site and hence some of the construction risks associated with Oxley Woods.

While prefabricated building systems are gradually being adopted, especially for local authority and student housing, such innovations in housing have still to be more widely accepted in the UK (Baldwin, 2015; NHBC, 2021).

Figure 5.13
Homeshell
demonstration
installation,
Royal Academy,
London, 2013. Lucie
Goodayle courtesy
of RSHP.

Figure 5.14
Y:Cube one-bed
studios designed
by RSHP and built
for the YMCA
using factory-built
stackable modules,
Mitcham, London,
2015. Copyright
RSHP. Courtesy of
RSHP.

### WHAT, IN SUMMARY, ARE THE MAIN LESSONS OF THE OXLEY WOODS PROJECT?

*Innovation is risky*, especially if several innovations are attempted at once.

*Division of responsibility* between concept and detailed technical design for manufacture and construction, even with good team communications, can lead to quality problems in the finished product. Thus, *early design freeze before production of innovative components begins is important to avoid subsequent problems.*

A major innovation, such as Oxley Woods, may be highly regarded by architects and the industry, but its wider adoption is likely to be hampered by subsequent quality and reliability problems.

To succeed with innovation, it is necessary to correct any initial problems, then continuously *improve, build upon, and develop* the original innovation.

In a conservative, risk averse industry and market, like housebuilding, *adoption of innovative designs and construction methods* is likely to be slow.

## REFERENCES

Archello (2009) *Design for Manufacture/Oxley Woods*. Available at: https://archello.com/project/design-for-manufacture-oxley-woods (Accessed: 6 July 2023).

Baldwin, M. (2015) 'A critical review of the prefabrication industry through an analysis of the Oxley Woods development'. School of Architecture, University of Kent. Available at: https://issuu.com/matthewedwardpeterbaldwin/docs/a_critical_review_into_the_state_of (Accessed: 12 June 2023).

Cahalan, P. (2013) 'Mark II: Can renowned architect Richard Rogers solve the housing crisis?', *The Independent*, 11 July. Available at: https://www.independent.co.uk/news/uk/home-news/mark-ii-can-renowned-architect-richard-rogers-solve-the-housing-crisis-8691228.html (Accessed: 12 June 2023).

Doggart, J. with Horton, A. and Skelton, T. (2017) *Milton Keynes – Energy Capital UK* (Lecture). MK50 CityFest, Milton Keynes, 26 June.

du Cros, A. (1938) *Wheels of Fortune. A salute to pioneers*. London: Chapman and Hall.

Dunlop, J.B. (1922) *The History of the Pneumatic Tyre*. Dublin: Alex Thom.

GHCP/Taylor Wimpey (2014) *Summary of defects analysis report Oxley Woods, Milton Keynes*. Bracknell: GHPC Group, April.

GHCP/Taylor Wimpey (2017) *Customer Handover Information. Oxley Woods Remedial Works*. Bracknell: GHPC Group, June.

HCA (2010) *Designed for Manufacture Lessons Learnt*. London: Homes and Communities Agency, March.

Historic England (2013) *22 Parkside*. London: Historic England. Available at: https://historicengland.org.uk/listing/the-list/list-entry/1409979?section=official-list-entry (Accessed: 12 June 2023).

Hopkins, K. (2015) 'Taylor Wimpey faces £12m repair bill for award winning estate'. *The Times*, 7 April. Available at: https://www.thetimes.co.uk/article/taylor-wimpey-faces-pound12m-repair-bill-for-award-winning-estate-fbkw8tgc9sg (Accessed: 12 June 2023).

MHCLG (2019) *Modern Methods of Construction. Introducing the MMC Definition Framework*. Ministry of Housing, Communities and Local Government Joint Industry Working Group report. Available at: https://www.cast-consultancy.com/wp-content/uploads/2019/03/MMC-I-Pad-base_GOVUK-FINAL_SECURE.pdf (Accessed: 12 June 2023).

NHBC (2021) *Modern methods of construction. Building on experience*. Milton Keynes: NHBC Foundation. Available at: https://www.nhbcfoundation.org/wp-content/uploads/2021/01/MMC_report.pdf (Accessed: 12 June 2023).

Roy, R. (2013) 'Creative design'. T217 *Design essentials*, Book 3. Milton Keynes: The Open University.

RSHP (2009) *Oxley Woods*. Rogers Stirk Harbour + Partners. Available at: https://rshp.com/projects/residential/oxley-woods/ (Accessed: 6 July 2023).

RSHP (2013) *Homeshell*. Rogers Stirk Harbour + Partners. Available at: https://rshp.com/projects/residential/homeshell/ (Accessed: 6 July 2023).

RSHP (2014) *Homeshell* (Brochure). London: Rogers Stirk Harbour + Partners.

RSHP (2016) *Y:Cube*. Rogers Stirk Harbour + Partners. Available at: https://rshp.com/projects/residential/ycube/ (Accessed: 6 July 2023).

# 6   Innovative products and buildings

## INTRODUCTION

In this chapter I consider two case studies. The first discusses an innovative product, a purpose-designed dog walking bag, and the entrepreneurial family business established to produce it. The second case discusses some innovative buildings designed by an established modernist architect. These are innovations that are new and original but not radically different from what exists somewhere in the world. These products or buildings represent valuable additions but are not highly influential in terms of changing knowledge or thinking in their field. As before, I will attempt to identify the factors and processes underlying their creation, development, and introduction to draw out some lessons for innovation success and failure.

## CASE STUDY: BARKING BAGS

This case study concerns the conception, design, development, and introduction of an innovative product – a range of purpose-designed bags for dog walkers. The project led to the establishment by Debra (Debbie) Greaves and her partner Robert Angell of *Barking Bags*, a small family business to produce and market the bags. I interviewed Debbie three times between October 2021 and November 2022 about the creation of the bags and her business. In 2022 the partners sold a 50 per cent share of the business to allow them to retire from day-to-day management and selling, to recover some of their initial investment, and benefit from future growth in the entrepreneurial business they founded.

### Background
Debbie spent most of her working life in in the public sector or working for charitable organisations, but she was no stranger to business. Her family had all been publicans and hoteliers in Yorkshire and from an early age Debbie grew up helping in the family business. She turned her back on the family tradition to train as a teacher but was surprised that when her parents retired that they asked her brother to take on the business, believing that that her politics and ethical values were not compatible with becoming a successful businessperson.

DOI: 10.4324/9781003354406-6

Debbie has long been involved in activities that require creativity, problem-solving, and entrepreneurship. She studied English and Drama at university and then worked as a school drama teacher and as a teacher trainer with Voluntary Service Overseas (VSO) in Ghana. Returning to the UK she had several paid and voluntary jobs. This included 12 years as co-ordinator of Global Centre Milton Keynes, a charity established to educate school students and raise awareness of the need for international development, fair trade, and addressing global poverty. She continued to train volunteers with VSO for two years, also co-writing a school qualification in Development Studies with her partner Rob. Applying for grants and reporting to funders became a key part of her work, in which business discipline and accountability were closely scrutinised. She argues that working for charities is often more challenging than working for business. As part of her work Debbie established, and for six years helped manage, *SUST!* a shop in Central Milton Keynes shopping centre selling fair trade food, clothing, and crafts. All these activities involved researching, raising funds, extensive networking, and coming up with ideas to get schools and the public to engage. She worked for many years as a fund-raiser for Northampton University and The Open University, jobs that also required research, creative ideas, problem-solving, and networking. Debbie has also been a trustee of a local international development charity and worked with other charities including MK SNAP, a charity helping adults with learning difficulties to develop skills through work training.

**What elements in Debbie's background are likely to have helped her as an innovator and entrepreneur?**

Her business *family background* and experience in a variety of jobs that involve *business, finance, management, and entrepreneurial skills.*

Experience as drama teacher, a profession that requires *creative thinking.*

The soft skills of *networking and collaborating with others* to achieve tasks and solve problems.

A clear willingness to *work hard, multitask, and transfer skills* between tasks.

*Experience as a fund-raiser* which involves persuading people to help meet joint goals.

Choosing jobs and tasks she is *motivated* to do, driven by a sense of *social responsibility and a desire to help people.*

### Barking Bags – Inspiration and concept

The original idea which led to Barking Bags was to create gainful employment for Debbie's daughter, who has Crohn's Disease and so could not work regular hours in the mainstream job market. In 2015 Debbie had acquired a puppy, Maisie, that she found was difficult to train. A trainer advised her to take Maisie for walks and take dog treats to reward Maisie for good behaviour. Walking the dog gave Debbie the mental space to think, research, and plan, on which she says potential innovators often fail to devote enough time. It got her thinking about how best to carry the treats, dog lead, water, toys, dog waste bags, and items such as keys and phone, an owner might need when out dog walking. Debbie looked around for a suitable utility bag, but an online search only came up with bags to carry small dogs or small bum bags. So, Debbie decided to mock up her own dog walking bag using a bag from a charity shop. She started by adapting the bag by adding a divider in the middle for treats and empty dog waste bags and pockets to hold a water bottle and full dog waste bags. When walking with Maisie, other dog owners made positive comments about her bag, including one who expressed surprise when Debbie put a full dog waste bag in what she thought was Debbie's handbag. These comments resulted in her modifying the first mock-up and producing another version using a commercial bag made from recycled leather pieces, which proved too costly and difficult to work with.

Debbie and Rob realised there was a potential market for a dog walking bag. So, they sought advice from the owners of a local pet shop, who gave them contacts in the industry to explore the business potential of this new product. They also did some informal market research by visiting the world's largest dog show, Crufts, which confirmed that there seemed to be nothing similar on the market, although handbags decorated with pawprints were selling well. Debbie and Rob then felt there was a potential market for a purpose-designed dog walking bag and set about creating a design and prototype (Greaves and Angell, 2021).

> **What can be learned from the genesis of the *Barking Bags* project?**
>
> A desire to provide employment for Debbie and Rob's daughter, who was challenged by a chronic health condition, and acquiring a puppy provided the *starting point*. Debbie's dissatisfaction (*constructive discontent*) with existing carrying bags provided the *motivation* to create something better.
>
> Taking time out during her dog walks enabled Debbie to *think, research, and plan* how to make a better bag.
>
> Thoroughly '*doing her homework*' before embarking on the project, through *online research* and by *seeking expert advice* from pet shops and local business networks.

### The design and development process

As neither Debbie or Rob were trained designers, in 2015 Debbie approached the Fashion Design tutor at the University of Northampton, where she worked

Debbie *acting as a user* to identify requirements for a dog walking bag and her ability to create a *rough mock-up* to test user-centred design ideas to meet those requirements.

Conducting some *informal market research* through industry contacts and at a major dog show to identify whether a gap in the market and a potential business opportunity existed.

as fund-raiser, whose students learned to design and make bags and other products in leather and textiles. Together with the tutors in the School for Fashion and Design she helped develop a brief for student project to design a dog walking bag. But due to university restructuring the project did not proceed. So, she looked for another suitable university and pitched her idea to Lee Mattocks, at the time Senior Lecturer and Head of the School of Design and Fashion at Nottingham Trent University. Mattocks was enthusiastic and he and Debbie first discussed who would own the intellectual property (IP) before they provided a group of students with a brief to design a dog walking bag.

The brief included a background narrative which said, for example, that the bag should be something that dog owners would be 'proud to carry', be capable of holding empty and full dog waste bags plus other dog and personal items, and be capable of being ethically produced at scale in different sizes. Other items in the brief specified that the bag be affordable, non-gender specific, made from environmentally friendly materials, and have 'slow fashion' brand appeal. Two students who produced good design drawings were given an award and Lee Mattocks was commissioned to use these as the basis for a prototype bag design (Figures 6.1 (a) and (b)). By 2018, with the help of the School's technical assistant, Mattocks had made a prototype.

### Production

Mattocks suggested potential UK makers for the bag, but their costs were far too high and would have made the business unviable. Through her fund-raising network Debbie remembered an Indian graduate of Northampton University, Sateesh Jadhav, director of a successful leather manufacturing company, called *Gaitonde*, based in Chennai, South India. After meeting Debbie in London, he agreed to take the prototype bag and get an initial run of 40 made in an artisan workshop managed by one of his employees (Figure 6.2).

### Market testing and launch

In May 2018, Debbie and Rob took the first batch of bags to a local dog show and sold out. They saw this as an early indicator that there could be a potential UK market for their product. Consequently, during 2018 they commissioned

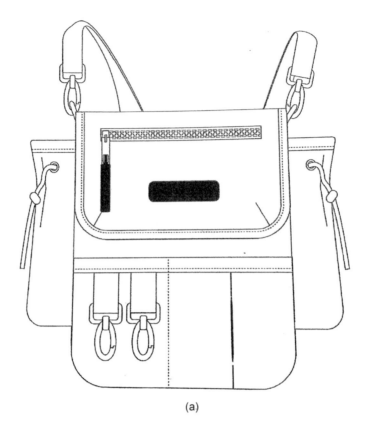

(a)

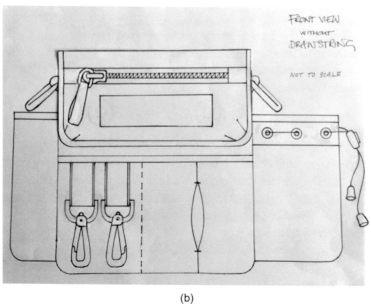

FRONT VIEW
WITHOUT
DRAWSTRING

NOT TO SCALE

(b)

Figure 6.1
(a) Laura Moseby's initial dog walking bag design, 2017. Courtesy of Debbie Greaves.
6.1 (b) Lee Mattocks's prototype design, 2018. Courtesy of Debbie Greaves.

Figure 6.2
Gaitonde artisan workshop, Chennai, South India making Barking Bags dog walking bags,
2022. Courtesy of Debbie Greaves.

**What can be learned from the process of design, development, and manufacture of the first *Barking Bags*?**

Debbie used her *networking skills* to identify individuals who could translate her idea and rough mock-up into a prototype commercial product and get it manufactured.

Debbie's ability to *specify user, market, and production requirements* in a brief for the product innovation was essential.

Debbie's ability to *collaborate* with design students and an academic/ professional designer to create a product based on her brief, and with an overseas manufacturer to make it at an economic price, enabled the project to progress.

Gaitonde to make more bags, booked a stand at a major London dog show, registered the design (IPO, 2018), and brainstormed possible names before registering 'Barking Bags' as a trademark. Backed by the partners' retirement funds, the Barking Bags business was launched at the London dog show at which sales and visitor and exhibitor feedback were very encouraging. As a result, Barking Bags were invited to exhibit at the 2019 Crufts dog show. Crufts, which typically attracts over 150,000 visitors, was seen by the partners as an opportunity to market the product and were pleased that investing about £1500 as an exhibitor was partly recovered through sales of over 500 of the original dog walking bags (Figure 6.3) priced at around £28 with a gross profit of £10–£12 per bag. At this point overheads were low; Barking bags were operating from home, there were no employees, advertising was though free social media channels, and the first website was free. All of this would change once the business began to expand, impacting on margins and profitability.

### Business development

While preparing for Crufts the partners started to develop the business. This included testing and approving a logo, producing a better website, and designing packaging. Marketing effort was increased via magazines, newspapers, and social media. Debbie used her networking skills to get help and advice from contacts and local business networks and to find local suppliers, for example for website design. As well as starting to sell online, Barking Bags continued to promote and sell their bags through dog shows. Exhibitors at these shows are generally very helpful, providing each other with advice, contacts, and feedback, which the partners found invaluable.

Figure 6.3
Original Barking
Bag design,
2018. Courtesy of
Debbie Greaves.

Figure 6.4
Debbie Greaves
and Masie with
an improved
Barking Bags
dog walking bag,
2023. Photograph
by the author.

**What can be learned from the launch of the product and the *Barking Bags* business?**

Sales of an initial production batch of Barking Bags seemed to confirm that there was *a potentially worthwhile market* for this innovative product.

The partners protected their *intellectual property* by registering the design and trademarking the Barking Bags name.

Advice, help, and recommendations from *local contacts, networks, and dog shows* were invaluable.

The partners had to *invest their own funds* to increase production, for marketing, and to develop their business on a professional basis with a logo, website, etc.

### *Design infringement*

In Summer 2019 at one of the shows the partners attended the Barking Bags stand was next to one selling dog coats and accessories. The owners of the neighbouring stand were typically friendly and helpful, and Debbie sold them a bag at cost price. Later, to the partners' surprise, someone congratulated

Barking Bags for winning one of the 2020 *PetQuip* Pet Product of Year Gold awards. Debbie and Rob were shocked to learn that another company had copied key features of the Barking Bags design and entered their bag (Figure 6.5) for PetQuip, a national award given by the International Trade Association of Pet Equipment Suppliers.

Very concerned that another company had copied their design, Barking Bags sought to resolve matters through a solicitor. The partners decided, despite the legal costs, time, and effort involved, they had to take action to stop sales of these copied walking bags and for infringement of their Registered Design (IPO, 2018). Fighting the case revealed some unresolved IP issues. Addressing these required Laura Moseley, who created the initial design, and Lee Mattocks, who developed the prototype, assigning their IP to Barking Bags (Gunnercooke, 2020a; 2020b). It cost Barking Bags about £20,000 to fight the case of which they recovered only about £8400. Such costs and effort usually deter designers and innovators whose products are copied from taking legal action. But Debbie and Rob were determined on moral grounds not to let someone else benefit from all their efforts.

Barking Bags learned that although design registration helps establish the ownership of a design, it does not necessarily prevent others from copying it. Registration simply gives the designer a stronger hand to challenge any infringement, while winning or coming to an agreement is likely to deter others from copying the design in the future.

Figure 6.5
Copycat dog walking bag (flap cut to prevent sales). Courtesy of Debbie Greaves.

Eventually the dispute was 'amicably resolved', but the legal agreement included a clause which prevents Barking Bags from disclosing information about the matter. The case clearly demonstrated the importance of IP to the partners. It led to the owners of the company at the heart of the infringement agreeing to cease selling and to destroy their stock of dog walking bags.

In 2021 Barking Bags entered their genuine product for a PetQuip award and although they did not win, they were finalists in two categories and went on to win a prestigious award from the Pet Industry Federation.

**What lessons can others learn from the infringement of the *Barking Bags* design?**

It is important, if they can afford to do so, for designers and innovators to *protect their IP* using, as appropriate, patents, trademarks, and registered designs.

Stopping others from copying a product or infringing an invention or design involves *high legal costs and much determination* and is not guaranteed to succeed. Whether the battle is worthwhile is a matter of judgement and finance.

### New product development

Barking Bags expanded their range with design variants and new products, often in response to feedback received at shows and on social media. For example, customers requested a padded carrying strap, reflective panels, an extendable side pocket for dog waste, and a waterproof inner lining and a bag with these enhancements was introduced (Figure 6.6). Barking Bags was also asked to produce, and launched, a vegan range. A half-size bag mainly aimed at men that could be worn on a belt was added to the range. By 2021 bags were available in waterproof fabrics and leather and in several colours and patterns.

Other new products planned at the time included a holiday bag to hold all a dog's needs when looked after by others and a bag for wheelchair users with assistance dogs.

### Ethics and sustainability

Throughout her career Debbie has tried to help disadvantaged people in the UK and abroad. This is reflected in the partners' attempts to make their business as ethically and environmentally responsible as possible, while being financially sustainable.

For example, both partners have visited the artisan workshop in India where their bags are made to satisfy themselves that the working conditions and wages are fair. Air freight was carbon offset and single-use plastic minimised. They produced blogs and newsletters that promoted ethical and responsible dog ownership. Many of the bags were packaged at MK SNAP, a local charity for adults with learning difficulties, as part of their work training. In 2021 they

Figure 6.6
Redesigned
Barking Bag with
an extendable
side pocket
for dog waste,
2020. Courtesy of
Debbie Greaves.

took on two young employees through the government's Kick Start programme designed to help young people into work.

Being true to one's values can be a challenge and the partners discovered that compromises must be made to make a success of a business. Growth came with additional costs: accommodation and staff, extra IT support, and input from professional web designers, social media, and marketing advisors. This means that the tight margins that they worked to could render the business unviable. So, the partners considered making a range of bags in China at a more competitive cost, alongside those handmade in India.

### Dragons' Den *and future plans*

In 2021 Barking Bags won one of the Pet Industry Federation New Business Awards (Figure 6.7) and were invited to appear on the BBC TV show *Dragons' Den* at which inventors and entrepreneurs pitch for investment from a panel of wealthy business angels in return for a share of the business. Preparing for the show involved assembling a dossier of evidence about Barking Bags, its finances, and its need for investment (Greaves and Angell, 2021).

On the show broadcast in January 2022 (BBC, 2022) Debbie and Rob were shown being offered an investment of £35,000 from Sara Davies, founder of a craft supplies business, for a 25 per cent share of the profits or sales value of their company. (The partners had known about Sara's offer in cash and/or help in kind since the programme was recorded six months earlier.) Feedback from the Dragons included doubts that a sufficiently large market existed for such a niche product when ordinary, perhaps more fashionable, bags could be used instead. Other comments were: at £35 retail the standard bag was too expensive but could be made for less in China, and it would be difficult to sell in retail outlets. However, the Dragons were impressed by Debbie's presenting skills and passion

Figure 6.7
Pet Industry
Federation New
Business of the
Year Award
2021. Courtesy of
Debbie Greaves.

for the product. So, Sara Davies made her offer on the basis that the bags were ideally suited to being demonstrated by Debbie on shopping television channels. When asked by Sara if she was willing to travel the world selling Barking Bags on television, Debbie's reply was enthusiastic, but on reflection she decided that she did not want to globetrot but might be willing to sell the bags on programmes produced in the UK.

For Debbie and Rob, the main benefit of appearing on *Dragons' Den* was excellent publicity and some useful advice from Sara Davies's team. The publicity led to an upsurge in sales, and they sold nine months' worth of stock in three days. Unfortunately, their workshop in India was unable to increase production quickly enough and many customers were unable to place orders. After the initial surge in sales, by mid-2022, given the difficulties of obtaining stock, inflation, and a cost-of-living crisis, Barking Bags began to lose money. By then the partners had decided not to accept Sara Davies's offer of investment, which involved selling via the QVC TV shopping channel and required extra capital than was on offer for stock. However, Sara's team provided useful advice and put them in touch with manufacturers in China. After several attempts, the Chinese manufacturers produced a prototype that was of sufficient quality and offered a considerable cost saving. But due to the COVID-19 pandemic they were unable to fulfil orders quickly and Debbie and Rob almost decided to close the business. But fortunately, through a consultant, they met two local entrepreneurs (founders of R&R Global Investments) and agreed to sell 50 per cent of what by then had become a limited company, Barking Bags Ltd. Their new shareholders agreed to invest cash and R&R's expertise into the company, retain the Indian workshop for making leather bags, and find lower cost suppliers elsewhere.

Under the new management the main range was rationalised to offer one standard design in different colours and materials. In response to customer feedback other ranges were also rationalised leading to the introduction of a compact 'Urban' bag designed to look like an ordinary shoulder bag with a dog waste bag dispenser (Barking Bags, 2023). R&R's IT expert is helping to promote the bags via social media. Debbie told me that, 'no matter how good your product is, to compete in a niche market social media are crucial to success'. For example, TikTok videos with animals can sometimes get millions of views.

R&R's strategy is to internationalise the business and develop new products with lower cost suppliers. It is likely that in future the bags will be machine-made in Turkey and China rather than hand-made in India, as the price charged by the Indian workshop plus transport costs does not produce a worthwhile profit on sales.

Debbie and Rob are both sad and relieved to be gradually withdrawing from the business they created. They plan to reduce their shareholding to 20 per cent with the intention of benefiting from future growth of a company, which they hope retains the ethical and environmental values they established from the beginning.

> **What general lessons can be learned from the evolution of the _Barking Bags_ business?**
>
> The founders of Barking Bags had the necessary _entrepreneurial and creative skills_ to specify and launch an innovative product and a small business.
>
> To develop and expand a new business it is necessary to _develop new products and improve on, and provide variants of, existing ones_. However, to reduce costs it may be necessary to _rationalise an over-diverse range_.
>
> An _ethically and environmentally responsible approach_ to business and its products can meet both moral and financial objectives but is challenging. For example, production of the bags will have to be moved from an artisan workshop to lower cost overseas suppliers to ensure that the business remains financially viable.
>
> For a small business nowadays, it is vital to make effective use of _social media_.
>
> _External investment and support_ are usually needed to further develop a business, its products, and financial position. Had new investors not come on board the business would probably have had to close.

## CASE STUDY: ROBERT DE GREY, MODERNIST ARCHITECT

The second case study in this chapter concerns the work of the Milton Keynes-based modernist architect, Robert de Grey, with a focus on the design of Milton Keynes Central Bus Station.

The former *Milton Keynes Central Bus Station* was designed by two Milton Keynes Development Corporation (MKDC) architects, Derek Yeadon and Robert de Grey, and completed in 1982–3. It is short walk across an open square from Milton Keynes Central train station, which was completed shortly before the bus station. The train station is located at the centre of a U-shaped group of modernist steel and mirror-glass buildings. The train and bus stations were part of the plan for Central Milton Keynes (CMK) (Figure 6.8) comprising contemporary , architect-designed pavilions set within a framework of grid roads with a modernist shopping building clad in mirror-glass at its core.

In September and October 2020, I interviewed Robert de Grey about his background and experience and his approach to and philosophy of design that led to his design of the bus station and other buildings. My interviews were supplemented by a recorded interview that Robert gave (de Grey, 2006) for a book about the planning, design, and construction of Central Milton Keynes (Hill, 2007).

### Background and education

Robert de Grey was born in 1948. His parents were both artists, his father was a landscape and figurative painter and his mother, Flavia Irwin, was an abstract painter. His father, Sir Roger de Grey, had been senior tutor of painting at the Royal College of Art and had taught David Hockney amongst other distinguished artists and was president of the Royal Academy of Arts from 1984–93. Robert's father was fascinated by buildings and pointed out interesting buildings during family drives to the south of France for holidays.

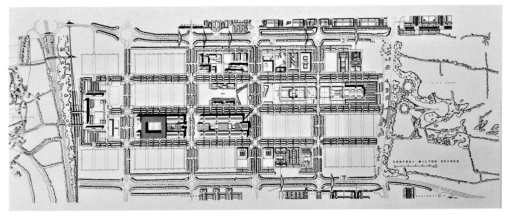

Figure 6.8
The plan for Central Milton Keynes, c. 1980. Buildings are set in a rectilinear road grid. The railway line and train and bus stations are at the western left-hand end, Campbell Park is at the eastern end, with one end of the shopping building next to the park. Photograph of plan licenced by and copyright of Homes England.

■ **Innovative products and buildings**

Robert was educated at Eton College and Cambridge University School of Architecture. He says that his architectural education became chaotic during the radical student uprisings of the late 1960s with the students challenging everything their tutors said. The experience made Robert very politically aware, while important elements of his architectural education happened through working with his fellow students outside the formal system.

### What can be learned from Robert's early experiences and education?

With both his parents being painters and his father's interest in buildings, Robert was from an early age steeped in *visual culture* and the *appreciation of buildings*. This background almost *destined him to be an architect*.

Robert's education during the radical student days of the late 1960s by tutors, who were to become prominent modern architects, as well as by his fellow students, exposed him to *radical ideas* and the desire for *social and political change*, including through *socially responsible architecture*.

### Career

After graduation from Cambridge, Robert worked for Birmingham City Architects' Department designing schools and public housing and working with residents on plans for deprived neighbourhoods. He was also part of the team submitting designs for a stadium, pool, and velodrome as part of Birmingham's bid to hold the 1982 Commonwealth Games. Although the bid was not successful, some facilities such as the 1976 Alexander Stadium were built. However, apart from projects such as the stadium, Robert felt that the opportunities for creativity and high-quality design suffered under the pressure of Birmingham's huge construction programme, which was mainly based on standardised house types and schools.

Robert therefore moved to Milton Keynes in 1977 to take up the opportunity of being employed by Milton Keynes Development Corporation (MKDC) by joining the team working on Central Milton Keynes. MKDC was staffed by many radical young professionals faced with the exciting challenge of planning and designing a new city. He said that contributing to the development of Milton Keynes was 'an opportunity of a lifetime, which is to influence the creation of a new city' (de Grey, 2006). He added that the job offered great scope for creative, human-centred design, 'I've always believed that... the interaction between people who are clear about what they want from building and an architect who's prepared to respond to that, produce better buildings' (de Grey, 2006).

Robert was impressed by the buildings designed by the City Centre team and how they were integrated with the infrastructure designed by the same team. He was more critical of the housing designed by the Central Area team which, for example, had open spaces in their middle, were three-stories high, had access through car ports, and, like so much of early MKDC housing, had technical faults, especially leaking flat roofs and inadequate heating systems. He felt that the early

Central Area housing, although beautifully detailed, felt like an example of architectural style being more important than the needs of residents, saying 'Good buildings are planted in the idea of responding to people's needs rather than a stylistic approach overriding those needs' (de Grey, 2006). He acknowledged that many of these issues were corrected in later Central Area housing estates.

Robert therefore was pleased to be in teams designing commercial and public buildings in the city centre. These included two 1980s offices, believed to be the UK's first atrium buildings, one of which became the headquarters of Milton Keynes Council until 2000, and Milton Keynes Central Bus Station (discussed below).

After resigning from MKDC in 1987, as the privatisation of its functions increased with the election from 1979 of Conservative governments under Margaret Thatcher, Robert joined Denton Tunley Scott, founded by other former Corporation architects. When Tunley left the practice, it became Denton Scott Architects until it folded in 1992–3. In 1993 Robert founded his own practice, The Architecture Studio, based in Milton Keynes and headed the practice until its closure in 2016. He continued to work from home as an architect.

### Influences

Among Robert's tutors at Cambridge were modernist architects, Richard MacCormac and Richard Rogers (mentioned in Chapters 2 and 5), who became internationally renowned. Robert's brother, Spencer de Grey, also trained as an architect at Cambridge and is Head of Design at the internationally known firm of modernist architects, Foster & Partners.

Robert admires two of the great 20th century architects: the German American architect Mies van der Rohe, one of the pioneers of modernism; and Frank Lloyd Wright, whose holistic designs aimed to be in harmony with their environment. Ted Cullinan is another influence who Robert admired for his pioneering ideas about ecology and sustainability embodied in, for example, the Downland Gridshell museum building, a lightweight structure formed of bent oak laths. Robert also admires the work of two Dutch architects, Herman Hertzberger and Aldo van Eyck, because of their emphasis on the human element in architecture and designing primarily for the users of a building.

### What can be learned from Robert's education and influences?

There seem to be two main currents.

The first is his *admiration for 20th century modernist architecture* with its minimalist, undecorated, functional forms, and use of industrial materials such as metal, reinforced concrete, and glass.

The second, which might sometimes conflict with the first, is his desire to design to *meet the needs of the users of buildings* and in *harmony with the site and the natural environment.*

### Milton Keynes Central Bus Station

Before completion of one of the city centre office buildings in 1980, another member of the City Centre group, Derek Yeadon, and Robert started designing Milton Keynes Central Bus Station on a site near Milton Keynes Central train station. The brief was to provide shelter for passengers using local bus services on the train station side of the building and for users of national or regional coaches on the other side. Facilities for passengers and bus company staff were also to be provided.

There were a few false starts, where different concepts were considered, and the brief evolved. Robert commented on the brief's 'lack of clarity from the client side, which wasted time' (de Grey, 2006). The concept changed, beginning as a major bus terminus, then as a large bus stop with a rear yard for buses and coaches, and finally to a canopy for sheltering passengers over an enclosure for facilities and offices.

The two architects' response to a revised brief came quite quickly. Their final concept proposed a large canopy with a central two-storey block to house passenger facilities, and on the first floor the bus company's offices and drivers' facilities. With the two-storey block under it, the canopy was high enough to allow double-deck buses to park underneath.

Derek and Robert then worked together on developing the concept design, sitting across a table, and making many sketches, until the design firmed up. Robert says working with Derek was one of the best experiences of his architectural career. Since then, he has always tried to collaborate with others to get both informal and formal feedback on his ideas and designs.

Many Milton Keynes city centre buildings had already been built in a modernist style, including the Shopping Building, completed in 1979, neighbouring offices and shops, and Milton Keynes Central train station. The bus station adopted the same design philosophy and style within the same 'architectural language'. This came from the design culture of the MKDC City Centre architects' group. They were strongly influenced by Mies van der Rohe, best known for his stone, steel, and glass German Pavilion for the 1929 Barcelona International Exhibition and for American skyscrapers of tall cube-shaped steel frames with tinted-glass facades. The bus station, Robert says, was not influenced by any specific building, but was Miesian in style, fitting into the urban landscape and road grid of the city centre. He said, 'I was working in a strong design-oriented group with very strong design ideas … you work within that framework' (de Grey, 2006). As David Lock, one of the senior planners of Milton Keynes, observed of the CMK architects' team, 'It was … a Messianic Task Force of extremely talented designers … they were all modernists … [who] didn't want to waste energy on unbelievers' (Hill, 2007, p. 45).

By the project's scheme (spatial coordination) phase the bus station design had been decided. It comprised an exposed steel framework of horizontal beams supported on columns with a large sheltering canopy over the core accommodation building, lit as much as possible by daylight. There were numerous details still to decide, down to the stainless steel rainwater pipes routed inside the canopy's support columns and furnishings. As a generous transport grant covered the building's cost, it was possible to specify high-quality materials such as granite cladding on the core building and on the walls and seating under and around the canopy. The bus station was built as drawn, down to the finest details.

**What were the main factors and processes resulting in the architects' conceptualisation, design, and development of _Milton Keynes Central Bus Station_?**

The starting point was a, vaguely defined, _brief_ from bus and coach operators and MKDC's decision to locate a bus terminus near Milton Keynes Central train station as part of completing one end of the CMK grid (Figure 6.8).

There were many _constraints in the brief_ which framed and drove the design. These included: the site and location, a requirement for bus and coach parking for an expected growth in demand, the need to accommodate passengers, bus company staff and their facilities, and to provide shelter for passengers and single- and double-deck buses.

Within the constraints of the brief, the _primary generator_ for the building was the requirement to fit the _modernist design culture_ of the CMK group. It had also to represent a significant contribution to the modernist group of buildings comprising the central train station and adjacent office blocks.

The _design and development process_ for the bus station was fairly typical of the phases involved in a significant architectural project. As the brief from the clients evolved, the two architects working individually at first and then creatively together, generated several _alternative design concepts_ through sketching and drawing. When the brief eventually firmed up, the concept settled on a steel frame structure with a core concrete pavilion under an overhanging canopy roof.

The concept was developed with input from structural engineers. The architects devoted great attention to the _technical and aesthetic details_ of the design to produce the working drawings for the building and its interior ready to proceed to construction.

The bus station was therefore designed and constructed to satisfy the final version of the brief. But soon after the bus station had been completed in 1982–3 (Figure 6.9), long-distance coaches travelling on the M1 no longer came through Milton Keynes but stopped at a new coachway off Junction 14. The routing of local bus services also changed with buses stopping outside the train station, thus creating the transport hub originally envisaged by the CMK team.

Figure 6.9
Milton Keynes
Central Bus
Station in use, c.
1983. Photograph
licenced by and
copyright of Homes
England.

The bus station therefore ceased fulfilling its original function. Since then, the building has been used for a variety of purposes, including: a night club, the 2005 *Buszy* skatepark used by professional and amateur street skaters, a multi-purpose youth centre, a winter night shelter support centre, a dance school, and a recording studio (Figures 6.10 (a) to (c)).

Despite this chequered history, following a 2013 English Heritage survey of bus stations, in 2014 it was listed at Grade II. The designation gave the following principal reasons for listing (Historic England, 2014),

> * Architectural interest: bus station in the form of a freestanding pavilion, that draws on seminal buildings by the acclaimed modernist architect Mies van der Rohe …; * Structural interest: deep projecting canopy slung from exposed steel girders supported on lightweight steel columns; * Use of materials: core building clad in Cornish Granite and detailed to an unusually high standard for a bus station; * Plan: internal and external naturally-lit waiting areas, where built-in seating and tables are treated sculpturally; * Contextual interest: designed as part of the transport hub to serve the new town of Milton Keynes.

The history section of the listing noted (Historic England, 2014),

> Bringing together facets of Mies van der Rohe's Barcelona Pavilion (Spain) and IIT Crown Hall, Chicago (US), the pavilion-like bus station embraces the modernist, Miesian philosophy applied throughout the new town. It was considered by *Building Design* on completion to be a strikingly simple building of stunning quality.

Figure 6.10
(a) The former
Milton Keynes
Central Bus Station
in 2021 with its
high-quality grey
granite cladding,
long after ceasing
to operate as a bus
station. Photograph
by the author.
6.10 (b) Milton
Keynes Central
train station viewed
from the former
Milton Keynes
Central Bus Station
in 2021. Note
the addition of a
mirror-glass lift and
staircase enclosure
at one end of
the bus station.
Photograph by the
author. 6.10 (c)
The remains of the
Buszy skatepark at
the former Milton
Keynes Central
Bus Station. The
group of three
modernist mirror-
glass-clad buildings
can be seen in
the background.
Photograph by the
author.

(a)

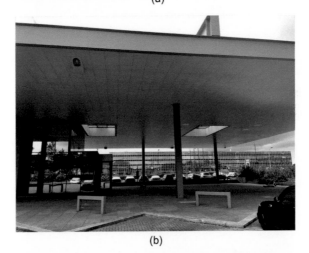

(b)

(c)

Although building energy efficiency was an issue when the bus station was planned, it did not feature much in the original design, hence it was single glazed with gas boilers for heating. Subsequently, a large solar photovoltaic array was installed on top of the canopy funded by a 2012 EU grant for energy innovation. Robert welcomed the environmental benefits but was unhappy about the aesthetic impact and managed to get the panels moved from the edge of the canopy so they could not be seen from the ground.

In September 2023 there was an exhibition titled 'Greentown 2023' at Milton Keynes Gallery in which Nottingham University architecture students displayed design proposals inspired by Milton Keynes urban form and architectural innovations, especially the unrealised plans drawn up in the 1970s to build a self-sufficient eco-community called 'Greentown' in the new city. The students' proposals included three designs which involved eco-redevelopment of the former bus station as headquarters for a revived Greentown project, a cultural centre, and a religious building for non-believers.

**How well has the former *Milton Keynes Central Bus Station* survived as external circumstances changed?**

Despite being awarded listed buildings status for its quality of design, finish, and construction, due to changing bus and coach operator requirements it ceased acting as a bus station a short time after its completion. Nevertheless, it has subsequently provided accommodation for a variety of other functions and support for a large solar photovoltaic array, and as the basis for eco-redevelopment to provide new functions, demonstrating the building's *versatility to be adapted* to meet changing needs.

### Subsequent architectural work
#### Rockwell Automation training centre
Before leaving MKDC in 1987, Robert was involved in the design of a variety of commercial and industrial buildings, including the award-winning Kiln Farm 7 Special Units completed in 1985. The units comprise four modernist pavilions of which he is rightly proud, two of which are occupied by Rockwell Automation (Figure 6.11). The units won a 1986 steel industry award for their simple, excellently detailed design and construction that effectively accommodates office and workshop functions.

#### Rowans Children's Centre
As noted earlier, in 1992–3 Robert founded his own architectural practice, The Architecture Studio. Among its projects was the design of one of the Labour government-initiated *Sure Start* centres: *The Rowans Children's Centre*, Fullers Slade, Milton Keynes, which was opened in 2006.

Figure 6.11
Rockwell Automation Training Centre, Kiln Farm, Milton Keynes, 2021. Photograph by the author.

The client was the local Sure Start Board, which did not have the capacity to produce a proper brief. In line with his belief in involving the users of a building in its design, Robert and his team attempted to make local residents the clients. However, when Milton Keynes Council (MKC) became the client, such direct involvement was no longer in favour. So instead, one of the Sure Start staff discussed likely user requirements with children's specialists at National Children's Homes on behalf of the residents. These requirements, together with numerous discussions with the Council during the design process, resulted in a modern building which Robert considers more humane and child-oriented than would have been created by a strict modernist philosophy. Nevertheless, it shares with the bus station the principle of 'enjoyable daylight', although built in white rendered blockwork rather than steel and glass (Figures 6.12 (a) and (b)).

With the urgency to consider environmental sustainability, Robert has increasingly placed emphasis on environmentally appropriate choices of materials and energy efficiency in the design of buildings and argued for prioritising walking, cycling, and public transport in urban design.

Consequently, since leaving MKDC, Robert became critical of key elements of the design of Central Milton Keynes. His major criticisms are that locating most of its buildings within a strict road grid and allowing cars to park in the centre has resulted in an environment of buildings surrounded by car parks that is uncongenial to pedestrians and public transport. He also feels that the highly planned centre lacks the disorder and animation of other cities that makes them interesting. He suggests that public transport be allowed into the core area with car parking at the periphery and has been involved in suggesting changes to improve the pedestrian experience (de Grey, 2006; Hill, 2007, p. 137).

Figure 6.12
(a) Rowans Children's Centre (now Family Centre), Fullers Slade, Milton Keynes, 2021. Photograph by the author.
(b) The Centre's Day Nursery. Photograph by the author.

(a)

(b)

**What can be learned from Robert's architectural work since leaving MKDC?**

Perhaps the main change has been a *departure from the strict modernism* of the CMK architects' group, while still using their rigorous design approach. His architecture shows a return to the user-centred design focus learned at Cambridge on designing buildings *with and for their users* and a growing concern with the *environmental sustainability* of buildings and cities.

This demonstrates Robert's ability to *adapt his ideas and practice* with experience, new knowledge, and changing external circumstances.

### *Political career*

As well as being an architect, Robert has had a powerful local political career. He was chair of Milton Keynes Labour Party for 14 years, a Labour member of Milton Keynes Borough Council in the 1980s and was elected again to Milton Keynes Council after it became a unitary authority in 1997. He regards politics, like architecture, as a creative activity as it involves producing and debating ideas and forming policies. He recognises that politics influences his architecture. For example, in the interview with me he said, 'architecture is about creating enjoyable places that bring people together and help undermine inequalities in society', and 'I put the people who will live and work in a building first rather than what would look good in a magazine.'

### *Robert de Grey's general approach to design*

In my second interview I asked Robert about his general philosophy and approach to design learned during his long experience as an architect. These are some of the observations he made.

> I don't start with a blank slate, for ideas, I look for patterns everywhere ... Architects are always looking at other architects' buildings and ideas in magazines, books, and now online. At worst they copy, at best they use an existing design and transform it.
>
> I try to find a solution drawing on experience, constraints and existing designs then challenge and test it against the brief, the site, function, aesthetics and budget.
>
> Constraints are good, they help to create a solution against an awkward constraint.
>
> Architects must communicate with themselves by sketching ideas on the backs of menus, etc. This then evolves into line drawings ... From the first exciting concept sketch to finished buildings through the RIBA [Royal Institute of

British Architects] process (RIBA (2020), see Chapter 1 Box 1.1] can take two to three years and is a complex team process.

I often challenge the brief as part of the process, for example by asking clients, do you really need this building? Often the brief is then changed by clients. The solution then evolves with further ideas that reinforce or modify the existing concept or is discarded. I often use the solution to explore the problem. The process is evolution and exploration, hence there are usually many design iterations in a team.

Architects must keep up with new technology, building materials and components through magazines, suppliers and online.

I don't use formal creativity techniques, the only one is informal brainstorming by sketching and discussing ideas in a group .... Physical models are useful; I've used fewer models than I'd like to have done after leaving MKDC, which had a model shop.

Buildings should evolve throughout the design process and the details, such as floor finishes and ironmongery, are very important.

Architects mature late when they have accumulated all the necessary technical, management and financial knowledge. However, experience is a two-edged sword as it makes one more likely to return to tried ideas and solutions.

Architects also need skills to be able to persuade clients and others and present projects clearly and be good project managers.

**What do Robert's work and observations about architectural design indicate about the factors, processes, and lessons likely to produce successful buildings?**

Over time Robert has accumulated a wide *'repertoire'* of architectural and other *knowledge, skills, past work, and experience* that he can draw upon for new projects.

He looks at and draws upon *other architects' work for inspiration and ideas* and tries to keep up with innovations in *materials, building components, and technologies*.

A starting goal for Robert's designs is his desire to meet the needs of *the client and users* of a building. Where possible he tries to *work with clients and the future users* of a building to identify their needs, wants, and demands.

Drivers of Robert's designs include *key constraints* such as the site and the budget, his preference for *modern(ist) architectural forms* and *sustainable buildings*.

Robert sometimes *questions the brief and may get clients to 'reframe'* the task or problem.

He, or the team of which he is a member, usually generate *several alternative concepts* before selecting one to develop. He sometimes uses informal *visual brainstorming* in a group to generate ideas and solutions.

The design process is a *lengthy, evolutionary, and iterative process* using sketches, drawings, and models and is typically based on the RIBA *Plan of Work* (RIBA, 2020).

Robert pays great *attention to the details*, technical and aesthetic, of any proposed design.

He likes *working in a team* with other individuals and/or organisations, especially with creative individuals and teams and in *organisations which support creativity and innovation*.

With experience, Robert has acquired essential *communication and project management* skills.

Robert's involvement in *Labour Party politics* interacts with his architectural work, for example in his belief that the design and financing of buildings and cities should help reduce social inequalities.

## REFERENCES

Barking Bags (2023). *The original and still the best dog walking bag!* Available at: https://barkingbags.co.uk/ (Accessed: 6 July 2023).

BBC (2022) *Dragons' Den.* Series 19, episode 4. BBC1 TV, 27 January. Available at: https://www.youtube.com/watch?v=knnwsm4ZThk (Accessed: 6 July 2023).

de Grey, R. (2006) 'Robert de Grey'. Interview by Roger Kitchen for the CMK Project. CD-ROM, CMK/001/031, 13 September. Milton Keynes: Living Archive.

Greaves, D. and Angell, R. (2021) *Barking Bags. Business Plan.* Unpublished, April.

Gunnercooke (2020a) *Laura Moseby and Barking Bags. Deed of Assignment.* Unpublished, November.

Gunnercooke (2020b) *Lee Mattocks and Barking Bags. Deed of Assignment.* Unpublished, November.

Hill, M. (2007) *The Story of the original CMK.* Milton Keynes: Living Archive.

Historic England (2014) *Former bus station, Station Square, Milton Keynes.* Available at: https://historicengland.org.uk/listing/the-list/list-entry/1416117 (Accessed: 16 June 2023).

IPO (2018) *Certificate of Registration for a UK Design. Dog walker's bag Design No.6039789.* Newport: Intellectual Property Office, July.

RIBA (2020) *Plan of Work 2020 Overview.* London: Royal Institute of British Architects.

# 7    Creative product designs

## INTRODUCTION

The examples and case studies in previous chapters have mainly concerned product and building innovations intended for commercial introduction or construction and where the creators were not also the makers. In this chapter I will consider some examples of creative product designs, most of which were not intended for the market, including designs created for educational purposes, and where the creators also produced what they designed. These examples cross into the territory of what has been called 'everyday creativity' or 'little-c' creativity (Kaufman and Beghetto, 2009), meaning creative actions undertaken by ordinary people in daily life, such as making a poster for a local event, creating recipes, or devising a garden planting scheme. In this chapter, however, the examples of creative product designs are at a professional, school student, and undergraduate design student level of design practice.

## CASE STUDY: NICHOLA CLARKE, DESIGNER AND ART TEACHER

The first case in this chapter concerns the work of Nichola Clarke, a former jewellery designer, now an art teacher. I interviewed Nichola in July 2020, with a WhatsApp messaging update in May 2023, about her background and professional experience in design and in teaching art to schoolchildren. We then focused on her creative process when conceiving, designing, and making a piece of contemporary jewellery and custom-designed greetings cards for friends and relatives.

### *Art and design background*

Nichola told me that she has been creative from a young age; an early memory was sprinkling talcum powder over a lace bedspread to create a pattern underneath. She enjoyed drawing and technical drawing at school, inspired by the encouragement of her art teacher. Friends often asked Nichola to draw their portraits. So, she decided to apply to art school and studied Foundation Art at Nene College (now University College Northampton) and Jewellery Design at Epsom School of Art and Design (now part of the University of the Creative Arts).

### *Jewellery design*

For two years after graduation, Nichola designed and made contemporary jewellery, such as neckpieces, broaches, and earrings. Nichola likes using layers of

DOI: 10.4324/9781003354406-7

materials in her designs and, arising from her interest in technical drawing at school, she appreciates the look of machines and mechanical objects.

Nichola provided me with descriptive and visual information about her creative process when designing and making a Perspex neckpiece. She started by making pen and pencil close-up drawings of mechanical objects, such as drill bits, cycle chains, wingnuts, and crank mechanisms (Figure 7.1 (a)). Her next step was to draw stylised versions of selected close-ups on paper. She then stitched cut or torn parts of the drawings on to a base (Figure 7.1 (b)). These 'observations' were then made into more distinct layered pieces by photocopying images on to tracing paper, which was then torn and stitched to a base with a sewing machine (Figures 7.1 (c) and 7.1 (d)). She then sandwiched samples of the more abstract pieces between a lower Perspex ring and upper Perspex shapes to form a prototype circular neckpiece (Figure 7.1 (e)). Perspex was her preferred material as it is easier to work and lighter than metal. The final stage was to develop the layered items into dark grey 3D elements, again sandwiched between a base ring and upper Perspex shapes, to produce the neckpiece ready for sale (Figure 7.1 (f)).

Nichola's process to produce an innovative piece of contemporary jewellery clearly shows that several stages of creative design iteration are involved. The initial drawing was inspired by her liking for mechanical objects with its images transformed in stages from 2D to increasingly 3D, using her liking for layering materials, while becoming more stylised and abstract. She then progressed to making a Perspex prototype of the neckpiece using the more abstracted layered designs before finalising the neckpiece with creatively transformed and more distinct 3D elements sandwiched between Perspex.

To sell her work, Nichola exhibited with and sold through Dazzle Contemporary Jewellery Exhibitions, which is still trading in 2023, over 40 years since its first show.

Nichola then landed her 'dream job' as a visual merchandiser for *Habitat*, a contemporary furniture, lighting, and homeware store. Her work involved creating layouts and placement of each new season's product collections in the store. Her layout and placement designs were to ensure that new products were located and displayed in the store so they would sell well.

### What can be learned from Nichola's background, education, and early career?

Nichola had an interest in *creative activities from a young age*, reflected in her liking for art and technical drawing at school and later gaining a degree in Art and Design.

Her early career continued to involve *creative work*, making her own jewellery designs and selling them via a contemporary designer jewellery outlet and designing store layouts.

■ **Creative product designs**

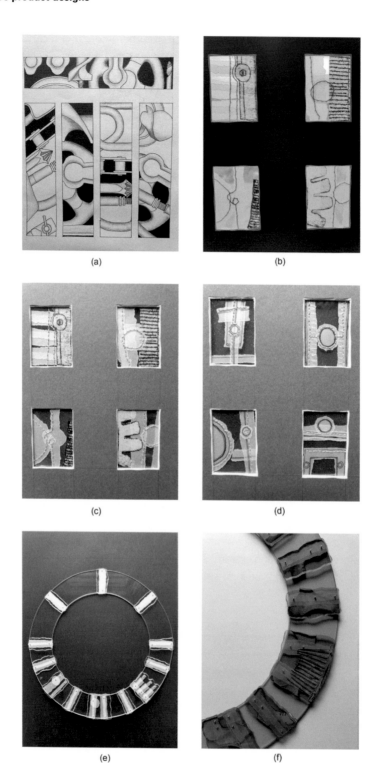

(a)

(b)

(c)

(d)

(e)

(f)

Figure 7.1
(a) to (f) Stages in the conception, development, and production of a contemporary Perspex neckpiece. Courtesy of Nichola Clarke.

Nichola's unique jewellery designs are driven by two *primary generators*: her liking for mechanical objects and the idea of layering materials. She also prefers to use Perspex as it is light and easy to work.

Her *iterative design* process is informed by her primary generators and involves *creative transformation and prototyping* of elements until a final product is completed.

### Art teaching career

After having her children, Nichola continued doing creative work with them, such as drawing and making items out of waste materials. Later she volunteered at a local primary school, which allowed her to make use of her creative skills. For example, one (English school) Foundation Year National Curriculum theme was 'Space' when she was closely involved in creating an outdoor 'Space World' area. This resulted in Nichola getting a teaching job at the school.

At the school Nichola specialises in teaching Art through working with four- to eleven-year-old children. To inform and inspire her teaching she draws on her previous work, including her courses in Foundation Art and Jewellery Design, her jewellery making experience, and her design work at Habitat. Recurrent ideas and methods from her previous work include cutting out, paper tearing, and stitching and layering of materials. Figure 7.2 shows textile work by Nichola's young art club students that make use of these ideas and methods.

Specific ideas often come from Nichola working with children on National Curriculum themes. For example, for an 'India' theme Nichola researched images, collected Indian textiles and beads, and made use of items such as puppets that were available at the school. She then worked with seven- to eleven-year-old children on making patterns for an exhibition at Milton Keynes Gallery inspired, for example, by the patterns on saris.

Nichola generally has an image in her head of how she wants school artworks to look but tries to let the children lead on the creative process and helps by making available proper art supplies and facilitates by providing guidance and supplying relevant objects and materials. For instance, a '2012 London Olympics' theme led to a whole school exhibition at Milton Keynes Central Library. For this project Nichola had an image in her head about how the large, finished work should look based on her favoured idea of using layers. Building on this idea, the first-year students made handprints for the inner layer, and the second-year group drew and painted faces for the second layer. Further layers working outwards involved words, pictures of track events, then field events, with an outer edge comprising silhouettes of London landmarks.

Figure 7.2
Coloured layered
and stitched work in
different materials
by Nichola's young
art club students.
Courtesy of Nichola
Clarke.

Apart from her recurrent ideas and methods such as layering, Nichola's sources of inspiration are ones she has always drawn upon, such as the colours, shapes, and patterns in the environment. Her training, design experience, and visits to art galleries provide further sources of ideas. For creativity Nichola told me, 'it's important not to have to be perfect. Relax don't worry, especially when working with children.'

### What lessons can be learned from Nichola's teaching career?

Nichola's uses (English school) National Curriculum themes as *starting points* for inspiring an art and design project or activity.

She *researches and 'immerses' herself* in the theme topic to gather ideas and materials to carry out a creative activity which addresses the theme.

She draws on her 'repertoire' of *accumulated knowledge, skills, and previous work* when working on a creative teaching activity.

Nichola *facilitates and guides her students* to do independent individual and group creative work by drawing on her own images of how the work might evolve, and by providing relevant materials.

### Greeting card designs

Nichola often uses her artistic and creative skills to design and make greetings cards for family and friends. Below are three examples of her creative process when designing and making the cards.

### Leaving card for two neighbours

When two well-liked neighbours, Sally and Trevor, moved away from the street where she lives, Nichola designed and made a leaving card to be signed by the street's other neighbours. The starting point for the design was Sally and Trevor's involvement in the street's Queen's Diamond Jubilee street party in 2012. This royal celebration immediately led to Nichola choosing red, white, and blue colours for the card. Her liking for paper cutting then resulted in her deciding to make cut-out silhouettes of her neighbours on black paper stuck on to the card. Sally was portrayed wearing a pinafore like the ones she made for the party's organisers. Trevor was shown holding balloons because he made balloon sculptures to entertain children at the party. Finally, she attached farewell messages in speech bubbles to the silhouettes.

### Birthday card for her mother

Nichola designed the card shown in Figure 7.3 (a) for her mother's birthday. She decided on a rose design because her mother liked roses and coloured the flower pink, lime, and pale blue based on her mother's living room colour scheme. Nichola employed her favoured cut-out method to make the flower's petals and leaves which were then stuck on to the card base.

Figure 7.3
Cards designed by Nichola Clarke. (a) 'Rose' birthday card for her mother, designed by Nichola Clarke. Courtesy of Nichola Clarke. (b) A neighbour's 80th birthday card, designed by Nichola Clarke. Courtesy of Nichola Clarke.

(a)

(b)

*A neighbour's 80th birthday card*
Nichola designed the card shown in Figure 7.3 (b) for a neighbour's 80th birthday. Her initial idea was another silhouette design like the leaving card mentioned above. However, she rejected this idea as being too complicated, but wanted to keep a sophisticated look to express the character of the recipient. Nichola used the cutting out method once again with the initial of the neighbour's name (Joy) at the centre plus several cut-out flowers and leaves reflecting Joy's love of her garden with a subtle number 80 in the centre of one of the flowers.

> **What can we learn from Nichola's creative process when designing and making greeting cards?**
>
> Nichola draws upon an *initial idea,* such as the Jubilee street party or a rose, from which to start the design.
>
> She uses *shapes, images, and colours* appropriate to the person or people the card is designed for.
>
> She often makes use of her liking for *cutting out* shapes in paper or other materials as the *construction method* for the card.

## CASE STUDY: OPEN UNIVERSITY STUDENT T-SHIRT DESIGNS

This final case concerns the creation of graphic designs by Open University (OU) students studying an online, first-year undergraduate course U101 *Design Thinking: Creativity for the 21st Century* (Open University, 2023). OU students, most of whom are mature and in employment, study part-time from home and do not require prior qualifications. They are therefore more representative of the general population than other university undergraduates. For their first assignment students had to create an original graphic design, print it on to a transfer sheet and then on to a T-shirt, which they photographed and then submitted to an online 'Open Design Studio' where it could be seen by other students and assessed by their tutors.

### Analysis of a large sample of T-shirt designs
An article on creativity in design written by two of the U101 Design Thinking course's authors, Peter Lloyd and Derek Jones, analysed 1038 student T-shirt designs from three years of the course. They studied the students' design processes, and the T-shirt designs they created. Both authors assessed 102 of the T-shirts for potential saleability (Lloyd and Jones, 2013). This student project was presented as an example of 'normal' or 'commonplace' creativity through which almost anyone can produce original designs from scratch given a suitable 'grammar' of creation, in this case a starting point for inspiration, a phased design process, and some essential materials. Then equipped with this design grammar, some techniques, and confidence gained from the experience, most people, Lloyd and Jones argue, should be able to go on to produce further creative designs.

For this assignment students were asked to use their own hands as a starting point and source of inspiration. They were guided to go through a four-phase systematic design process involving:

1.  *Exploration* by considering (a) different parts of their hand, (b) a story about their hand involving an object, and (c) possible hand gestures.
2.  Creation of at least three *design concepts* based on the explorations.
3.  *Selection and development of a concept*, then production of and printing a *final design*.
4.  *Evaluating* their product.

If necessary, they could trace around photographs as a method of drawing.

Analysis of the designs by Lloyd and Jones showed that the most common source of inspiration was a hand gesture, resulting in the creation of images of various gestures such as thumbs up or making a heart shape with the hands. Next most common was a story around an object related to hands, which produced images such as pens and pencils, a guitar, and mobile phones. Different designs created by the students involved one or more images, the inclusion of words, and different placements of images and/or words. As the students were able to view other students' designs online before submitting their work for assessment, some used the opportunity to develop their concepts stimulated by designs produced by others.

The analysis revealed that this student creative design project, with the design process grammar provided by the course, produced a striking range and variety of T-shirt graphic designs, including some which Lloyd and Jones judged to be potentially saleable. Before they started most of the students had little or no previous design experience and many were very unsure of their ability to undertake a creative task or even to produce simple drawings.

### Some recent student T-shirt designs

To bring the project up to date I obtained four T-shirt designs produced to the same brief by recent U101 students together with their accounts of their creative thinking and design processes.

The 'Lhandscape' T-shirt shown in Figure 7.4 (a) was a development of the design produced by a student for her original assignment. The student's starting point was a close-up photograph of her upturned palm. The photograph reminded her of the shape of three hills, which gave her the idea for a design concept that gave the impression of a landscape. She made some tracings and drawings from the photograph and then simplified and stylised them. She wrote,

I then used symmetry and repetition of this shape to look like a landscape of hills. I tilted the shape to give a more organic feel to the design, then researched colours and colour meanings and added my choices to the design. The [Lhandscape] text was to pull the design together as I liked the play on words (Quinn, 2023).

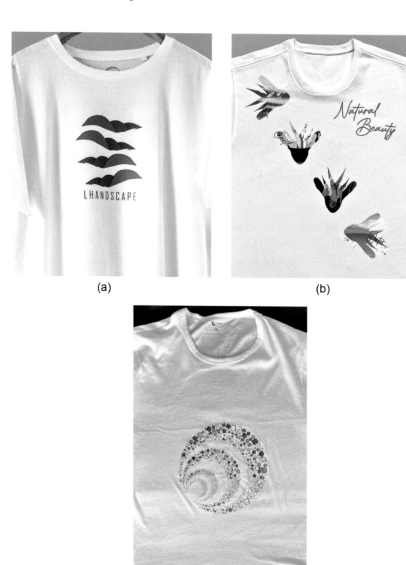

(a)

(b)

(c)

Figure 7.4
(a) 'Lhandscape' T-shirt, designed by Jacqueline Quinn, Open University U101 student. Courtesy of Jacqueline Quinn. 7.4 (b) 'Natural Beauty' T-shirt, designed by. Rhiannon Davies, Open University U101 student. Courtesy of Rhiannon Davies. 7.4 (c) 'The Circle of Life' designed by Tom Gibbard, Open University U101 student. Courtesy of Tom Gibbard.

The second T-shirt, shown in Figure 7.4 (b), was also a development of the original design which started from a photo of the upper side of the student's hand with her fingers and thumb outstretched. She traced around the photo and, using principles learned from the course about abstraction, produced a simplified drawing. Using a lightbox, she rotated and superimposed the image on the first drawing to produce a symmetrical composition. Early on this student decided that she wanted her T-shirt design to spread a positive message, conveying the 'natural beauty' of the wearer and the Earth. Different orientations of the superimposed composition she thought resembled various beautiful natural objects: a deer's head, a bird in flight, flames, and a fish. Further creative transformation led to the concept of these objects representing the four elements: Earth, Air, Fire, and Water. She produced and coloured the final four images digitally with image manipulation software that she had taught herself to use and added the text for Natural Beauty and the Earth, Air, etc. labels for the images using the same software (Davies, 2023).

The third T-shirt, shown in Figure 7.4 (c), exemplifies an even more trans-formative creative process. The starting point was three white marks the student observed under his index fingernails, which reminded him of the dots on domi-noes and playing the game with his grandmother as a child. Now as a father, he has taught dominoes to his two children. This gave him the idea of 'the circle of life' with each generation passing knowledge and memories to the next. He then conceived a design concept to represent this idea by four circles, each one representing a person at different stages of life. This concept evolved into crescents, the outer one being his grandmother and the inner one his youngest child. The number of coloured elements in each crescent, representing knowl-edge and memories, indicates life already lived and the monochrome elements the years of life remaining. The student generated this coloured image digitally but for technical reasons had to print it on to the T-shirt in monochrome and col-our the elements by hand with the colours chosen to express each individual's personality (Gibbard, 2023).

A fourth T-shirt design 'The Working Hand' (not illustrated) represents a more straightforward creative design process employed by many U101 students. This student started by simply looking at her hands and observing their forms. She chose her right hand with its palm facing forward and fingers together. She wanted to create a design that conveyed the message that she works with her hands and uses tools (Wright, 2023). This resulted in a design comprising four straight-edged fingers placed side by side with rounded ends and stylised fingerprints. The index finger has a hammerhead outline above its fingertip and the other three fingers have, respectively, outlines of a screwdriver, a ruler, and a spade within the finger shapes. The dark blue fingers and orange tool shapes are contained within a light blue square.

### Discussion

Analysis of the outputs of this Open University student design project by Lloyd and Jones (2013) and the accounts of the processes that some recent U101 stu-dents used when creating their T-shirt designs, demonstrate that given a starting point, a design process or grammar, plus some design skills, novice designers can create worthwhile, even potentially saleable, designs. Familiarity with the types of images that appear on existing T-shirts and viewing the designs created by other students before having to finalise their designs of course also helped. The guidance and support provided by the U101 *Design Thinking* course gave the students some of the approaches and methods that professional and experienced designers, architects, and design engineers have acquired from their education and design work and apply routinely, even almost intuitively, when undertaking a project (Roy, 2013). These approaches and methods include exploration to understand a problem and find sources of inspiration; gathering information;

considering existing solutions; sketching, drawing, digital and physical modelling; and team working. These approaches and methods may typically be applied during a phased process of concept creation, concept selection and development, and detail design for production or construction.

The students' work lends support to the creativity theories of Weisberg (1993) introduced in Chapter 1 and illustrated in Figure 1.5. Weisberg argues that creativity and innovation are not mysterious activities or the work of geniuses but the result of applying ordinary thinking processes and in-depth knowledge to build on previous ideas, typically triggered by a source of inspiration and forms of associative thinking such as the use of analogies. Although the designs produced by some U101 students were more original and better executed than those produced by others, indicating a role for differences in ability and/or prior experience, almost all were able to create acceptable designs relevant to the task with some showing significant originality.

As novice designers become more experienced and confident in using the approaches and methods used by professionals, they should be able to tackle more complex tasks involving higher levels of innovation, if they possess or acquire the domain knowledge and skills that the task requires and are prepared to work hard at finding and realising a creative solution.

**What does the example of a graphic design project undertaken by mainly novice design students indicate about the development of creative design skills?**

People with little or no design experience can produce worthwhile creative designs given guidance on a *starting point and a systematic design process or 'grammar'*, after learning some basic design skills.

Some of the designs produced by novice design students indicate processes of *transformational creative thinking* and the use of *manual and digital design skills* learned for the project, with a proportion judged to be potentially saleable. Other student's designs represent a more straightforward creative process.

As novice designers become more confident in using the approaches normally used by professional or experienced designers, they should be able to tackle more innovative projects given the *opportunity and motivation, relevant knowledge and skills,* and a *creative design process.*

## REFERENCES

Davies, R. (2023) Email to Robin Roy, 24 June.

Gibbard, T. (2023) Email to Robin Roy, 24 June.

Kaufman, J.C. and Beghetto, R.A. (2009) 'Beyond Big and Little: The Four C Model of Creativity', *Review of General Psychology*, 13(1), pp. 1–12.

Lloyd, P. and Jones, D. (2013). 'Everyday creativity in design process', *Art, Design & Communication in Higher Education*, 12(2) pp. 247–63.

Open University (2023) *Design thinking: creativity for the 21st century*, U101 Level 1 undergraduate module. Available at: https://www.open.ac.uk/courses/modules/u101 (Accessed: 6 July 2023).

Quinn, J. (2023) Email to Robin Roy, 24 June.

Roy, R. (2013) 'Creative design', T217 *Design essentials,* Book 3. Milton Keynes: The Open University.

Weisberg, R.W. (1993) *Creativity: Beyond the myth of genius*. New York: W.H. Freeman.

Wright, E. (2023) Email to Robin Roy, 28 June.

# 8 Guidelines for successful creative design and innovation

## INTRODUCTION

In this chapter I will identify general patterns associated with success, and lack of success, in creative design and innovation. These patterns are based on my analysis of the examples and case studies discussed in Chapters 2 to 7, which are summarised in the text boxes in those chapters. I will then attempt to translate those patterns into guidelines and lessons for individuals, teams, and organisations wanting to produce successful new products, buildings, and innovations and reduce the risk of failures. A set of criteria for assessing whether the products, buildings, and innovations discussed in the book were considered successful, or unsuccessful, were given in the Introduction to Chapter 2.

### Limitations of the guidance

The guidelines and lessons in this chapter are intended to be useful to designers, engineers, architects, product and innovation managers, and entrepreneurs, and to teachers and students of those subject areas. *However, it is important to note that these guidelines and lessons do not claim to be comprehensive.* For example, they only touch upon the business management, marketing, manufacturing, construction, and financial aspects of design, architecture, new product development, and innovation, as these are well-covered by the existing literature.

Although the examples and cases cover the spectrum from revolutionary innovations, such as the smartphone, to creative product designs, such as an item of contemporary jewellery, and innovators ranging from multinationals like Apple to small businesses and individual designers, they are inevitably selective. In addition, it was not possible to provide a full account of the often long and complex histories of every example or case. And, as I noted in Chapter 1, analysis of a limited number of examples and case studies can only identify patterns that may be *associated with* rather than provide scientific or statistical proof of the *causes* of success and failure in creative design and innovation. Nevertheless, many of the guidelines and lessons provided in this chapter find support in the literature on creativity, new product development, and design and innovation management that were referenced or summarised in Chapter 1 and in my previous book on consumer product innovation (Roy, 2016).

DOI: 10.4324/9781003354406-8

### Structure of this chapter

To structure this chapter, I compiled the material associated with success and failure in creative design and innovation illustrated by the book's examples and case studies to identify the topic areas they covered. This resulted in this chapter being divided into the following sections:

1. The socio-technical and market context.
2. Creative individuals and organisations.
3. The motivation to create and innovate.
4. Starting points and inspirations for creativity and innovation.
5. Effective creative design and innovation processes.
6. Characteristics of successful products, buildings, and innovations.
7. Intellectual property protection.
8. Continuing improvement and innovation.
9. Unsuccessful products, buildings, and innovations.

Then, within each section I outline factors, processes, or lessons associated with success or failure and illustrate them with brief examples summarised from Chapters 2 to 7 (shown in bulleted text). Finally, at the end of each section I offer 'Guidelines for success'. These are summaries (shown in boxed text) of guidelines and lessons associated with successful creative design and innovation for that section's topic area. This structure should become clear as you read. Depending on your interests, this chapter may be read as a whole or dipped into. This might mean focusing on selected sections or concentrating on the 'Guidelines for success' at the end of each section.

## THE SOCIO-TECHNICAL AND MARKET CONTEXT

New products, buildings, and innovations are influenced, stimulated, or hampered by the socio-technical and market context in which they are conceived, developed, introduced, and used. This section will discuss some of the significant contextual factors revealed by the examples and cases in this book and provide some guidelines on how to take account of those factors.

### Contextual factors affecting innovation

New products, buildings and innovations often depend on *enabling technologies* that allow for their creation or improvement. These technologies may be new or long established and are often developed outside an organisation or industry, sometimes with government support. For example:

- The development of integrated circuits and microprocessors from the 1950s enabled the creation of portable mobile phones and eventually smartphones like the *iPhone*. US military research provided the foundation for many of these technologies (Mazzucato, 2013).

The success of a new product or innovation depends on the organisations and systems that supply services and components and manufacture, distribute, and sell it. These *complementary assets* are necessary to enable the item to function and reach widespread adoption or *diffusion*. For example:

- Mobile and smartphones depend for their operation on successive generations of digital cellular radio networks and on global supply chains for production, distribution, and sales.

Consumer preferences and behaviours are an important factor in driving innovation. Consumers may demand new features or uses for a new product or innovation that were not anticipated by its originators, and its ability to meet these demands will affect its success. For example:

- Users demanded a wide variety of third-party 'apps' for the iPhone. When Apple allowed such apps for the iPhone 3G onwards to be downloaded from its App Store, it ensured the innovation's success and facilitated the emergence of a major app industry.

The state of the market and competition also impacts the success of new products and innovations:

- The popularity of digital music players on mobile phones threatened the market for Apple's iPod music player and iTunes service. This initially stimulated Apple to partner with Motorola and Cingular to develop an 'iTunes phone'. When this product proved unsuccessful, Apple focused on the development of the iPhone series capable, among many other functions, of downloading and playing multimedia content from iTunes.

Changes in society, such as shifts in demographics and cultural values, can create new consumer needs, wants, and demands. Products and innovations that align with these changes are likely to have a greater chance of success. For example:

- A fashion for cycling, including among women, in the late 19th century helped to grow an industry to manufacture 'safety' bicycles pioneered by the *Rover Safety*. This in turn provided technologies and businesses for the fledgling motor industry.

Government regulations, policies, and funding can stimulate or hamper innovation, depending on the incentives they create for businesses and consumers. For example:

- The oil crisis in the 1970s led to increased support for innovations in energy conservation and renewable energy, which waned and then grew again with the climate emergency in the 21st century.

Environmental problems and increased environmental awareness can stimulate creativity and innovation that aims to address the problems. For example:

- Growing environmental consciousness in the 1960s and 1970s inspired architect Derek Taylor to focus on wind power and sustainable architecture, leading to his creation of innovative designs and concepts for vertical-axis wind turbines and zero and positive carbon buildings.

Industries and markets vary in their willingness to adopt new ideas and technologies. For example:

- Conservative, risk-averse industries and markets, like UK housing, are resistant to, or slow to adopt, innovative designs and methods, such as prefabricated and zero carbon homes. This contrasts with industries and markets, such as consumer electronics, that are receptive to innovations in design and technology.

### Guidelines for success: The socio-technical and market context

Designers, architects, engineers, and others need to keep abreast of technological advancements in their own and related fields to ensure that **enabling technologies, components, and materials** on which their new product, building, or innovation depends are available and economically viable when required.

Innovators need to ensure that the **complementary assets** – the technological systems, services, components, and supply chains – required to introduce the innovation on to the market or into use can either be provided by others or set up in time by the innovating individual or organisation.

Innovators should **monitor the changing market and social context** for social and market changes, trends, and fashions that offer opportunities for innovation and to identify products with which any planned new product or innovation would have to compete.

Innovators should consider **regulatory and political factors,** such as national and international regulations and government policies and funding, that may affect the new product, building, or innovation. Understanding these factors can help innovators anticipate potential barriers and opportunities when attempting to innovate.

**Environmental problems** – such as the climate and biodiversity crises; the depletion of material and water resources; air and water pollution; and unsustainable transport systems and buildings – **provide opportunities for**

**innovation**. Innovators can seek opportunities in the green economy and contribute to addressing these critical and urgent environmental issues.

Innovators should consider the likely **acceptability of their new product, building, or innovation** in the industry and market in which it is intended to be introduced. Are the industry, market, and potential users receptive or resistant to innovation? What barriers to innovation are likely to arise, and how might they be overcome?

## CREATIVE INDIVIDUALS AND ORGANISATIONS

Creative individuals, groups, and organisations tend to share certain characteristics. This section identifies some of these characteristics from the book's examples and cases and provides some guidelines and lessons on how to foster creativity.

### *Creative individuals*

Chapter 1 reviewed some of the literature on creative individuals, whether they are born creative, or became creative because of their background, psychology, knowledge, or opportunities. What is the evidence from the book's examples and case studies?

The *background* of creative individuals is often significant:

- Sir Jonathan (Jony) Ive had an interest from childhood in drawing and making, and in designed objects, how they work, what they are made from, and how they are made. This background contributed to him becoming a world-renowned industrial designer.
- The practical family backgrounds of both Jack Kilby and Sophie Wilson led to their early interest, education, and careers in electronics and eventually to their breakthrough ideas and innovations in integrated circuits and microprocessors.
- Derek Taylor's family background in making buildings and other objects and Robert de Grey's family of artists and architects directed and prepared them for creative careers in architecture and design.

Creative individuals who succeed as innovators often possess certain *personality traits*, such as great self-belief, determination, and drive. They often question conventional ideas. It was said, for instance, of the Young British Artists of the 1990s, such as Damien Hirst and Rachel Whiteread, that 'A determination to defy convention led to an explosion of creativity' (BBC, 2022). Examples from the case studies include:

- James Dyson required great determination and persistence to develop a mass-market cyclone vacuum cleaner in the face of rejection by manufacturers and financiers and to fight attempts by other manufacturers to copy his patented dual cyclone technology.

- Steve Jobs was said to possess a 'reality distortion field' and believe that he was a 'chosen' or special person to whom normal rules did not apply on what he and his teams at Apple could achieve (Isaacson, 2011, pp. 118–9).

Creative individuals have usually had to acquire *deep knowledge, skills, and expertise* in the domain in which they successfully create and innovate. Malcolm Gladwell (2008, p. 41), with his rule of '10,000 hours' of practise, popularised the idea that a very high level of expertise is essential before an individual or group can produce major creative work. Gladwell also emphasised it is necessary for the individual or group to have had the *opportunity* to practise a skill and acquire knowledge over a long period, citing examples such as The Beatles and Bill Gates. Such individuals typically also have interests outside their area of expertise that together provide *a 'repertoire' of deep and wide knowledge.* For example:

- Jony Ive acquired extensive knowledge of materials, product architectures, and manufacturing processes, and a wide interest in and knowledge of art and design, that enabled him to design elegant, user-friendly, and functional products.

If necessary, creative individuals will *learn or acquire any domain-specific knowledge* required to undertake an innovation project. For example:

- Dyson said that through deep study someone can quickly become sufficiently knowledgeable in any subject required to solve a problem. He therefore immersed himself in available knowledge of cyclone technology before realising that he needed to carry out his own experimental research and development to design a working prototype cyclone vacuum cleaner.

Successful creative innovators are willing to *work extremely hard*, if necessary for years, to achieve their goals – in Edison's well-known saying, 'Genius is one percent inspiration, ninety-nine percent perspiration.' For example:

- Dyson took four years to develop his first prototype cyclone vacuum cleaner and fifteen years of persistent technical, design, and business effort before his first mass-produced cyclone cleaner, the *DC01*, was launched.

Such dedication, however, can come at a cost to personal and family life:

- Frank Canova, who led the team that developed the IBM *Simon Personal Communicator* smartphone, worked such long hours that he only managed to see his new baby while still at work (Merchant, 2017, p. 34).

- It took over two years for Apple engineers and designers, working under relentless pressure, to develop the iPhone. Several of the team said later that they toiled at the expense of their health and family relationships (Merchant, 2017, pp. 375–6).

Creative individuals who succeed at innovation must usually possess *good interpersonal and business or entrepreneurial skills*, such as the ability to raise funds, convince others to support their work, and negotiate deals:

- Dyson had to employ his abilities and experience in business, negotiation, and raising finance to develop, make, and introduce his innovations in cyclone vacuum cleaners.
- Debbie Greaves, who conceived of and prototyped a purpose-designed dog walking bag, had good interpersonal, networking, and fundraising skills learned through working in the voluntary sector. These skills enabled her and her partner to establish a business to get the product designed and manufactured.

Creative individuals must usually *collaborate with others* to develop and refine their ideas through to innovation. For example:

- Dyson developed his first commercially successful cyclone vacuum cleaner, the *G-Force*, by working with engineers and managers in a Japanese company with a strong culture of innovation. He went on to develop the first mass-market cyclone clearer by working with his own small team of engineers and designers.
- Dunlop partnered with financier Harvey du Cros to commercialise and manufacture his invention of the pneumatic cycle tyre.

### Innovative organisations

As was discussed in Chapter 1, there is an established literature on innovative organisations, their strategies, characteristics, and how they are led, organised, and managed, so this will not be covered here.

However, it is worth noting the complementary relationship between creative individuals and innovative organisations, since creative individuals best thrive in organisations that encourage and support new ideas. For example:

- Jony Ive emphasised the importance of the innovative culture at Apple which allowed for fragile new ideas to be explored and then developed if they showed promise.
- Derek Taylor was only able to pursue his innovative ideas on wind power and sustainable buildings when he joined the creative environment of like-minded people at the Architectural Association and then the Open University.

### Guidelines for success: Creative individuals and organisations

**What can individuals do to enable them to produce creative and innovative work?**

While there is little that an individual wishing to create and innovate can do about their family background or their innate personality or talent, there are some elements of creative ability that they can foster.

Innovators should acquire a **deep and wide 'repertoire' of knowledge, skills, and expertise** relevant to the projects they undertake. This may start with a personal interest from childhood in a subject area which is then fostered through formal and informal education, employment, and experience. This takes time, but if a project requires specific new knowledge and skills, these might be rapidly acquired through **concentrated immersion in and study of**, and preferably some practical experience in, **the relevant domain**.

While a creative idea might come quickly (or not) translating the idea into an innovation usually requires dedicated and **persistent hard work**. This might take months or years, often with many technical, practical, and financial setbacks and barriers to overcome. So, the potential innovator must be willing and prepared for that task.

**Collaboration with other people** to provide the knowledge, skills, and expertise that an individual might lack and to share the hard work of innovation is usually essential to succeed. If the project is within an organisation there is likely to be a small or large team involved depending on the scale of the project and the range of expertise required.

Creative individuals often need to **work within a creative organisation** to make effective use of their abilities.

Most innovation projects require, as well as technical expertise, the application of **interpersonal, business, or entrepreneurial skills**.

## THE MOTIVATION TO CREATE AND INNOVATE

People, as individuals or within organisations, want to create something new for a variety of reasons. As noted above, innovation usually involves hard work often over a long period and with many setbacks. Hence there is a need for an individual, team, or organisation to have the necessary *motivation* to carry out the task. This motivation may come from many possible sources.

One of the most common motivations to innovate is what has been called *'constructive discontent'* (Bansal, et al., 2022). That is dissatisfaction arising from experience with existing situations or artefacts leading to a desire to improve them. For example:

- Dyson found from experience that, among other faults, conventional wheel-barrows sank into soft ground and that bagged vacuum cleaners lost their suction during use. This motivated him to invent, design, manufacture, and sell a wheelbarrow with a ball-shaped wheel that did not sink, and cyclone vacuum cleaners without a bag to clog with dust.

Another common source of motivation is a *general goal or broad problem* that an individual or organisation believes needs addressing. For example:

- Derek Taylor strongly felt that environmental problems that threaten the earth's survival urgently require solutions. This led him to a lifetime of research in, and invention and design of, innovative wind turbines and zero and positive carbon buildings.

Motivation often also arises through the desire to *solve a specific problem* or to *address a specific goal or need*:

- Martin Cooper considered that a portable cell phone was needed to free users from AT&T's fixed car-based phones, which eventually resulted in Motorola introducing the world's first portable mobile phone.

The motivating problem or need can be *personal*:

- Dunlop was motivated to invent and prototype a pneumatic cycle tyre by his son's desire to beat his friends in races on the uneven cobbled Belfast streets.
- Debbie Greaves found that no suitable bags existed to carry all she needed when walking her new puppy. This led her and her partner to establish a business to develop, make, and sell purpose-designed dog walking bags.

Spotting a *market opportunity* or *recognising a latent demand* for a new and bet-ter product is another source of motivation. For example:

- Frank Canova believed that a need and a latent demand existed for a mobile phone that combined the functions of a telephone and personal digital assistant. This motivated him to persuade IBM management to support the creation of such a product and devote two years of dedicated teamwork to the development of the *Simon Personal Communicator*.

*Winning a competition* may sometimes provide a strong motivation for innovation. For example:

- Marks Barfield were motivated to design their *Bridge of the Future* by a Bridges and Infrastructure ideas competition sponsored by a civil engineering magazine and won first prize.

Underlying some of the motivating forces may be the wish for *financial gain, business growth, profit, or status*. Such motivations were typically unstated in the examples and case studies, probably because they were implicit or might have been considered less worthy than trying to make better products, meeting social needs, or solving environmental problems.

***Guidelines for success: The motivation to create and innovate***

Innovators can **acquire the necessary motivation** needed to overcome the challenges involved in innovation from one or more sources:

A desire to **improve the world**.

To **improve unsatisfactory artefacts** (from constructive discontent).

To **solve a general or specific problem**.

To **meet a personal need**.

To **enter or retain a market**.

To **win a competition**.

For **personal, business, or financial gain**.

## STARTING POINTS AND INSPIRATIONS FOR CREATIVITY AND INNOVATION

Creativity, of course, requires inspiration but there are other starting points for creativity and innovation revealed by the examples and case studies.

An important starting point is an initial *'big idea'* or *vision* that drives the invention, design, or innovation process. For example:

- Jobs provided his teams with the vision of a smartphone operated entirely via a touchscreen. He considered that multitouch technology developed for a tablet computer – a previous 'big idea' which would later result in the *iPad* – should be first applied to a smartphone for which there was a larger market.

■ **Guidelines for successful creative design and innovation**

For many projects the starting point are the requirements in a client's *brief or specification*:

- RSHP architects created the pre-technical concept design for the *Oxley Woods* prefabricated eco-homes in response to the multiple requirements of a Design for Manufacture competition to design homes that could be built for £60,000 or less, excluding land.
- Derek Yeadon and Robert de Grey were given the brief by Milton Keynes Development Corporation to design a central bus station near the city's main train station to provide shelter and accommodation for passengers and bus company staff and which complemented the existing modernist buildings around the site.

Sometimes a problem or brief may be 'reframed' to provide a new starting point:

- The problem of flooding in London was reframed as one of developing an openable Thames flood barrier rather than continuing to build higher river walls or embankments.

Architects, and other designers, often use ideas and forms from *existing arte-facts* or *geometrical shapes* that they admire to provide the core idea that drives a design. Such starting points have been called 'primary generators' (Darke, 1979). For example:

- When searching for ideas for the design of college building, the architect Richard MacCormac had the image of a 'belvedere' (a structure command-ing a view) which he said, 'stabilised the whole concept' (Parry, 1990).

A liking for certain *styles, designs, or fashions* often provides another starting point:

- Ive's design of the *iMac G3* computer echoed the 'blobject' aesthetics fash-ionable in design circles at the time.
- De Grey and most of his colleagues in Milton Keynes Development Corporation's architects' department in the 1970s and 1980s were devotees of modernist architecture.

Designers, engineers, and architects often prefer using certain *materials* and/or *production methods*:

- Ive liked to design Apple products to be made from plastics and aluminium.
- Art and design teacher, Nichola Clarke, when working as a jewellery maker, preferred to make products from Perspex, which is light and easy to work.

Admired *people, publications, products, or buildings* may provide the driving force behind designs and innovations:

- Jobs and Ive admired elegant, usable, and functional designs, such as the consumer products designed by Dieter Rams for the German company Braun.
- Taylor's thinking and work was inspired by people and publications with radically alternative ideas for society and technology, notably Buckminster Fuller and *The Whole Earth Catalog*.
- De Grey admires the work of Dutch architect Herman Herzberger because of his focus on designing for the users of a building.

Another source of inspiration maybe the *ideas and work of particular social groups or movements*. Eno (2009) calls this the 'scenius' in which creative individuals and groups work and inspire each other. For example:

- Barbara Hepworth and Ben Nicholson were part of a group of other artists, designers, and architects living in and around Hampstead, North London who inspired, collaborated, and competed with each other.
- Taylor's ideas for wind turbines and sustainable buildings powered by renewable energy arose from him being a member of the emerging UK Alternative Technology movement.

A *chance event or accidental discovery* may provide the starting point for an important innovation:

- The very low power requirement of a RISC microprocessor was discovered by accident when its creators, Wilson and Furber, were testing it.

A *flash of insight* or *'lightbulb moment'* may sometimes provide a breakthrough. The idea may arise while thinking about a problem or, unexpectedly, after 'sleeping on it', as proposed in the 'incubation/illumination' theory of creativity (Wallas, 1926). For example:

- Kilby had the idea for integrated circuits when he had the opportunity, while alone at work, to think about how to connect the increasing number of components in electronic circuits.
- The breakthrough that led to Noyce's rival integrated circuit arose when a colleague working on how to protect transistors from failure had the idea, while relaxing in the shower, of covering a silicon circuit with a layer of silicon oxide containing tiny windows.

The examples and case studies also revealed many other sources of inspiration for inventions, new products, and buildings, some of which resulted in innovations.

Several ideas resulted from *transferring ideas, objects, components, or technologies from one field to another* – a form of 'associative thinking'. For example:

- Fraenkel's river current turbine derived from his idea, based on a knowledge of fluid dynamics, of transferring the technology of wind turbines to operate underwater so greatly increasing turbine output.
- Dunlop's thinking when conceiving his pneumatic cycle tyre was said to involve transferring his knowledge of rubber veterinary appliances to an air-filled tyre.

Other ideas resulted from considering *physical or biological analogies* – another form of associative thinking. For example:

- Charles Draper, who conceived the flood control gates with a D-shaped cross-section for the *Thames Barrier*, was inspired by an analogy with the similar mechanism of a gas stopcock.
- J.K. Starley created a bicycle that made best use of the rider's effort by thinking that pedalling a bicycle was like climbing a ladder.
- Marks Barfield's Bridge of the Future was inspired by the vertebrae of a dinosaur seen in London's Natural History Museum.

*Comics, films, books, or other media* may provide sources of ideas and inspiration:

- Martin Cooper said he was inspired to create a portable mobile phone by the two-way wrist radio portrayed in the 1940s *Dick Tracy* comic strips.
- The iPhone's multitouch interface was inspired by several sources, reportedly including the gesture-controlled screen in the science fiction film, *Minority Report*.

An *external trigger* may provide the inspiration. For example:

- Gafni's cardboard bicycle was inspired by him hearing about someone who had made a cardboard canoe.

*Observations of the environment* – for example of people, objects, plants, and landscapes – is another common source of inspiration. For example:

- Dyson's visit to the French lavender fields inspired the novel lavender and pink colours of his G-Force cyclone cleaner.

A new product, building or design may sometimes be inspired by designers or architects expressing *symbolic meaning* through an innovation. For example:

- Marks Barfield's *London Eye* observation wheel, built to celebrate the Year 2000, was conceived to symbolise the turn of the Millennium.

*Guidelines for success: Starting points and inspirations for creativity and innovation*

**How may designers, architects, engineers, or others find starting points and inspirations for creative design and innovation?**

**Starting points** can be:

A **big idea or vision**.

A **project brief or specification**.

From **reframing a problem**.

Sometimes by **chance** or **accidental discovery**.

**Inspirations** tend to come from something that stimulates the ideas and thinking of individuals or groups, including:

A **liking for certain styles, forms, or materials**.

Admired **people, publications, or objects**.

The ideas of **social and environmental groups or movements**.

Through **associative thinking**, involving the **transfer of ideas** from one field to another or thinking of physical or biological **analogies**.

An **external trigger**.

**Observations of the environment.**

**Films, books, or other media.**

Attempts to express **symbolic meaning**.

A '**lightbulb moment**' when thinking, relaxing, or sleeping on a problem.

Innovators need to be **open to these many possible ways** of starting a creative design and innovation project, and for getting inspiration for new ideas, concepts, and designs.

## EFFECTIVE CREATIVE DESIGN AND INNOVATION PROCESSES

There are many models of the innovation process in which design provides the bridge between creative ideas and a new product, building, or innovation. Four such models were shown in Figures 1.1 to 1.3 and Box 1.1 in Chapter 1. However, the processes that may result in new products, buildings, or innovations shown by the book's examples and case studies do not always neatly fit these models. But the processes generally follow an *iterative*, phased pattern moving from an idea, brief, need, or problem, through concepts and solutions represented in increasing detail, to a product, building design, or innovation ready for introduction or construction, and then into use.

### Research and feasibility

Most innovation projects require an initial phase of exploration, research, and investigation. This may involve defining and understanding a problem and establishing technical feasibility. For example:

- Through practical investigations Dyson realised that existing vacuum cleaners lost suction because their bags clogged as they filled with dust. While constructing an industrial cyclone to filter paint powder in his wheelbarrow factory, Dyson had the idea of a bagless vacuum cleaner that used the cyclone principle. He then conducted an experiment to test the feasibility of his idea and found that a small cardboard cyclone could work on a vacuum cleaner.

Assessing user requirements and potential market demand is often also part of this phase. For new or innovative products, formal or informal *market research* can be conducted to identify user needs, demands, and wants and to assess whether a potential market exists. For revolutionary and radical innovations, *conventional market research is usually inappropriate* as potential users cannot express needs and preferences for something about which they have no knowledge or experience. Sometimes, *creative market research* methods, such as designer-user workshops, may be used to explore users' responses to future innovation concepts, but whether a potential market exists may have to depend on the innovator's vision, belief, or intuition. For example:

- Development of the iPhone depended on Jobs's vision, and the cyclone cleaner on Dyson's belief, that a market existed for their revolutionary and radical innovations.
- For a much less innovative product, Greaves said 'doing her homework' before developing her first dog walking bag was vital to establish whether a gap in the market and a potential business opportunity existed. She conducted informal market research through online searches and by seeking advice from pet shops, industry contacts, and at dog shows.

### Creative idea generation

The previous section identified many sources of inspiration for creative ideas, such as existing artefacts, geometrical shapes, associative thinking, observation, a lightbulb moment, or chance discovery. This idea may only emerge after several alternatives have been considered in the mind of the creator, or during team or group discussions, but then becomes the single core idea that is pursued further in the creative design and innovation process. Some design and innovation process models, however, suggest that the process involves a deliberate phase of *divergent* exploration and generation of alternative ideas and concepts, followed by *convergent* selection of one or more options for further development.

Repeated phases of idea generation and selection are then required as a project develops. The book's case studies indicate that an explicit diverge/converge process sometimes takes place but may be less common than the process models, such as the Funnel-Bugle and Double Diamond innovation process models in Chapter 1, suggest. But there are some examples:

- Draper's creative idea of rotating gates with a D-shaped cross-section as a method of flood control for the Thames Barrier was only chosen for development after several alternative concepts had been considered by an expert technical group.
- Before the iPhone project proper began, a group of engineers and designers spent a long time, through brainstorming, information searching, and regular discussions, exploring the 'search space' to find better methods than mice and keyboards for human-computer interaction. This eventually led to construction of a mock-up to simulate a multitouch screen, which became the basis of the iPhone's interface.
- Later during the iPhone's development, software engineers generated many novel design concepts for its virtual keyboard before Jobs decided on a standard typewriter keyboard layout. Then to make a standard keyboard layout useable on a touchscreen many methods for displaying the keys were created and tested before software that enlarged the keys when pressed was selected and implemented.
- The architect Robert de Grey said in my interview with him that he and Derek Yeadon worked together on the design of *Milton Keynes Central Bus Station* making many sketches of possible concepts before a design emerged as the one they selected for development.

*Brainstorming* was the only idea generation technique mentioned in the case studies, despite the availability of many other creativity techniques such as mind mapping, morphological analysis, and random stimuli (see e.g., VanGundy, 1988). For example:

- The *Compare the Meerkat* advertising campaign was conceived by Darren Walsh as a result of a brainstorming session around the Compare the Market brand name which led to the word 'market' becoming 'meerkat' when pronounced in a mock Russian accent.
- Robert de Grey told me in his interview that he did not use formal creativity techniques except for 'informal brainstorming by sketching and discussing ideas in a group'.

But although professional designers, engineers, and architects rarely use formal creativity techniques, when learning these students subjects often find the techniques useful when stuck during problem exploration, idea generation, and concept selection (Roy, 2013).

### The design, development, and innovation process

Once an idea, concept, or initial design has been created and selected, it must be developed in increasing detail until ready for production or construction. This is typically an *iterative, evolutionary process* with successive phases of testing and modification.

The designers, engineers, and architects in the book's examples and case studies typically followed this iterative design and development process, evolving through increasingly detailed 2D and 3D representations and models appropriate to the product or building (see e.g., Evans and Pei, 2010). For example:

- Gafni developed his cardboard bicycle through a series of sketches, computer models, and prototypes before eventually succeeding in making a rideable machine.
- Industrial designers and engineers at Apple developed the iMac G3 computer through sketches, drafts, and mock-ups, including the key stage of embodying Ive's design concept as physical models and prototypes that could be worked on individually and in a team.

Novice designers should be able to produce worthwhile creative product designs when provided with a starting point for inspiration and a systematic design process or design 'grammar' to follow. For example:

- First-year undergraduate Open University design students, most of whom had no prior design experience, produced original graphic designs for printing on T-shirts some of which were judged to be potentially commercially saleable. The students developed their designs through creative thinking, photographing, drawing, and modelling within a systematic design process.

### Elements of the design, development, and innovation process

Within the creative design and innovation process various approaches and methods may be applied to develop an idea or concept.

Designers, engineers, and architects often develop new products, buildings, and innovations by *adapting, developing, or combining existing technologies, products, or components*:

- The iPhone's multitouch screen was developed from existing products; at the concept phase by adapting the technology of a trackpad for people with hand injuries, then at the detailed phase by adapting the technology of a Sony touchscreen music player.
- In the *Oxley Woods* eco-housing development, the *Ecohat* solar-heated ventilation system was developed from an existing mechanical ventilation system.
- Starley's *Rover Safety* bicycle was designed by integrating existing cycle components – tangent-spoked wheels, roller chains, and hollow metal frames – in a new configuration which resulted in a greatly improved design.

- Derek Taylor's *Energy Showcase* house was designed by putting together the principles, designs, materials, and components of existing ultra-low energy houses to create a new positive carbon design.

*Human or user-centred design* is an essential approach when designing products, buildings, or innovations for people. For example:

- Dyson applied user-centred design to the *Ballbarrow* and his cyclone vacuum cleaners to address their usability problems, based on his personal experience of using conventional wheelbarrows and vacuum cleaners.
- The architect Robert de Grey tries to work with clients and the future users of a building to identify and meet their wants, demands, and needs.
- Debbie Greaves acted in the role of a user to identify the requirements for a dog walking bag. She then created a rough mock-up to test a design that met those user requirements before handing her design concept over to a professional designer for development.

*Industrial design* is another vital discipline when creating products and innovations, especially for consumer markets. For example:

- Cooper asked Motorola's industrial designers to create concepts of what a portable mobile phone should look like to attract potential users before his team developed the phone's electronics.
- To create the external form of the iPhone, Ive's industrial design team produced many concepts and tested prototypes for usability, eventually choosing a form based on his and Job's original vision of a design dominated by the screen.

*Technical and user testing* is a key stage in the development process to ensure that the product or innovation is functionable and useable:

- The virtual keyboard was one of the few elements of the secretive iPhone project that was tested with a sample of potential users before further development.
- In Dyson's company the results of technical and user testing are applied to modify and improve designs during development until they are ready for production.

Great attention to *detail design* is vital to ensure that a new product, building, or innovation meets all its technical, user, and production or construction requirements. For example:

- Ive's team paid painstaking attention to the technical, user, and aesthetic design details of the iMac G3 computer before its introduction.
- Dyson's design and engineering team spent enormous effort on every technical, user, and aesthetic detail of the DC01 cyclone vacuum cleaner to ensure that it offered unique functions and ease of operation, was visually innovative, and allowed for economic manufacture.

Design and development for *appropriate and economic use of materials and manufacture* is another key element of a successful new product or innovation project. For example:

- Norcross's lighting designs are finalised to meet commercial cost and manu-facturing requirements through application of her detailed knowledge of materials and manufacturing processes.
- The iPhone as a successful innovation depended on deep knowledge within Apple of materials and product manufacturing via global supply chains.

For some case studies *sustainable or eco-design*, that is designing to reduce the adverse environmental impacts of a new product, building, or innovation, was a major factor in their conception and development. For example:

- Dyson's company attempts to reduce the environmental impacts of its prod-ucts, especially by designing for energy efficiency. This is because energy use produces most of the environmental impacts of electrical products throughout their lifecycle.
- Taylor's design and construction of buildings such as The Energy Showcase and his creation of the *AeroSolar Dek House*™ were driven by sustainable and eco-design principles.
- RSHP's concept design of the Oxley Woods eco-housing development aimed to achieve high energy efficiency, construction using low environ-mental impact materials, and flexibility to changing user requirements to extend their useful life.

### *Guidelines for success: Effective creative design and innovation processes*

**What are the key elements of an effective creative design and innova-tion process?**

Establishing the **technical feasibility** of a radical new idea or concept is often required at the start of the innovation process. This may be done by conducting a **critical experiment** with a **physical model** or **mock-up** to establish basic functionality.

Moving through **systematic phases of iterative development** – from problem, need, idea, or brief, via increasingly detailed representations, models, and prototypes, to a final design ready for production, construc-tion, and introduction – is more likely to result in a successful outcome.

For **new or innovative products**, formal or informal **market research** is usually needed to understand user requirements and assess potential mar-ket demand before starting a project.

For **revolutionary and radical innovations, conventional market research is usually inappropriate** as potential users cannot express needs and preferences for something about which they have no knowledge or experience. Whether a potential market exists may have to depend on the innovator's belief or intuition. Sometimes, **creative market research** methods, such as designer-user workshops, may be used to explore users' responses to future innovation concepts.

When there is a brief, need, or identified problem to be solved, **exploring the search space** by deliberately generating **alternative ideas or solution concepts** can be a crucial step. More often, however, **a core idea or concept** (or '**primary generator**') that drives the creative design and innovation process has emerged in the mind of the creator, or during team or group discussions, stimulated by the many possible sources of inspiration.

Ideas and concepts may be developed many ways, including by **adapting existing products** or by **combining existing technologies, products, or components** into new configurations.

For products to be used by people, the application of **human-centred design** and **industrial design,** focusing on user requirements, useability, and on form, style, and appearance, is vital to ensure that the product is easy to use and attractive.

**Technical and user testing** of a new product or innovation during development, and modifying it as necessary, is important to ensure its functionality, usability, and quality.

Great attention to **detail design of all elements and components** of a new product, building, or innovation is also vital to ensure functionality, usability, market appeal, and quality.

Considering **materials and manufacture** from the early stages of the development process is essential to ensure the new product, building, or innovation can be produced or constructed economically, efficiently, and to quality.

Reducing the adverse environmental impacts of new products, buildings, and innovations through **sustainable or eco-design** is increasingly important to address growing environmental problems and crises.

## CHARACTERISTICS OF SUCCESSFUL PRODUCTS, BUILDINGS, AND INNOVATIONS

The classic text on how rapidly an innovation is adopted is *The Diffusion of Innovations* by Everett Rogers (2003). Rogers identified five characteristics of an innovation that help or hinder its adoption into the market or social use. These are *relative advantage* (whether the innovation is perceived as better than what already exists); *compatibility* (whether it is perceived as being compatible with the values, experiences, and needs of potential adopters); *complexity* (whether it is perceived as being difficult to understand and use); *trialability* (whether it can be tried on a limited basis); and *observability* (whether the results of adopting it are visible to others). Rogers (2003, p. 17) says that the three most important characteristics are relative advantage, complexity, and compatibility, so those are the ones focused upon here. For example:

- The iPod was a highly successful product because it offered advantages not provided by rival digital music players ('a thousand songs in your pocket') in an elegant, user-friendly series of designs; it met emotional and aesthetic as well as functional needs (Fadell, 2022).
- The iPod's success also depended on Apple's introduction of the iTunes Store from which music could be easily downloaded to the iPod using software compatible with both Macintosh and the more widely owned Windows computers.
- The early iPhone series offered many advantages over other smartphones available at the time it was introduced, including their unique multitouch screen, ease of use, touchscreen keyboards and icons, an increasing number of apps, all packaged in highly desirable designs from an admired brand.
- Dyson's cyclonic vacuum cleaners offered several unique advantages that attracted buyers. These included no loss of suction as the machines filled with dust, no need to replace dust bags, low dust emissions, and innovative-looking, user-centred designs.
- Starley's Rover Safety bicycle, as well as being safe to ride, proved itself to be faster, more comfortable, and convenient than other types of cycle still being made in the late 19th century. It was also aesthetically simple and attractive to consumers, including women cyclists, despite initial ridicule by adherents of high-wheel 'penny-farthing' bicycles.
- The Oxley Woods prefabricated eco-homes were rapidly sold to their initial buyers for several reasons including their environmental credentials, low running costs, innovative modern design, and light-filled interiors.

### Guidelines for success: Characteristics of successful products, buildings, and innovations

**The book's case studies confirm what is already familiar from the marketing and innovation literature.**

To succeed a new product, building, or innovation should offer potential adopters **one or more unique advantages** not provided by existing products or services. However, such innovations should also be **compatible** with supporting technologies and services, and **not too complex** for consumers to understand and use.

**Aesthetics, emotional appeal, and brand reputation** will also affect the success of the product.

## INTELLECTUAL PROPERTY PROTECTION

Intellectual property (IP) protection – patents, trademarks, and registered designs (design patents) – is a crucial element of many innovation projects. The creators of most of the book's examples and case studies involving new technology or design have obtained some form of IP protection, and several have had to take legal action against those attempting to infringe their IP. For example:

- Apple has over 300 patents on the iPhone. In 2018 Apple won a court case which alleged that its main smartphone competitor, Samsung, had infringed eight iPhone technical and design patents (Kastrenakes, 2018).
- Dyson risked much to defend his cyclone vacuum cleaner patents and designs against copying. A case against a US company, Amway, which had launched its own design of cyclone vacuum cleaner, involved Dyson in legal costs which threatened his company's survival. Fortunately, settlement of the case gave him the funds to develop the mass-market DC01 cleaner. Dyson then won a case against Hoover in 2000 after it launched a bagless cleaner with three cyclones.
- Dunlop applied for a patent on his pneumatic cycle tyre in 1888, unaware that Robert Thomson had already patented a pneumatic tyre in 1846. Dunlop's patent was later declared invalid until Thompson's patent expired in 1890, which permitted his tyre to be legally commercialised.
- Derek Taylor patented and trademarked his *Aeolian Roof*™ building-integrated wind and solar system. Taylor, however, can be wary of collaboration if there is a risk of his ideas being copied or his patents being infringed because the cost to an individual of renewing and defending patents is usually prohibitive.
- Debbie Greaves and her partner had to take legal action to stop another small business copying the Registered Design of their dog walking bag. Legal action cost the partners much more than they recovered, but they were determined not allow others to benefit from their efforts.

### Guidelines for success: Intellectual property protection

It is crucial for inventors, designers, and innovators **to protect their IP** if they can afford to do so using, as appropriate, patents, trademarks, and registered designs.

Stopping others from copying a product or infringing an invention usually involves **high legal costs and much time and determination**. Whether a case is worth fighting is a matter of judgement and the availability of finance.

## CONTINUING IMPROVEMENT AND INNOVATION

Few new products, buildings, and innovations will continue to succeed without further improvement, adaptation, or variation after their first introduction or construction. The book's case studies provide several illustrations of the need for continuing improvement, adaptation, and innovation. For example:

- The first Motorola portable mobile phone had to be improved using new technologies to produce designs that were less expensive, smaller, lighter, and with a longer battery life, before the company's mobile phones could become mass-market products.
- Since launch the iPhone has undergone continuous improvement and innovation, ranging from incorporating radical new technologies to making minor design improvements. Continuing innovation and improvement through 12 generations and multiple variants over 16 years has ensured the iPhone's continued market success and enabled it to compete with rival touchscreen smartphones that followed it.
- Dyson's company invested in developing generations of new and improved cyclone vacuum cleaners as competitors introduced their own cyclonic and bagless cleaners. The company also exploited its expertise and technology in further innovations, including cordless and robot vacuum cleaners, and other air movement products such as fans, hand and hair dryers, and air pollution filtering headphones.
- As a result of changing bus and coach operator requirements, Milton Keynes Central Bus Station ceased operating as a bus station soon after completion. The former bus station has subsequently provided accommodation for a variety of other functions and support for a large solar photovoltaic array, and inspired student architects to propose eco-redesigns of the building to meet new needs, thus demonstrating the building's versatility to be adapted to meet changing requirements.
- Debbie Greaves and her partner's business developed a range of new and variant designs of dog walking bags, in response to feedback from customers. Subsequently, to reduce costs, the range was rationalised to offer two standard designs in different colours and materials.

### *Guidelines for success: Continuing improvement and innovation*

To maintain the success of a new product or innovation it is necessary to continue to **innovate, develop new products, and improve upon and provide variants of existing ones**. However, to reduce costs it may be necessary to rationalise an over-diverse range.

For continued innovation success it is necessary to monitor and respond to **feedback from users, suppliers, and others**, to innovate in response to

**competition**, and make use of **new materials, components, and technologies** as they become available.

If possible, it is desirable to create designs which are sufficiently **flexible to permit improvement and adaptation** after introduction or construction.

## UNSUCCESSFUL PRODUCTS, BUILDINGS, AND INNOVATIONS

There are many reasons why a new product, building, or innovation may not be introduced or built, fail to be adopted, or exhibit significant problems after introduction or construction. Christensen (2016), for example, has shown that most new products and innovations fail to reach the market or diffuse into use. The book's examples and case studies illustrate some of the reasons for innovation failure, limited success, or the need for major modifications before the new product, building, or innovation may be considered a success.

The first group are examples of innovation failure:

- Gafni's cardboard bicycle failed to become a commercial innovation. The prototypes were too expensive to attract customers and potential customers were unsure how reliable and durable a cardboard bicycle would be compared to a conventional bicycle. A subsequent attempt at crowdfunding did not raise sufficient funds to develop a cardboard bicycle for volume production.
- Dyson's company has developed a few innovative products which failed to be introduced. The products discussed in the case study are the Dyson electric car, which was not produced because it would have been too expensive to compete with vehicles from established car manufacturers, and a prototype robot vacuum cleaner which was too heavy, complex, and costly to be a commercial proposition.
- Despite a demonstration of its effectiveness, progressing Taylor's building-integrated wind and solar Aeolian Roof™ beyond an experimental prototype has not so far been possible. A major obstacle has been that it is difficult to raise sufficient funding to develop radical housing innovations into practical designs, especially given the risk-averse and conservative property market.
- The problems that affected the Oxley Woods eco-housing development clearly demonstrate that *innovation is risky*, especially if *several innovations*, such as prefabricated construction, the use of recycled materials, and inclusion of the Ecohat heat recovery system, *are attempted simultaneously*. This, together with a division of responsibility between architectural concept design and technical design for construction, resulted in poor detailed design and workmanship. This led to water

penetration and rot which eventually required complete refurbishment of the development.

- Thompson's pneumatic tyre for heavy vehicles, which predated Dunlop's pneumatic cycle tyre, was a *premature innovation* that failed for several reasons. Enabling technologies, especially suitable materials to make a durable tyre, were not available at the time. It also had deficiencies, such not being easily removable for replacement or repair, and there was insufficient demand for a pneumatic tyre for horse-drawn vehicles to make it a commercial proposition. Successful innovation of the pneumatic tyre had to wait for the introduction of safety bicycles equipped with Dunlop's improved pneumatic tyres, and subsequently the introduction of motorcycles and cars that required pneumatic tyres.

A second group are examples of limited innovation success:

- The first real smartphone, the 1994 IBM Simon Personal Communicator, had limited commercial success. It was a premature innovation, because the technologies needed to make it fully portable, functionable, and easy to use did not exist at the time. Its high price also limited its market.
- The 'iTunes phone', an attempt by Apple in partnership with Motorola and Cingular to develop a mobile phone with an integrated music player to prevent rival mobile phones limiting sales of Apple's iPod music player, was not a success because of its limited storage capacity and its clumsy user interface and design compared to the iPod.
- Dyson's *Contrarotator* dual drum washing machine was withdrawn after five years of production because it was not perceived by consumers to have sufficient relative advantage over conventional washing machines to allow it to be sold at a price that made a profit.
- RSHP's improved prefabricated housing designs such as the Y:Cube apartment blocks for the YMCA, based on what was learned from the Oxley Woods development, have to date only been built on a limited scale given the conservative housing industry and market.

The third group are innovations requiring improvement or adaptation after introduction:

- The original iPhone only had a limited market because of its high price, relatively slow 2G cellular communications, and limited range of apps. It was replaced about a year later by a lower priced, faster 3G version with GPS and support for third-party apps.
- Dunlop's pneumatic cycle tyre needed improvement by incorporating innovations, including Welch's detachable tyre and Wood's inflation-deflation valves, before it gained widespread adoption.

*Guidelines for success: Avoiding unsuccessful products, buildings, and innovations*

**How can designers and innovators avoid limited success or failure of a new product, building, or innovation?**

By ensuring that **enabling materials, components, and technologies** to develop and introduce the new product, building, or innovation are available when needed. (Also see the section on Contextual factors).

By ensuring that there is an **existing or latent market** for the new product or innovation and that it offers **worthwhile relative advantages or unique benefits** over what already exists. (Also see the section on Characteristics of successful products, buildings, and innovations).

By ensuring that **sufficient funding** is available or can be raised to develop the product, building, or innovation, and then to make and introduce it.

By ensuring that the new product or innovation can be offered at an **affordable or competitive price** and provides **value for money**.

By ensuring that the new product, building, or innovation offers sufficient **reliability, quality, and durability**.

By not incorporating **too many innovative elements at once** as this increases the risk of technical failure and reliability or quality problems in use.

By realising that revolutionary and radical innovations **may be expensive and imperfect at first**, often with a limited market, but can provide the basis for technological and design improvement and wider market success.

By learning from **problems and failures** which can provide lessons and information which can help create successful future new products, buildings, and innovations.

## REFERENCES

Bansal, S., Venaik, A. Upveja, S. and Saritha S. (2002) (eds.) *Constructive Discontent in Execution. Creative approaches to technology and management.* Florida: Apple Academic Press.

BBC (2022) *Sensationalists. The bad boys and girls of British art.* Episode 2. BBC2 TV, 4 November.

Christensen, C.M. (2016) *The Innovator's Dilemma.* Boston: Harvard Business Review Press.

Darke, J. (1979) 'The primary generator and the design process', *Design Studies*, 1(1), pp. 36–44.

Eno, B. (2009) 'Brian Eno on Genius, And "Scenius"'. *Synthtopia*, 9 July. Available at: https://www.synthtopia.com/content/2009/07/09/brian-eno-on-genius-and-scenius/ (Accessed: 29 June 2023).

Evans, M.A. and Pei, E. (2010) *ID Cards. A taxonomy of design representations*. Loughborough University. Available at: https://www.idsa.org/wp-content/uploads/IDSA%20iD%20Cards.pdf (Accessed: 30 June 2023).

Fadell, T. (2022) *Build. An unorthodox guide to making things worth making*. London: Bantam Press.

Gladwell, M. (2008) *Outliers: The story of success*. London: Allen Lane.

Isaacson, W. (2011*) Steve Jobs*. London: Little Brown.

Kastrenakes, J. (2018) 'Apple and Samsung settle seven-year-long patent fight over copying the iPhone'. *The Verge*, 27 June. Available at: https://www.theverge.com/2018/6/27/17510908/apple-samsung-settle-patent-battle-over-copying-iphone (Accessed: 6 July 2023).

Mazzucato, M. (2013) *The Entrepreneurial State. Debunking public vs. private sector myths*. London: Anthem Press.

Merchant, B. (2017) *The One Device. The secret history of the iPhone*. London: Bantam Press.

Parry, E. (1990) 'MacCormac Jamieson Pritchard', *Architects' Journal*, 19 and 26 December, pp. 28–9.

Rogers, E.M. (2003) *The diffusion of innovations* (5th edition). New York: Free Press.

Roy, R. (2013) 'Creative design'. Book 3, T217 *Design Essentials*. Milton Keynes: The Open University.

Roy, R. (2016) *Consumer Product Innovation and Sustainable Design. The evolution and impacts of successful products*. Abingdon, Oxfordshire: Routledge.

VanGundy, A.B. (1988) *Techniques of structured problem solving* (2nd edition). New York: Van Nostrand Reinhold.

Wallas, G. (1926) *The Art of Thought*. New York: Harcourt.

# Index

Note: Information in figures and tables is indicated by page numbers in *italics* and **bold**, respectively.